SINGER

Home Decorating Projects Step-by-Step

RD PRESS

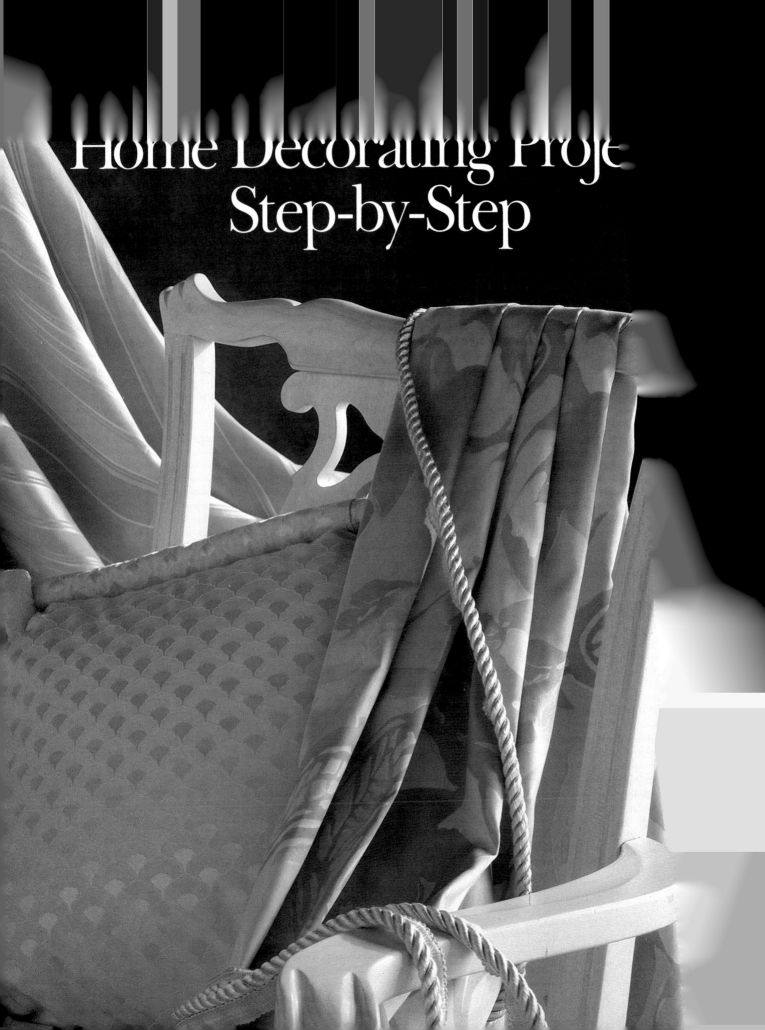

Home Decorating Proje
Step-by-Step

Contents

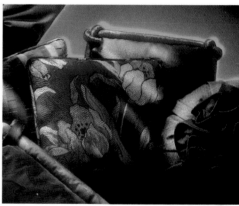

Singer Home Decorating Projects Step-by-Step
draws pages from the individual titles of the
Singer Sewing Reference Library.

Pages 46 and 47 also appear in *Singer Sewing
Step-by-Step.*

Canadian Cataloguing-in-Publication Data
Main entry under title:

Singer home decorating projects step-by-step.

Includes index.
ISBN 0-88850-305-9

   1. Machine sewing. 2. House furnishings.
I. Reader's Digest Association (Canada).

TT705.S55 1992 646.2'1 C92-090260-X

Published in Canada in 1992 by:
The Reader's Digest Association
  (Canada) Ltd.
215 Redfern Avenue
Montreal, Quebec H3Z 2V9

The Reader's Digest Association (Canada)
Ltd. is a licensed user of the trademark RD
Press.

CY DECOSSE INCORPORATED
Chairman: Cy DeCosse
President: James B. Maus
Executive Vice President: William B. Jones

Created by: The Editors of Cy DeCosse
  Incorporated, in cooperation with the
  Sewing Education Department. Singer is a
  trademark of The Singer Company and is
  used under license.

Printed on American paper by: R. R. Donnelley
& Sons Co. (0992)

92 93 94 95 96 / 5 4 3 2 1

How to Use This Book

Any successful sewing project for the home requires two things: a thorough understanding of basic sewing skills and the specific information needed to create projects from curtains to slipcovers. *Singer Home Decorating Projects Step-by-Step* provides both. Now you can update or revitalize any room in your home, or simply add a finishing touch.

Getting Started

This section helps you plan your project. It gives basic information on colors, patterns, and fabrics, as well as on measuring, marking, and cutting. Basic seams and sewing techniques are also clearly explained and illustrated.

Home Sewing Projects

The sections of this book deal with general projects, such as curtains, pillows, slipcovers, and table coverings, and projects for specific rooms, such as the bathroom and the bedroom.

The Windows section includes designer window treatments as well as basic information on hardware selection, covering and installing mounting boards, and sewing casings and hems. Learn how to make flip top and tie top curtains for a casual look. Or for a more formal look, try bishop sleeve or hourglass curtains, rod-pocket swags and cascades, or pleated draperies. Add rosettes to tiebacks, swags, or pillows for a creative accent. Swags, shades, and a wide variety of top treatments such as stagecoach valances, handkerchief valances, sunburst curtains, and covered poles and finials complete this section.

Bathroom Decorating projects include shower curtains and valances, sink and vanity skirts, and embellished towel ideas.

The Pillows section begins with plain or corded pillows; includes many with a designer flair, such as

sash, butterfly, knotted-corner, and reversible rosette pillows; and ends with four quick ideas for pillow covers.

Sewing for the Bedroom features projects like comforter covers, some with matching pillow shams, and bed skirts to complete the look. Other projects include a reverse sham bed cover, a daybed dust skirt and tufted cover, and a padded headboard. The styles range from basic to very elegant.

Slipcovers is a comprehensive section that takes you from pinfitting to laying out, cutting, and sewing slipcovers and cushions. You will also learn to make boxed cushions with decorative welting, cushion ties and tabs, and easy slipcovers for folding chairs.

The Tables section presents decorative ideas for placemats, table runners, and table linens, utilizing techniques such as mitering, fagoting, and satin stitching.

The final sections of the book inspire true creativity. They include Finishing Touches, which covers trims, bows, knots, fabric screens, and decorating with lace; Creative Touches, a section devoted to fabric painting, screen printing, transparent appliqués, cutwork, and monograms; and Decorating with Quilts, a "grand finale" of a section that teaches you the basics of making quilts by machine. Small beginning projects using easy techniques require only basic sewing skills.

Step-by-Step Guidance

From beginning to end, the step-by-step instructions make your sewing-for-the-home projects easy and understandable. Whether you are an experienced sewer or a beginner, you will find this book to be a help and an inspiration. Use it for many successful home decorating and sewing projects.

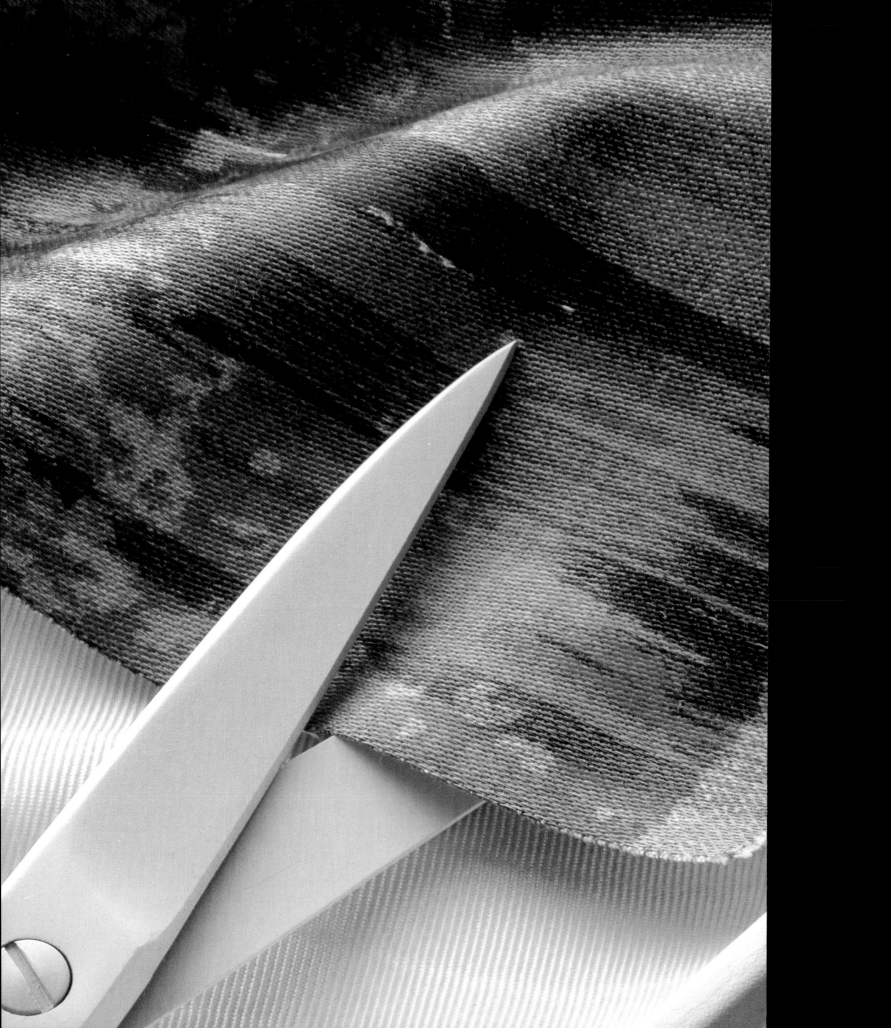

Getting Started

PS-15

PL-14

PL-15

PS-15

Planning Your Project

The first step in planning any project, no matter how large or small, is to analyze the room in which the project will be placed. Think about what you like in the room and what you want to change. If possible, collect samples of any carpeting, fabric, wallpaper, or paint that will remain in the room. Then bring the samples with you to the fabric store, to help you coordinate the old and the new.

You may want to look through recent decorating magazines for ideas to inspire you in updating your room. Pictures can help you decide on a style you like. Rooms with several print fabrics tend to appear cozier and smaller. Rooms with mostly solid colors tend to look restful and larger. The colors you select can also have an effect on the way you feel. Bright, strong colors are more cheerful; muted colors, more relaxing.

Keep in mind that there is no right or wrong way to coordinate the decor of a room. Some general guidelines can help you make good decisions, but your own feelings and preferences are the most important consideration. Salespeople or designers may give helpful suggestions, but be sure to follow your own instincts if you are not comfortable with their ideas.

Learn about the various types of decorating fabrics that are available (pages 16 and 17). Bring home samples of the fabrics you are considering before making your final decisions. Place the samples where they will be used in the room. If a fabric will be used for a valance, place it at the top of the window. Be sure to check the fabrics during daytime and evening hours, since natural and artificial light affect the way colors match or coordinate. Leave the samples in place for a few days to be sure you are comfortable with your decisions. Your initial reactions may change.

Planning the Colors & Patterns

When planning the style of a room, try to visualize the colors and patterns of your sewing projects and how they will be used in the room. Avoid using equal amounts of all the fabrics. Use the primary fabric for about two-thirds of the room furnishings, use a secondary fabric for about one-third, and use accent colors in small amounts. The size of the fabric samples should be in proportion to how they will be used, such as large samples for draperies, small samples for accent pillows.

Vary the textures in the room. Nubby or textured fabrics and surfaces, mixed with smooth ones, add interest. For example, textured sheers contrast with a shiny brass pole.

How to Plan a Coordinated Decor

1) Select the primary patterned fabric. This will be the main fabric and will be used for about two-thirds of the fabric in the room. Select a print that will coordinate with existing furnishings, such as carpeting.

2) Add a secondary patterned fabric that includes some of the colors from the primary fabric. The secondary pattern is used for about one-third of the fabric in the room. Striped fabric works well as a secondary pattern, but florals or plaids may be used, if desired. Vary the scale of the pattern so it is different from the primary print.

3) Add accent patterned fabrics to be used in small amounts. These fabrics can introduce another color from the primary fabric. Or you can add texture by selecting fabrics such as lace; some prints have a textural appearance, even though the fabric has a smooth surface.

4) Select solid-colored fabrics to unify the patterned fabrics and give visual relief. Choose colors you want to emphasize from the other fabrics.

Mixing Patterned Fabrics

Plaid fabric was selected as the primary pattern, because a tailored style was desired. A traditional paisley print was chosen as the secondary pattern to soften the look and repeat the colors in the plaid. The striped fabric adds a bright accent.

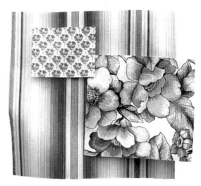

Floral patterns are traditionally the basis for a romantic look. A coordinated fabric group designed by the manufacturer was used for this decorating scheme. The soft colors of the prints are accented with a brighter solid color.

Geometric designs give a more active, contemporary look. These patterned fabrics have a rich textural appearance and an interesting mix of color. The solid-colored accent fabric emphasizes one of the colors in the prints, while its ribbed texture contrasts with the smooth finish of the patterned fabrics.

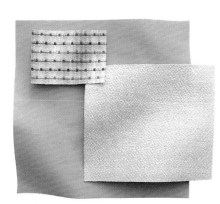

Solid-colored fabrics were selected as the primary and secondary fabrics, giving a more passive look to the room. The colors are compatible, yet offer contrast. Texture has been used to provide variety. For an accent fabric, a novelty weave was used to tie in the colors of the solid fabrics.

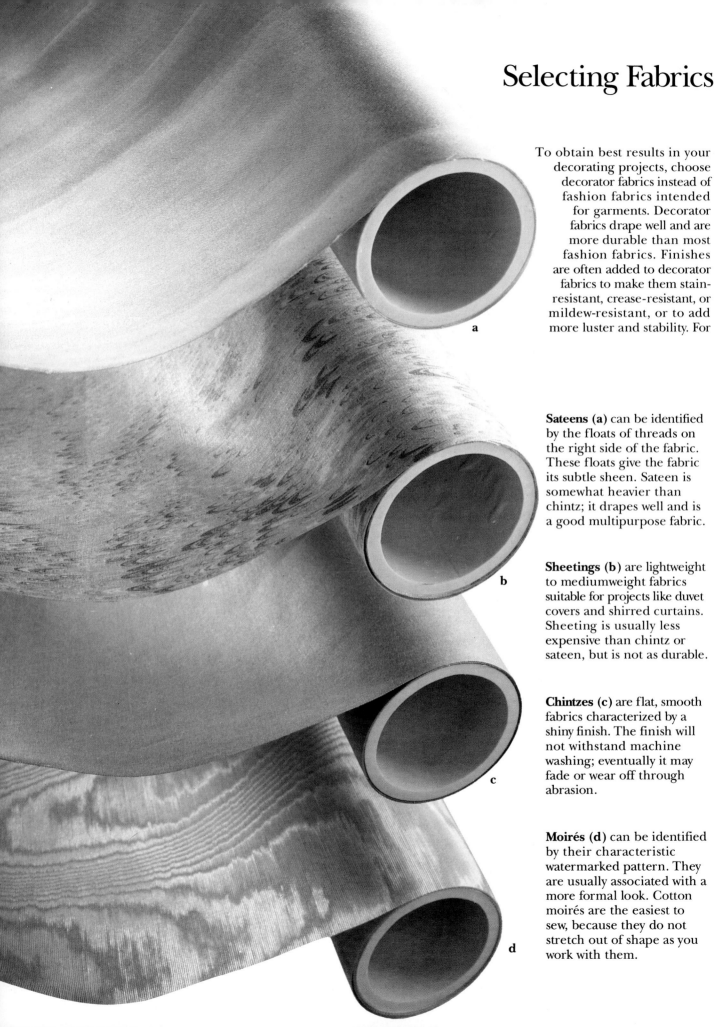

Selecting Fabrics

To obtain best results in your decorating projects, choose decorator fabrics instead of fashion fabrics intended for garments. Decorator fabrics drape well and are more durable than most fashion fabrics. Finishes are often added to decorator fabrics to make them stain-resistant, crease-resistant, or mildew-resistant, or to add more luster and stability. For

Sateens (a) can be identified by the floats of threads on the right side of the fabric. These floats give the fabric its subtle sheen. Sateen is somewhat heavier than chintz; it drapes well and is a good multipurpose fabric.

Sheetings (b) are lightweight to mediumweight fabrics suitable for projects like duvet covers and shirred curtains. Sheeting is usually less expensive than chintz or sateen, but is not as durable.

Chintzes (c) are flat, smooth fabrics characterized by a shiny finish. The finish will not withstand machine washing; eventually it may fade or wear off through abrasion.

Moirés (d) can be identified by their characteristic watermarked pattern. They are usually associated with a more formal look. Cotton moirés are the easiest to sew, because they do not stretch out of shape as you work with them.

best results, do not preshrink decorator fabrics. Washing may remove the finishes, change the fabric's hand, or fade the colors. Dry cleaning is recommended to keep the finished projects looking their best. Several types of fabric may be used in one room. When different fabric types are used, the various surface textures add interest and variety to the decor.

Sheers (a) are lightweight fabrics that add softness to a window treatment and allow light to filter into the room for a bright, airy look. They usually have plain weaves or linenlike textures.

Laces (b), available in many patterns and weights, add texture to the room decor. When used at the window, lace lets in light. Lace may also be used for room accessories, such as tablecloths and pillows.

Duck (c) and lightweight canvas are coarsely woven and have a flat finish. Medium to heavy in weight, they are durable fabrics suitable for casual decorating.

Novelty weaves (d) have woven-in patterns or designs. They add texture and interest to the decor of a room.

Timesaving Fabrics

Whether you are planning a large or small home decorating project, the choice of fabric can save you time in the long run. When looking for fabrics that are timesaving, use these general guidelines.

Prints bring style and the impression of detailing to quick sewing projects. They also provide a built-in color scheme for attractive room settings, hide any imperfect stitches, and show soil or wear less quickly than plain fabrics. Choose allover or small-scale prints rather than larger motifs that must be matched at the seams, centered, or balanced, and you will save fabric as well as time.

Coordinated prints give you a custom look quickly. These fabrics may have coordinated borders or a companion print, such as a stripe, that can be cut apart for trims, tiebacks, and ruffles. Specialty groups include decorative panels that look like handcrafted patchwork or appliqué for shortcut wall hangings and pillows. There are also preprints designed for easy-to-make home accessories, such as kitchen appliance covers, placemat and napkin sets, holiday accents, and nursery items.

Dull or matte finish fabrics absorb rather than reflect light; therefore, they do not require the perfection in sewing or draping needed for fabrics with luster or sheen.

Wide fabrics are best for large projects, such as window treatments, bed coverings, and tablecloths; the wider the fabric, the fewer the seams that are needed. Most home decorating fabrics are at least 54" (140 cm) wide to keep seams to the minimum, but some sheers are 110" (280 cm) or wider so you can eliminate seams entirely. For seamless window treatments, choose fabric wide enough to make headings and lower hems on the selvage edges so the lengthwise fabric grain runs across the window.

Flat bed sheets come in generous sizes that are often large enough for seamless projects. In addition, many sheet styles have borders or applied trims that can be used as prefinished project edges or cut apart to make small items, such as tiebacks.

Reversible fabric, which has no apparent right or wrong side, allows you to eliminate linings and backings. Both fabric faces are attractive on many sheers, jacquard weaves, synthetic suedes, and woven plaids. Create a reversible fabric by using two fabrics back to back. Glue, fuse, or machine-baste wrong sides together.

Lace is suitable for many decorating projects; it does not ravel or require hems or linings. Take advantage of lace border designs by using them as ready-made edges. For window treatments, choose lace that has one edge prefinished as a border and the other prefinished with openings for a curtain rod.

Knits are usually wide enough to minimize seaming; they drape well and may not require hemming. Use velour for pillows, and lightweight tricot for full sheer curtains.

Plaids and stripes have built-in timesaving features. For cutting, measuring, and marking, the lines of a woven plaid or stripe are always on a straight grain. Check to be sure that a printed geometric is printed on-grain or it will be difficult to work with.

Notions & Equipment

Fusible web saves time when used to apply trim or make hems as well as to anchor seam allowances inside a casing for easy curtain rod insertion.

Glue stick is a fast way to position trims, hems, backings, and linings for stitching.

Liquid fray preventer seals the exposed and cut edges on non-sew slits cut into curtains or valances for inserting a rod or brackets.

Overlock machine makes neat, fast hems and edge finishes on ruffles, shades, tablecloths, runners, placemats, and napkins. Also use the overlock machine to sew sheer fabrics without puckers and to sew long, straight seams on curtains, draperies, or bed coverings in minutes.

Rotary cutter is ideal for cutting straight pieces, such as ties, ruffles, bindings, and trimming strips.

Bias tape maker uniformly folds the raw edges of fabric strips as you press. Use it for bias binding, curtain tabs, decorative tapes, and custom band trims. Tape makers come in four sizes to make folded strips ½", ¾", 1", or 2" (12, 18, 25, or 50 mm).

Fabric adhesive, such as craft or white glue, can be used to anchor a shade hem to a lining or to close an opening left for turning a project right side out.

Tapes with self-styling cords are stitched flat to fabric and pulled to shirr, smock, pleat, or fold fabric automatically. Tape is a fast, easy way to make decorative headings on curtains, draperies, valances, and dust ruffles. Ring tape and shade tape are other self-styling tapes. Ring tape has plastic rings sewn at 6" (15 cm) intervals; shade tape has cord tacked loosely at intervals. Both can be used to form swagged hems quickly.

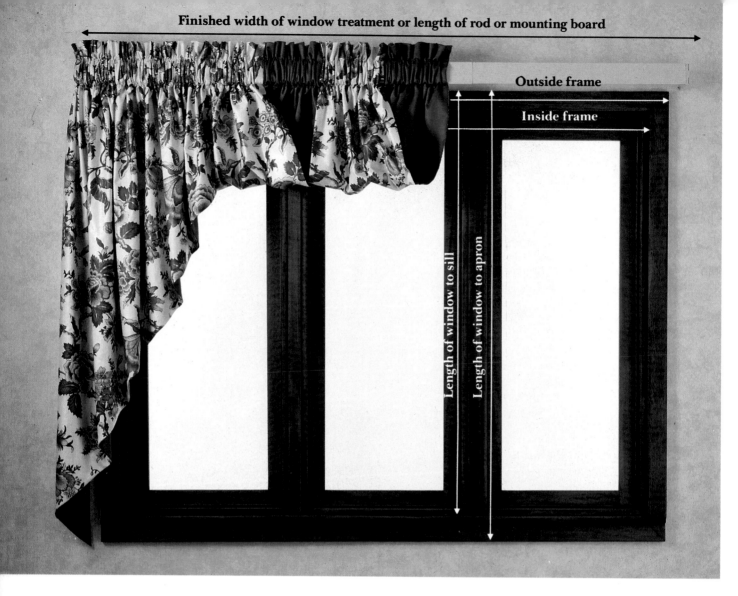

Finished width of window treatment or length of rod or mounting board

Outside frame

Inside frame

Length of window to sill

Length of window to apron

Measuring Windows

Before measuring the windows, select the style of the window treatment and the hardware. Decide where the window treatment will be positioned and install the hardware, so accurate measurements can be taken.

Hardware, including curtain rods, swag holders, and mounting boards, can be mounted inside or outside the window frame. For an inside mount, install the hardware inside the top of the window frame so the molding is exposed. For an outside mount, install the hardware at the top of the window frame or on the wall above the window. When the hardware is mounted above the window frame, visual height is added to the window treatment. Cascades and side treatments can be mounted so they cover part of the wall at the sides of the window, adding visual width. When window treatments are mounted onto the wall, more glass can be exposed, letting in more light.

Draperies can be either sill-length, apron-length, or floor-length. For good proportion, valances and swags are often one-fifth the length of the window

or the completed window treatment. Cascades are often one-third or two-thirds the length of the window. Avoid dividing the window treatment in half visually.

To determine the finished length of the window treatment, measure from the top of the curtain rod or mounting board to the desired length of the window treatment; if the window treatment will have a heading above the rod, add the length of the heading to this measurement. To determine the finished width, measure the length of the drapery rod. For some window treatments, it may also be necessary to measure the width of the return, or the distance that the rod projects out from the wall.

Use a folding ruler or metal tape measure for taking accurate measurements; cloth or vinyl tape measures may stretch or sag. If you are making window treatments for several windows in the same room, measure and record the measurements for each window separately, even if they appear to be the same size.

Measuring Beds

When measuring a bed for a duvet or comforter, measure the bed over the blankets and sheets that will normally be used. The measurements will be larger than the mattress size, but this ensures that the bed covering will fit correctly. Measure the width of the bed from side to side across the top, and measure the length from the head of the bed to the foot.

Duvets or comforters reach 1" to 4" (2.5 to 10 cm) below the mattress on the sides and at the foot of the bed. Determine the drop length of the duvet or comforter by measuring the distance from the top of the bed to the desired position for the lower edge of the duvet. The drop length is usually 9" to 12" (23 to 30.5 cm), depending on the mattress depth.

When measuring for a bed skirt, measure from the top of the box spring to the floor; then subtract ½" (1.3 cm) for clearance.

Drop length of duvet

Drop length of bed skirt

Estimating Yardage

Because fabric widths vary, the yardage requirements for decorating projects cannot be calculated until the fabric has been selected. After you have taken the necessary measurements and determined the finished size of the project, you will need to figure the cut length and cut width of the project.

To determine the cut length and cut width of a fabric that does not require matching, add the amounts needed for any hems, rod pockets, headings, ease, seam allowances, and fullness to the finished size of the project. For example, if you are sewing a gathered valance, add the amount needed for rod pockets, headings, and hems to the finished length; then add side hems, seam allowances, and fullness to the finished width. If the fabric requires matching, you will need to allow extra fabric (page 24).

Frequently a decorating project will require more than one width of fabric. To determine the number of fabric widths required, divide the cut width of the project by the width of the fabric.

To calculate the amount of fabric you will need, multiply the cut length of the project by the number of fabric widths required; this is the total fabric length in inches (centimeters). Divide this measurement by 36" (100 cm) to determine the number of yards (meters) required.

Rod-sleeve valance (page 90) is made from striped fabric that has been railroaded, changing the direction of the stripes. The stripes run on the lengthwise grain on the fabric, but are turned horizontally on the railroaded valance. The curtains were not railroaded, so the lengthwise grain of the fabric runs lengthwise on the curtain.

Railroading Fabrics

Many fabrics can be railroaded, or cut so the lengthwise grain will run horizontally on the finished project. This is possible when the cut length is shorter than the fabric width. Railroading is often used for cutting fabric for valances, bed skirts, and short curtains to eliminate seams and save sewing time.

If the fabric is patterned, check to see that the design can be turned sideways. Flowers with stems, birds, and other one-way designs cannot be turned sideways. Striped fabrics may be railroaded, but stripes on the lengthwise grain will run horizontally if the fabric is railroaded.

Yardage requirements are calculated differently when fabric is railroaded. To determine how many yards (meters) of fabric you will need, divide the cut width by 36" (100 cm). Depending on the project, railroading may require more or less fabric.

Sunburst curtain (page 96) has been railroaded to prevent seams. Seams would be noticeable in the sheer fabric when light comes through the window.

Handkerchief valance (page 88) has been railroaded to prevent seams, which would detract from the overall appearance of the valance.

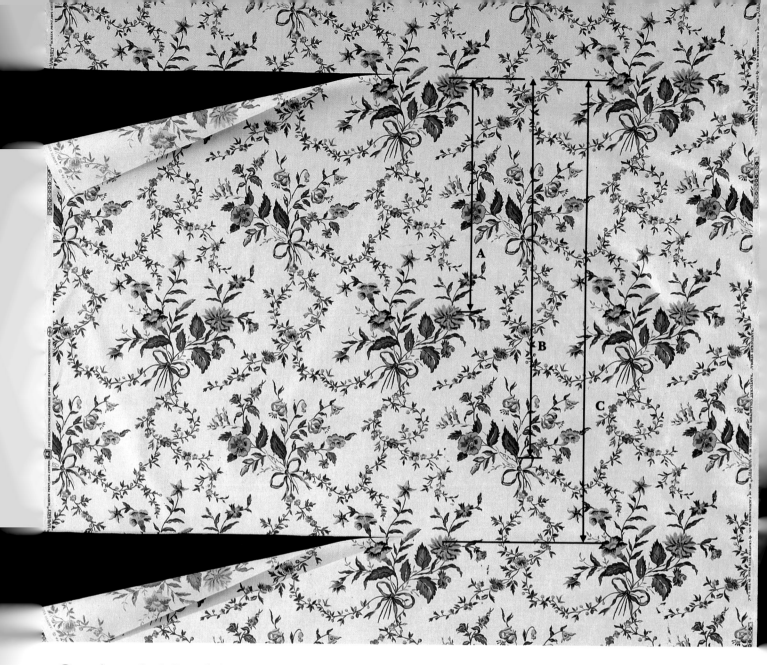

Cutting & Matching Patterned Fabrics

For professional results, always match the pattern of a fabric at the seamlines. Extra yardage is usually needed in order to match the pattern.

The pattern repeat (**A**) is the lengthwise distance from one distinctive point on the pattern, such as the tip of a particular petal in a floral pattern, to the same point in the next pattern design. Some patterned fabrics have pattern repeat markings (+) printed on the selvage. These markings mark the beginning of each pattern repeat, and they are especially helpful for fabrics that include several similar designs.

Add the amounts needed for any hems, rod pockets, headings, ease, seam allowances, and fullness to the finished length, to determine how long the lengths of fabric need to be (**B**). Then round this measurement up to the next number divisible by the size of the pattern repeat. This is the cut length (**C**). For example, if the pattern repeat (**A**) is 19" (48.5 cm), and the finished length plus hems, rod pockets, and other allowances (**B**) is 30" (76 cm), the actual cut length (**C**) is 38" (96.5 cm). To have patterns match from one panel to the next, each panel must be cut at the same point on the pattern repeat.

To calculate the amount of fabric you will need, multiply the cut length by the number of fabric widths required for the project; add one additional pattern repeat so you can adjust the placement of the pattern on the cut lengths. This is the total fabric length in inches (centimeters); divide this measurement by 36" (100 cm) to determine the number of yards (meters) required.

How to Match a Patterned Fabric

1) **Position** the fabric widths, right sides together, matching the selvages.

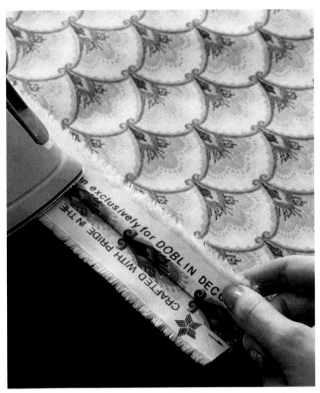

2) **Fold** selvage back at one end until pattern matches. Lightly press foldline.

3) **Unfold** selvage. Pin on foldline; check the match from right side.

4) **Reposition** pins perpendicular to foldline; stitch on foldline. Trim away selvages. Trim fabric to finished length plus hems, rod pockets, and other allowances, as calculated opposite.

Machine Stitching

Most home decorator sewing can be done entirely by machine with a straight or zigzag stitch. Although machines vary in capabilities, each has the same basic parts and controls. Consult your machine manual to review the threading procedures and to locate the controls that operate the principal parts.

Tension, pressure and stitch length and width are the main adjustments that create perfect straight or zigzag stitching. Choosing the appropriate needle and thread for the sewing project and fabric also helps to create quality stitching.

Tension is the balance between the upper and bobbin threads as they pass through the machine.

When tension is perfectly balanced, the stitches look even on both sides of the fabric because they link midway between fabric layers. Tension that is too tight causes seams to pucker and stitches to break easily. Tension that is too loose results in weak seams.

Pressure regulates the even feeding of fabric layers. When pressure is too heavy, the bottom fabric layer gathers, forcing the upper layer ahead of the presser foot. This unevenness can make a difference of several inches at the end of a long seam, such as one on a curtain. Pressure that is too light may cause skipped stitches, crooked stitching lines and weak, loose stitches.

Stitch length is controlled with a regulator that is on an inch scale from 0 to 20, a metric scale from 0 to 4, or a numerical scale from 0 to 9. On the metric and numerical scales, higher numbers form a longer stitch, lower numbers a shorter stitch. For normal stitching, set the regulator at 10 to 12 stitches per inch (2.5 cm). This setting is equivalent to 2.5 to 3 on the metric scale, and 5 on the numerical scale.

Needle, size 80/14, is used for general-purpose sewing on mediumweight fabrics. Because the firm weave and glazed finish of many home decorator fabrics dull a needle quickly, change the needle often. A bent, blunt, or burred needle damages fabric. Prevent damage to the needle by removing pins from the seam as you come to them. Never sew over pins or let them get under the fabric where they may come in contact with the feed dogs.

Thread for general-purpose sewing is suitable for most home decorator projects. Use an all-purpose weight. Choose all-cotton, all-polyester, or cotton-wrapped polyester thread that matches the fiber content of the fabric. For balanced tension, use the same type of thread in the bobbin and the needle.

Thread the machine correctly; incorrect threading can cause a stitch to be too loose or too tight. To rethread the machine, remove the spool completely and begin again, in case the thread has tangled in the tension or over the spool pin.

Use a scrap of fabric to test the tension, pressure, and stitch length before starting to sew. To check the balance of the tension, you may want to thread the machine with different colors for upper and bobbin threads so the stitches are easier to see.

Perfect Straight & Zigzag Stitching

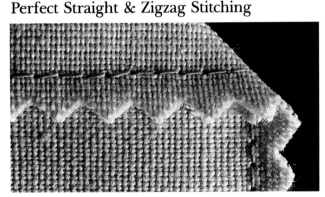

Straight stitches should link midway between fabric layers so stitches are the same length on both sides of fabric. Adjust tension and pressure so stitches do not break easily and the seam does not pucker.

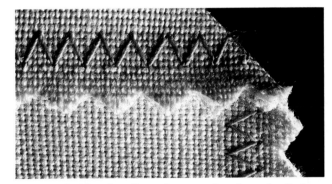

Zigzag stitching is adjusted correctly when the links interlock at the corner of each stitch. Stitches should lie flat. Adjust the zigzag width and density with the stitch length and width regulators.

Machine Stitching Terms

Bastestitching (a) is the longest straight stitch on the machine: 6 on the inch scale, 4 on the metric scale, and 9 on the numerical scale. Some sewing machines have a separate built-in bastestitch **(b)** that makes two stitches to the inch (2.5 cm). Use it for speed-basting straight seams.

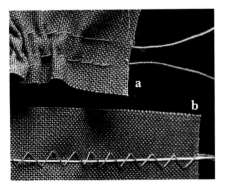

Gathering stitch is done with two rows of bastestitching placed ½" (1.3 cm) and ¼" (6 mm) from the fabric edge. Loosen tension, use heavier bobbin thread, and pull up bobbin thread to form gathers **(a)**. For long areas of gathers, zigzag over cord, string, or dental floss without catching cord in the stitch **(b)**. Pull up cord to gather.

Edgestitching is placed on the edge of a hem or fold. The straight-stitch foot and straight-stitch needle plate aid in the close control needed for this stitching. The narrow foot rides on the folded edge, and the small hole of the needle plate keeps fragile fabric from being drawn into the feed dogs.

Basic Seams & Techniques

All seams in home decorator sewing are ½" (1.3 cm) unless otherwise specified. To secure seams, backstitch at each end of the seam by stitching in reverse for ½" (1.3 cm). Four seam techniques are used in home decorator sewing.

1) Plain seam is suitable for almost every fabric and sewing application when you plan to enclose the seam or cover it with a lining.

2) French seam eliminates raw edges in exposed seams. Use it whenever a seam is visible on the wrong side or is subjected to frequent laundering.

3) Interlocking fell or self-bound seam, like the French seam, completely encloses raw edges. For this seam, sew on the wrong side of the fabric. Use the narrow hemmer attachment as a timesaver.

4) Overedge or zigzag seams are plain seams with a zigzag finish to prevent raveling. Use them on heavy, textured fabrics that are too bulky for French or self-bound seams. Or use an overlock or serger seam, and allow ¼" (6 mm) seam allowances.

Long straight seams tend to pucker in some fabrics. To prevent this, use taut sewing, pulling equally on the fabric in front of and in back of the needle, and let fabric feed through the machine on its own. Do not stretch.

Ruffles are used often in home decorating. There are three easy ways to do this, as shown on page 30. Other sewing techniques sometimes needed are applying ribbon or trim (page 31), mitering corners (page 32), and making bias strips (page 32) and double welting (page 33).

How to Sew a Plain Seam

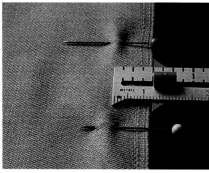

1) Pin right sides of fabric together, placing pins at right angles to seam line for easy removal. If using basting tape, place it at the raw edge and do not stitch through it.

2) Use seam guide to sew even seams. Backstitch to secure; then stitch seam, removing pins as you come to them. Backstitch at end of seam. Lift presser foot and remove fabric by pulling 2" to 3" (5 to 7.5 cm) of thread to the left.

3) Clip threads close to the end of seam. Press seam open or to one side. If seam is on the selvage, clip selvage diagonally every 1" to 6" (2.5 to 15 cm) to prevent the seam from puckering.

How to Sew a French Seam

1) Pin fabric *wrong* sides together. Stitch a scant ¼" (6 mm) seam. Press seam allowance to one side. For narrower finished seam, trim seam allowance to ⅛" (3 mm).

2) Turn fabric panels right sides together to enclose the trimmed seam allowance. Stitching line should be exactly on fold.

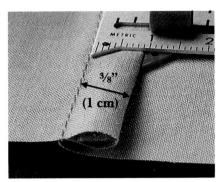

3) Stitch ⅜" (1 cm) from folded edge, enclosing first seam. Press the seam to one side. If first seam was trimmed, stitch ¼" (6 mm) from the edge.

How to Sew an Interlocking Fell Seam

1) Pin fabric, right sides together, with edge of top layer ½" (1.3 cm) from edge of bottom layer. Stitch ¾" (2 cm) from edge of bottom fabric layer.

2) Fold and press ¼" (6 mm) on seam allowance of bottom layer so that it meets edge of top layer. Fold and press again, covering the stitching line.

3) Edgestitch close to fold. Press seam to one side, holding fabric taut to eliminate puckering. Or use narrow hemmer for final stitching (page 34).

Three Ways to Sew an Overedge Seam

Zigzag plain seam. Stitch ½" (1.3 cm) plain seam. Zigzag seam allowances together close to raw edge. This eliminates trimming the seam, but results in a wider seam. Press seam to one side. This is the easiest overedge seam to sew and is suitable for most fabrics.

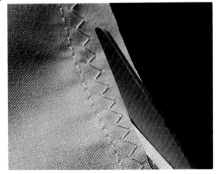

Zigzag narrow seam. Stitch ½" (1.3 cm) plain seam. Zigzag seam allowances together, stitching with wide zigzag close to stitching. Trim seam allowances close to zigzag stitching. This seam requires time for trimming. It can be used as an alternative to French seams.

Overedge seam. Trim seams to ¼" (6 mm) before stitching. Then stitch seam with built-in overedge stitch. This makes a straight seam and zigzags over cut edge in one step. Use this seam on medium to heavyweight fabrics which ravel.

Three Ways to Gather Ruffles

Zigzag. Stitch ⅜" (1 cm) from raw edge over a strong, thin cord such as string, crochet cotton, or dental floss. Use wide zigzag setting so cord does not get caught in stitching. Pull up cord to gather.

Ruffler attachment. Make a test strip, and adjust ruffler to desired fullness. Measure test strip before and after stitching to determine length of fabric needed. Before ruffling lightweight fabrics, zigzag ⅜" (1 cm) from edge with widest zigzag to give ruffler teeth something to grasp.

Shirring foot. 1) This foot is designed to lock fullness into every stitch, assuring evenly spaced shirring. Set stitch length for a long stitch; the longer the stitch, the greater the fullness. Use balanced tension.

2) Tighten tension, and hold index finger behind presser foot for more fullness with shirring foot. Fabric piles up against finger. Release finger, and repeat until entire edge is gathered.

How to Sew and Attach a Ruffle with a Heading

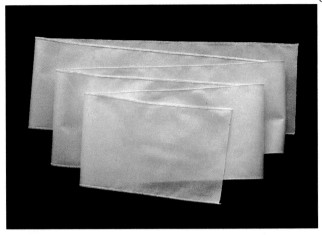

1) Hem both edges of strip to be ruffled with narrow double hem or overlock rolled hem. Use narrow hemming foot for ⅛" (3 mm) hem.

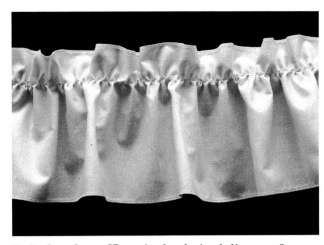

2) Gather the ruffle strip the desired distance from upper edge, using any gathering technique opposite.

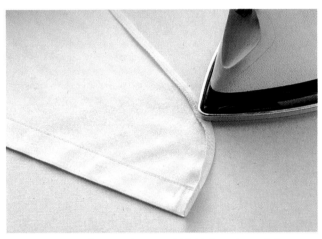

3) Overlock edge, and press ½" (1.3 cm) to right side. Or turn and stitch double ¼" (6 mm) hem on *right* side of the edge where ruffle will be applied.

4) Place wrong side of ruffle on right side of the fabric, with the gathering line on the hemline. Stitch ruffle in place. Allow extra fullness at corners.

How to Apply Ribbon

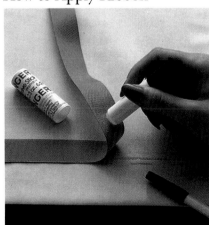

1) Mark trim location, using marking pen with water-soluble or disappearing ink. Use glue stick to hold trim in position.

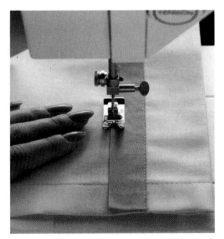

2) Stitch both sides of the ribbon trim in the same direction to prevent diagonal wrinkles.

How to Apply Braid Trims

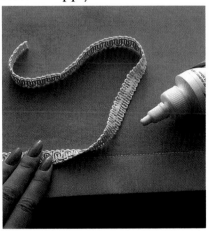

Glue a braid trim in place when stitching is not desirable.

How to Miter Corners on an Outside Edge

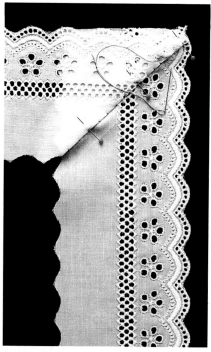

1) Place two lengths of trim, right sides together and edges even. Fold top trim at right angle to form diagonal at corner; press.

2) Slip-baste the two pieces together on the diagonal fold. Unfold trim.

3) Stitch on the line of slip basting on the wrong side. Trim the seams, and finish the edges.

How to Use a Bias Tape Maker

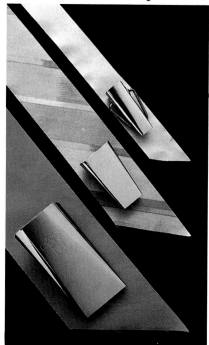

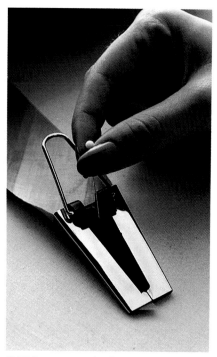

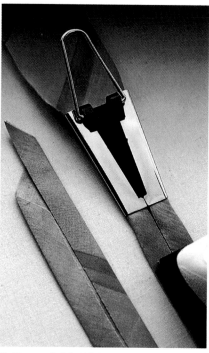

1) Cut bias strip scant 1" (2.5 cm) for ½" (1.3 cm) bias tape; cut 1⅞" (4.7 cm) for 1" (2.5 cm) tape; or 3¼" (8.2 cm) for 2" (5 cm) tape.

2) Trim one end of bias strip to a point. Thread point through wide end of tape maker, bringing point out at narrow end. Insert pin in slot to pull point through. Pin point to pressing surface.

3) Press folded bias strip as you pull tape maker the length of strip. Tape maker automatically folds raw edges to center of strip to create uniform bias tape.

How to Make Double Welting

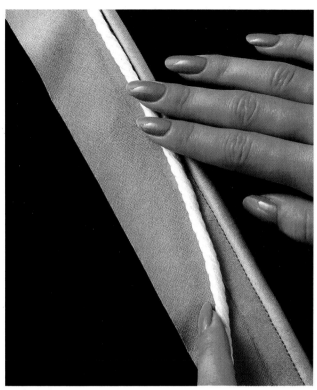

1) Place ⁵⁄₃₂" cording on wrong side of 3" (7.5 cm) fabric strip. Fold fabric over cording, with ½" (1.3 cm) seam allowance extending. Stitch with zipper foot next to cording.

2) Place second cording next to first welt. Bring fabric over second cording.

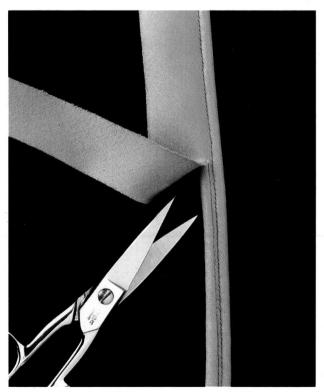

3) Stitch between the two cords on previous stitching line. Loosen tension and use zigzag foot riding on top of the welting.

4) Trim off excess fabric next to stitching for clean edge finish. Raw edge is on the back of the finished double welting.

Timesaving Accessories

Many home decorator sewing projects require long seams or hems. There are several machine attachments and special feet that speed hemming, binding, ruffling and straight stitching. Some of these accessories come with the machine; others are available from your machine dealer.

Before buying special-purpose attachments, find out if your machine has a high, low or slanted shank. Consult the machine manual if you are not sure what type of shank your machine has. Snap-on presser feet will fit any machine with a snap-on, all-purpose shank.

Special-purpose foot is used for decorative stitching and machine embroidery. The plastic foot lets you see the stitching easily, and a groove under the foot allows for a build-up of thread. Use the foot for general-purpose sewing and special tasks such as closely-spaced zigzag overedge.

Zipper and cording foot is used for inserting zippers, applying snap tape and for making and applying cording. It adjusts to either side of the needle, allowing stitching to be placed close to bulk on one side of the seam.

Even Feed™ foot feeds top and bottom layers of fabric at the same rate, ensuring that seams start and end evenly. This foot helps keep plaids and other matched designs aligned in long seams. Use on heavy, bulky or quilted fabrics, as with insulated shades.

Narrow hemmer automatically double-folds the fabric edge and stitches a ⅛" (3 mm) hem without pressing or pinning. The foot is useful for hemming and for stitching interlocking fell seams.

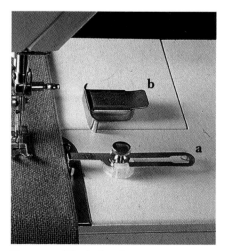

Seam guide helps keep seam allowances even. It attaches to the bed of the machine (a) and adjusts for seam widths up to 1¼" (3.2 cm). A magnetic seam guide (b) attaches to any metal machine bed.

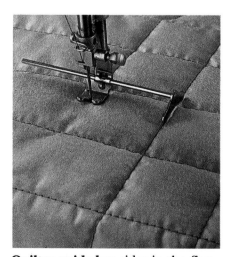

Quilter guide-bar rides in the first row of stitching to form perfectly parallel quilting lines. Use it for topstitching or channel quilting. The bar adjusts to widths up to 3" (7.5 cm) and can be used on either side of the needle.

Ruffler Attachment

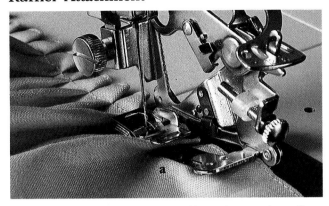

Ruffler attachment automatically gathers strips of light or mediumweight fabric. Stitch length affects fullness; short stitches give more fullness and longer stitches give less. Gather one layer of fabric (a).

Or gather one layer and attach it to another layer of fabric in one step (b). Insert fullness at every stitch, or at 6 or 12-stitch intervals. Use this attachment for ruffles on curtains, pillows or dust ruffles.

Blindstitch Hem Foot & Guide

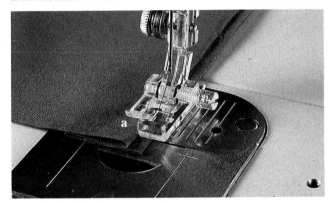

Blindstitch hem foot is used with the built-in blind hemming stitch. The foot (a) positions the hem for sewing with straight and zigzag stitches which are

barely visible on the right side. Blindstitch hem guide (b) is used with the general-purpose foot to position the hem for blindstitching.

Binder Attachment

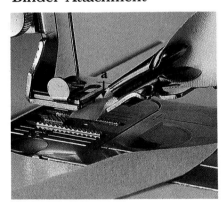

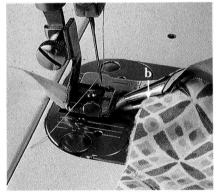

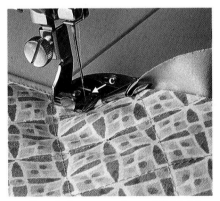

Binder attachment is used to fold and attach bias bindings in one step. First, cut a sharp point at end of bias strip. Feed the point through scroll on foot (a). Pull point through

so strip folds to the inside. Sew a few stitches to hold bias fold in place. Insert fabric to be bound into slot between scroll edges (b). Adjust position of foot so that

needle stitches on edge of fold (c). Guide fabric gently as you stitch. Use the binder attachment for finishing edges of any fabric.

35

Hand Stitching

Almost all sewing for home decorator projects can be done on the machine, but sometimes hand stitching is necessary. Closing seam openings on pillows, attaching trims and finishing hems are tasks which may require delicate hand sewing.

To make hand stitching easier, run the thread through beeswax to make it stronger and prevent it from snarling. Use a long needle for the running stitch. Hemming and tacking are usually easier with a short needle.

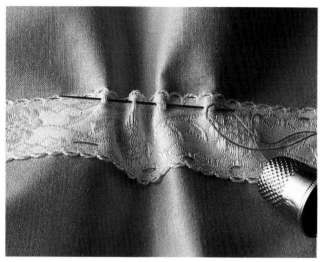

Running stitch is a straight stitch used for temporary basting, easing, gathering or stitching seams. Work from right to left, taking several stitches onto needle before pulling it through. For easing or gathering or for seams, make stitches ⅛" to ¼" (3 to 6 mm) long. For basting, make stitches ½" to ¾" (1.3 to 2 cm) long; use longer stitches for speed-basting.

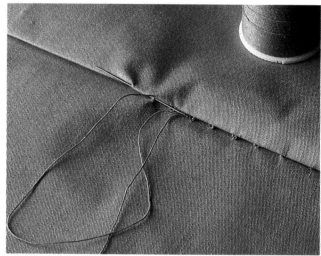

Slipstitch is a nearly invisible stitch for hems, seam openings, linings or trims. Work from right to left, holding folded edge in left hand. Bring needle up through fold and pull thread through. Then take a tiny stitch in body of fabric, directly opposite point where thread came out. Continue taking stitches every ¼" (6 mm).

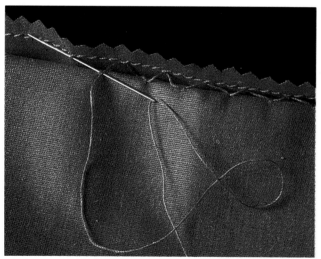

Blindstitch makes a hem that is inconspicuous from either side. Work from right to left with needle pointing left. Take a tiny stitch in body of fabric. Roll hem edge back slightly and take next stitch in underside of hem, ¼" to ½" (6 mm to 1.3 cm) to left of first stitch. Do not pull thread too tightly.

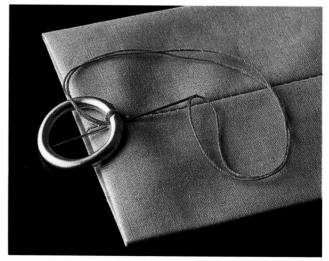

Tacking is used to attach rings and weights, secure linings or hold facings in place. Using double thread, take two or three stitches in the same place, one on top of the other. Secure with a backstitch. When tacking through more than one layer of fabric, do not sew through to outside layer.

Padded Work Surface

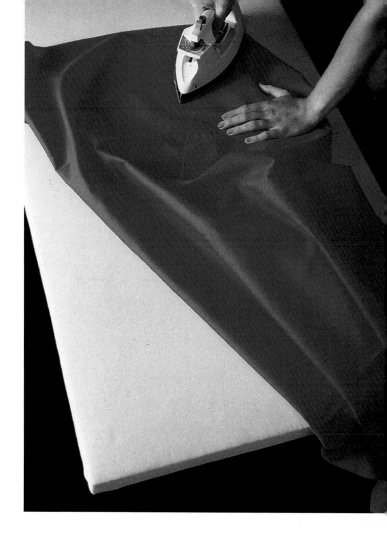

Make a padded work surface to lay out an entire panel for cutting, measuring, squaring off ends and pressing. The square corners and ample width make it easier to work with square and rectangular shapes. Fabric does not slide on the muslin-covered surface; you can also pin into it and press directly on it.

For small projects, use the *square* end of a regular ironing board as a work surface.

Use a steam-spray iron for all your pressing needs. To press fabric, lift and lower the iron in one place. This up-and-down motion prevents fabrics from stretching or distorting. Let the steam do the work. To make sharp creases or to smooth a stubborn wrinkle, spray the fabric with water or spray sizing.

YOU WILL NEED

Hollow door or ¾" (2 cm) plywood, approximately 3' × 7' (.95 × 2.16 m), set on saw horses.

Padding, cotton batting (not polyester), table pads or blankets, ¼" to ½" (6 mm to 1.3 cm) thick, enough to overlap door or plywood 6" (15 cm) on all sides.

Muslin or unpatterned sheet, approximately 6" (15 cm) larger than door or plywood on all sides.

How to Make a Padded Work Surface

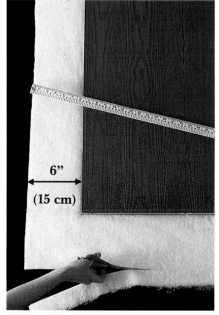

1) Place layers of padding on the floor or on a large, flat surface. Center the door on top of the padding; cut padding 6" (15 cm) larger than the door on all sides.

2) Fold padding over one long edge of the door and tack with 4 or 5 staples. Pull padding on opposite edge and tack. Repeat on both ends. Secure with staples 3" (7.5 cm) apart.

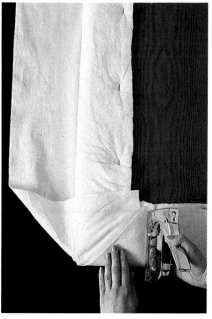

3) Center padded door on top of muslin. Wrap and fasten with staples 3" (7.5 cm) apart. Turn right side up and spray muslin with water. As it dries, muslin shrinks slightly so cover fits tightly.

Windows

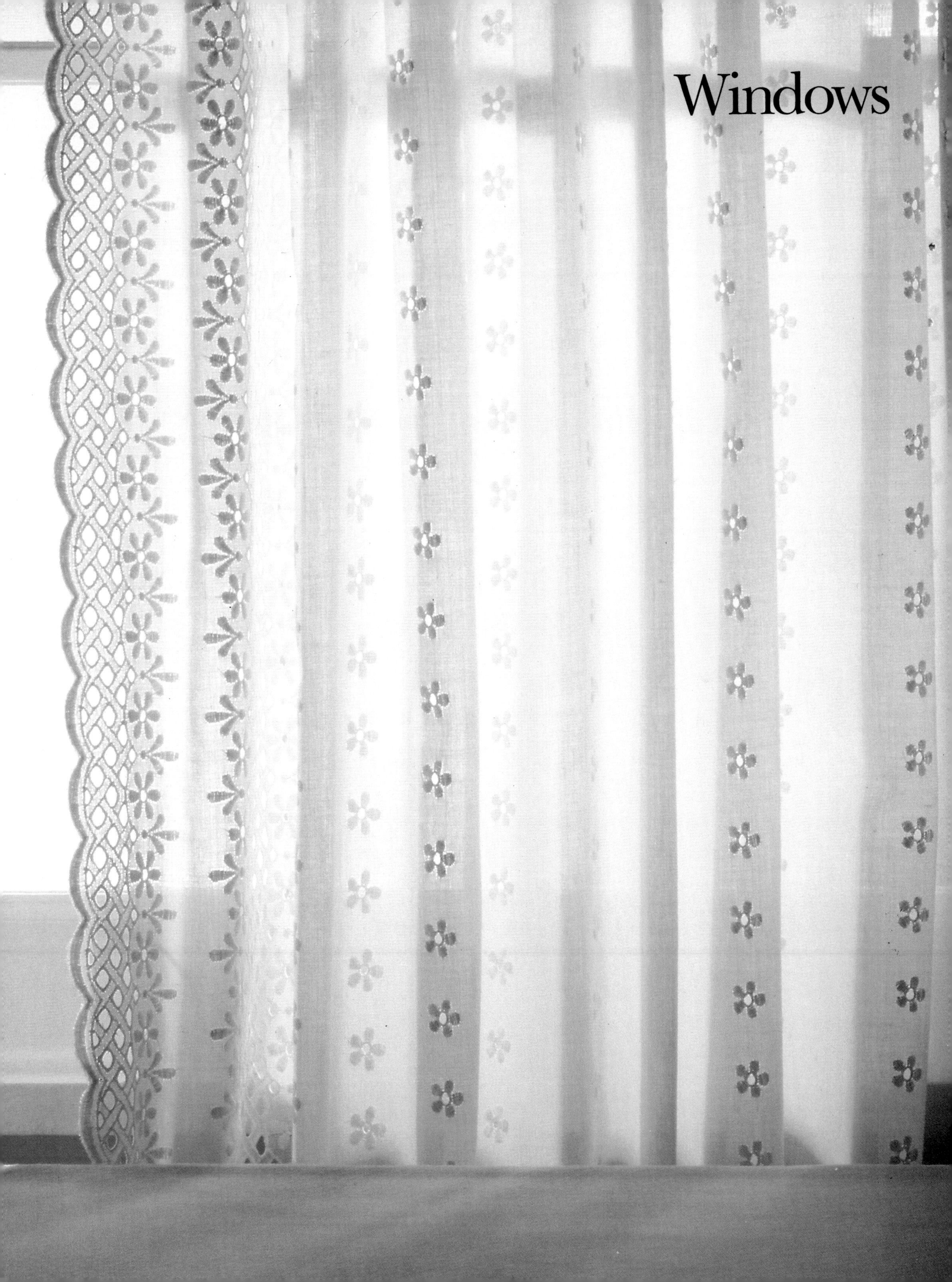

Hardware

Select the drapery hardware before measuring for the window treatment, because the cut length of the fabric will vary, depending on the drapery rods.

Support drapery rods with brackets to prevent the rods from bowing in the middle. The brackets are usually positioned at intervals of 45" (115 cm) or less, across the width of the window. Whenever possible, screw the brackets into wall studs. Use molly bolts if it is necessary to install brackets between wall studs into drywall or plaster.

How to Install a Drapery Rod Bracket Between Wall Studs Using Molly Bolts

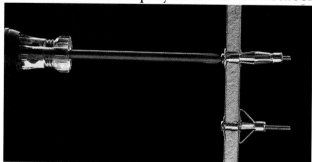

1) Hold drapery rod bracket at desired placement; mark hole locations. Drill 5/16" (7.5 mm) holes into drywall or plaster; for heavy window treatments, use two molly bolts for each bracket. Tap long molly bolt into drilled hole. Tighten screw; molly bolt expands as it is tightened.

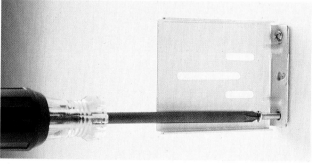

2) Remove screw from molly bolt; insert screw into drapery rod bracket. Align screw to installed molly bolt. Screw bracket securely in place.

Basic Rods

Curtain rods **(a)** are used for simple rod-pocket curtains and valances. When lace or sheer fabric is used, select a curtain rod of clear or opaque plastic to prevent it from showing through and detracting from the fabric.

Wide curtain rods **(b),** known as Continental® and Dauphine® rods, available in both 2½" (6.5 cm) and 4½" (11.5 cm) widths, add depth and interest to the rod pockets of shirred curtains and top treatments. Corner connectors are used to make these rods suitable for bay windows and corner windows. The connectors allow you to sew a continuous window treatment, without interruptions or breaks in the treatment at the corners.

Flexible ⅜" (1 cm) plastic tubing **(c),** found in the plumbing department of hardware stores, can be shaped to fit the curve of arch windows.

Decorative Pole Sets

Contemporary metal pole sets **(d),** or Cirmosa® pole sets, can be used for multiple-rod treatments, such as the rod-sleeve valances on page 90. These drapery rods, also available for traverse draperies, have metallic and pearlized finishes in several colors.

Traditional brass pole sets **(e)** come in various sizes and finial styles. Brass hardware is used for rod-pocket curtains and valances as well as with draped swags or pole swags. Brass rods in smaller diameters can be bent for use in bay windows.

Wood pole sets **(f)** with plain or fluted poles are available in finished or unfinished wood. Finials in various styles give the wood poles a decorator look. The poles and finials may be covered with fabric, or painted.

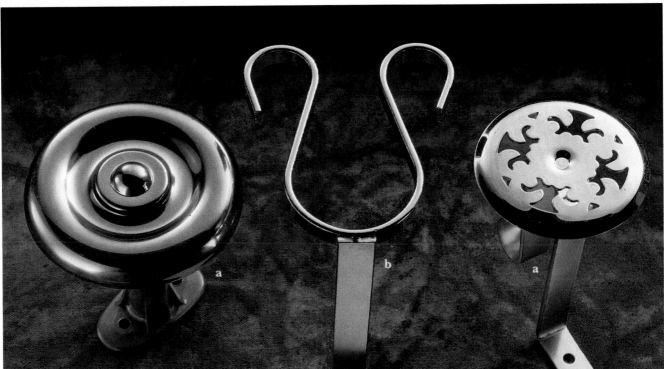

Drapery accessories are used to secure the draped fabric in swag window treatments and in tieback draperies. Tieback holders **(a)** with projection arms or stems are used instead of fabric tiebacks to hold curtains in place. They may also be used for scarf swag window treatments (page 67). Swag holders **(b)** are also used for scarf swags when rosettes are desired.

Covering & Installing Mounting Boards

Some window treatments are mounted on boards instead of being hung on drapery rods. For a professional look, cover the mounting board with fabric. This gives it a more finished appearance and protects the window treatment from being snagged by unfinished wood.

The mounting board is cut to the finished width of the window treatment and may be mounted inside or outside the window frame. For an inside mount, the board is attached inside the window frame, using #8 gauge 1½" (3.8 cm) pan-head screws. Predrill the holes for the screws, using a ⅛" (3 mm) drill bit.

For an outside mount, the board is installed at the top of the window frame or on the wall above the window. For clearance, the board is cut wider than the outside measurement of the window frame or undertreatment, and it projects out from the wall farther than the window frame or undertreatment. Angle irons are used to install the mounting board. The angle irons must be a little shorter than the width of the mounting board. Whenever possible, screw the angle irons into wall studs, using pan-head screws and predrilling the holes for the screws, using a ⅛" (3 mm) drill bit. If it is necessary to install angle irons between wall studs into drywall or plaster, use molly bolts to ensure a secure installation. To prevent the mounting board from bowing in the middle, position angle irons at 45" (115 cm) intervals or less.

Supplies include mounting board (**a**), angle irons (**b**), pan-head screws (**c**), and molly bolts (**d**).

How to Determine the Size of the Mounting Board

Inside mount. Cut 1" × 1" (2.5 × 2.5 cm) mounting board ½" (1.3 cm) shorter than inside measurement of window frame, to ensure that the board will fit inside the frame after it is covered with fabric.

Outside mount. Cut mounting board 2" (5 cm) longer than width of undertreatment or window frame and at least 2" (5 cm) wider than projection of undertreatment or window frame.

How to Cover the Mounting Board with Fabric

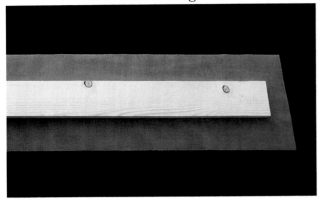

1) Cut fabric to cover mounting board, with width of fabric equal to distance around board plus 1" (2.5 cm) and length of fabric equal to length of board plus 4½" (11.5 cm). Center board on wrong side of fabric.

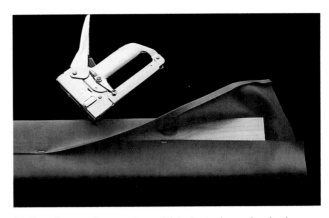

2) Staple one long edge of fabric to board, placing staples about 8" (20.5 cm) apart; do not staple within 6" (15 cm) of ends. Wrap fabric around board; fold under ⅜" (1 cm) on long edge, and staple to board, placing staples about 6" (15 cm) apart.

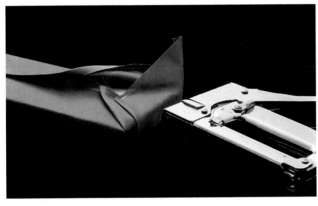

3) Miter fabric at corners on side of board with unfolded edge of fabric; finger-press. Staple miters in place near raw edge.

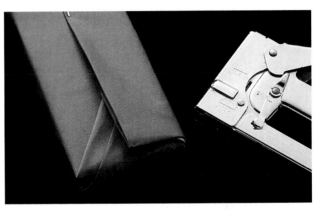

4) Miter fabric at corner on side of board with folded edge of fabric; finger-press. Fold excess fabric under at end of board; staple near fold.

How to Install a Mounting Board Using Angle Irons

1) Screw angle irons into covered mounting board, using #8 gauge ¾" (2 cm) pan-head screws. Hold board at desired placement, making sure that it is level; mark screw holes on wall or window frame, using pencil.

2) Remove angle irons from board. Secure angle irons to wall, using ⅛" (3 mm) L (long) molly bolts (page 40) or ¾" (2 cm) pan-head screws.

3) Mount window treatment onto mounting board, using staples. Place mounting board on installed angle irons. Screw angle irons into mounting board.

Curtain Basics

Curtains are a traditional favorite for window fashions. They are flat, nonpleated panels, so they are easier to clean and press than many other window treatments.

Curtains are often made of lightweight or sheer fabrics. Heavier fabrics such as linen, chintz, or textured or polished cotton look best for formal, floor-length curtains. Lighter, crisper fabrics work well for casual, sill-length, and cafe curtains. Sheer curtains are usually two and one-half to three times the fullness of the finished width; heavier fabrics require only double fullness.

Mount curtains at windows on stationary rods or poles. Rods may be plain, covered with shirred fabric between the curtain panels, or wide and flat such as Continental® and cornice rods. Take window measurements (page 20) after style and hardware have been selected.

Casings, also known as rod pockets, are hems stitched in place along the upper edge of curtains. The hems are open at both ends so a curtain rod or pole can be inserted. This is the most common way to hang curtains, cafe curtains, and valances (page 80).

Headings are optional on curtains. The heading creates a decorative ruffle above the casing along the upper edge of the curtain. It may be done in contrasting fabric or include binding on the top edge.

Linings add weight and body to curtains. Although a lining may not be necessary, it can improve a curtain's appearance, give it a custom look, protect it from fading, and provide some insulation.

Tie top curtains (page 51) have fabric ties instead of a casing along the upper edge. These curtains are used with decorative brass or wooden poles.

Ruffled curtains have a graceful appearance. Ruffles may be added to many curtain styles and may have a heading or be plain.

Tiebacks (page 62) are separate fabric strips that hold curtains open and emphasize the drape of the curtain. Tiebacks can be straight, shaped, or ruffled and are usually stationary on panel curtains.

Shower curtains (page 104) are flat, one-piece, hemmed curtains with evenly spaced holes along the upper edge for hanging with hooks or rings.

Shirred pole covers (page 47) can be used to cover a plain pole that shows between curtain panels. They can be made with or without a heading and should match the casing or heading on the curtain panels.

Hourglass curtains (page 54) for door windows have casings both top and bottom and are stretched between sash rods. Add a rosette (page 65). Cafe curtains can also be made this way.

Casing Styles for Curtains

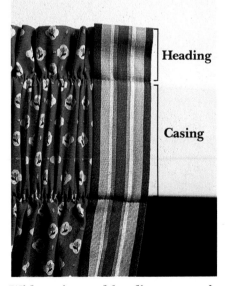

Simple casing is stitched along the upper edge of the curtain. It may be used for sheer curtains that hang behind draperies, a valance or cornice.

Heading creates a ruffled edge above casing. Headings are from 1" to 5" (2.5 to 12.5 cm) deep, depending on curtain length and weight of the fabric.

Wide casing and heading are used with a Continental or cornice rod. They are well suited for floor-length curtains, where casing and heading depth should balance with curtain length.

How to Sew a Simple Casing

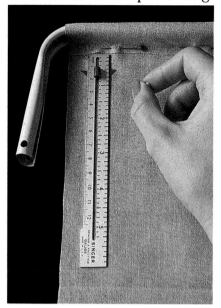

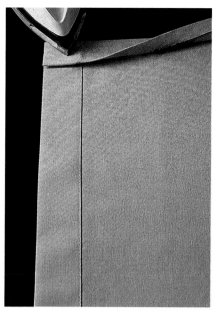

1) Determine casing depth by loosely pinning a curtain fabric strip around the rod. Remove rod and measure the distance from the top of the strip to the pin. Add ½" (1.3 cm) to be turned under.

2) Press under ½" (1.3 cm) along upper cut edge of curtain panel. Fold over again and press to form a hem equal to amount measured in step 1.

3) Stitch close to folded hem edge to form casing, backstitching at both ends. If desired, stitch again close to the upper edge to create a sharp crease appropriate for flat or oval curtain rods.

How to Sew a Casing with a Heading

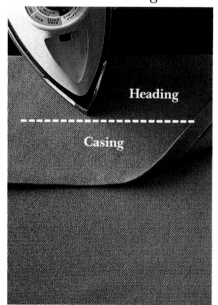

1) Determine the depth of the casing as directed in step 1, above. Determine the depth of heading, opposite. Press under ½" (1.3 cm) along upper cut edge of the curtain panel. Fold and press again to form hem equal to casing plus heading depth.

2) Stitch close to folded edge, backstitching at both ends. Mark heading depth with a pin at each end of panel. Stitch again at marked depth. To aid straight stitching, apply a strip of masking tape to the bed of the machine at heading depth, or use seam guide.

3) Insert rod through casing and gather curtain evenly onto rod. Adjust heading by pulling up the folded edge so the seam is exactly on the lower edge of the rod. A wide heading may be made to look puffy and more rounded by pulling the fabric out on each side.

How to Sew a Continental® or Cornice Rod Casing with a Heading

1) Measure window after rod has been installed to determine total length. Add 15½" (39.3 cm): 5½" (14 cm) for the casing and seam allowance, 8" (20.5 cm) for the double-fold hem, and 2" (5 cm) for 1" (2.5 cm) heading. For a deeper heading, add twice the desired heading depth.

2) Turn under ½" (1.3 cm) on upper edge of curtain and press. Fold over again 6" (15 cm) for casing and heading. Stitch 1" (2.5 cm) from upper folded edge to form heading. Stitch close to folded edge to form casing.

3) Insert rod through casing and gather curtain evenly onto rod. Hang on installed brackets. For a wide heading, use two Continental or cornice rods, installed one above the other. Add 10" (25.5 cm) for second casing.

How to Make a Shirred Pole Cover

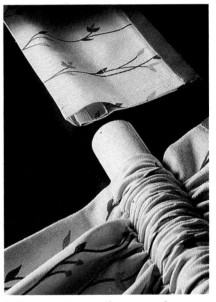

1) Cut fabric two and one-half times the length of pole area to be covered; cut width equal to circumference of pole plus 1½" (3.8 cm). For pole cover with a heading, add amount equal to twice the heading depth.

2) Stitch ½" (1.3 cm) hems on short ends. Fold strip in half lengthwise, right sides together, and pin long edges together. Stitch ½" (1.3 cm) seam. Press seam open. Turn cover right side out.

3) Press cover so that seam is at back of pole. To form heading, stitch again at appropriate distance from upper folded edge. If desired, add narrow binding to upper edge, opposite. Gather pole cover onto rod between two curtain panels.

Customizing Casing-top Curtains

Bindings, borders, ribbon or contrasting returns give casings individuality and style. These decorative touches customize casings and require little additional sewing time.

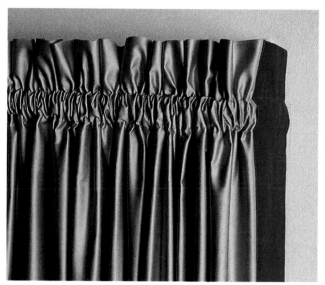

Contrasting returns. Cut fabric strips the width of return plus 1" (2.5 cm), and the cut length of curtain. Allow for ½" (1.3 cm) side seam on one edge of the curtain. Press under ½" (1.3 cm) on one long edge of strip. Pin right side of strip to wrong side of curtain, unpressed raw edges even; stitch. Press strip to right side; fuse or edgestitch edge to right side of curtain. Finish curtain.

Narrow binding. Construct basic curtain. Cut 2½" (6.5 cm) strip of fabric with length equal to finished width of panel plus 1" (2.5 cm). Press under ½" (1.3 cm) on one long side and each short end. Pin unpressed edge to upper edge of curtain, right sides together; stitch. Press folded edge of binding over upper edge. From right side, stitch in the ditch.

Edgestitched ribbon banding. Cut fabric trims two times the finished width of banding, length equal to cut length of curtain. Press and stitch 1" (2.5 cm) double-fold side hems on curtain. Press trim, wrong sides together and raw edges meeting at center. Pin trim with outer edge covering side hem stitching line. Edgestitch trim close to folded edges. Finish curtain.

Fused border. Construct basic curtain. Cut fabric trim two times the width of finished band, and the finished length of curtain plus 1" (2.5 cm). Press trim wrong sides together and raw edges meeting at center; press under ½" (1.3 cm) on short ends. Cut strips of fusible web slightly narrower than finished trim; insert between curtain and trim. Fuse in place.

Hems

If you have measured, figured and cut accurately, your curtains should fit windows perfectly once they are hemmed. For the neatest and easiest hems, follow the procedure used in professional workrooms: sew the lower hems first, the side hems next, and casings and headings last.

Side and lower hems of unlined curtains are almost always double to provide strength, weight and stability. The easiest way to make a double-fold hem is to press it in place on an ironing board or padded work surface. Use a seam gauge to measure each fold. As you make the fold, pin the fabric to the padding, placing the pins so they do not interfere with pressing. If side edges are on the selvage, cut off selvage or clip it every 1" to 6" (2.5 to 15 cm).

Curtains hang better when hems are weighted or anchored. Sew small weights into the hems at the lower corners and bottoms of seams to keep the curtain from pulling or puckering. Use heavier weights for full-length curtains, lighter weights for lightweight fabrics and shorter curtains.

How to Sew Double-fold Hems

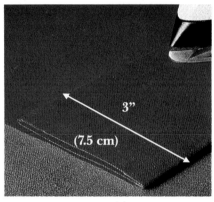

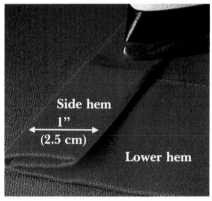

1) Turn a scant 3" (7.5 cm) to wrong side on lower edge of curtain. Pin along cut edge. Press fold. Turn under another 3" (7.5 cm), pin and press in place. Finish lower hem using one of the methods below.

2) Turn a scant 1" (2.5 cm) to the wrong side for side hems. Pin and press. Fold under another 1" (2.5 cm); pin and press. Tack weights inside the second fold at side corners, if desired.

3) Press the side hems in place. When the hems have been pressed, finish them with straight stitching, machine blindstitching or fusible web.

Three Ways to Finish Curtain Hems

Straight-stitch on folded hem edge, using 8 to 10 stitches per inch (2.5 cm). When stitching three layers of fabric, lessen pressure slightly and stitch slowly.

Machine blindstitch to make stitches almost invisible on right side. After pressing, fold hem back to right side, leaving a fold of fabric ⅛" (3 mm) from hem edge. Set machine to blindstitch. Adjust zigzag stitch to take tiny bite into curtain only.

Fuse hem in place. Tuck strip of fusible web between pressed hem and curtain. Follow manufacturer's instructions for fusing, using damp press cloth for additional steam. Most fusibles require 15 seconds for permanent bonding.

Flip Top Curtains

To create this one-piece curtain that looks as if it has a separate valance, select fabric with no apparent right or wrong side. For sheer and lightweight fabrics, use triple fullness across the window. To save time, do not piece panels together; using the full fabric width, sew each panel separately. Install all the panels on a single curtain rod or pole, arranging the sides of the panels so they fall inside the draped fabric folds.

To determine the length of each curtain panel, add a total of 24" (61 cm) to the finished length, measured from the top of the rod. This amount includes allowances for a 2" (5 cm) heading, and a rod pocket casing 2" (5 cm) deep to fit a 1½" (3.8 cm) diameter curtain rod. The finished length of the valance from heading to hem is 14" (35.5 cm).

To prepare each panel for the flip top heading, make double side hems. If the selvages have a finished look, side hems can be omitted on the inner panels.

How to Make a Flip Top Heading

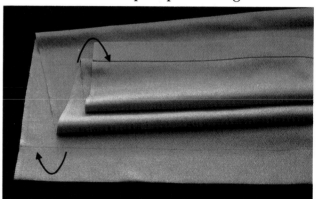

1) Stitch a double hem toward *right* side at top of curtain panel. Stitch a double hem toward *wrong* side at lower edge of curtain.

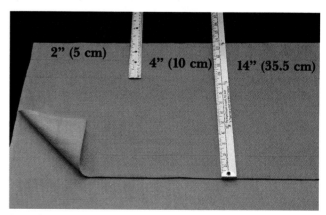

2) Fold top of panel over to right side to create valance 14" (35.5 cm) long. Mark stitching line 2" (5 cm) from fold for heading and 4" (10 cm) from fold for rod pocket. Stitch on marked lines.

Tie Top Curtains

Refreshingly casual, a tied heading is appropriate for sill-length or full-length curtains. Make ties from matching or coordinating fabric, or save time by using 1½" to 2" (3.8 to 5 cm) wide ribbon.

For the curtain, use 1½ to 2 times the finished width for fabric fullness. To determine the finished length, measure from bottom of the rod to the desired length. Allow enough extra fabric for double side and lower hems, plus ½" (1.3 cm) seam allowance at the top of each panel. Also cut a 4" (10 cm) facing as long as the finished width of the panel. To prepare each panel for the tie top heading, make double side hems and a double lower hem.

For each tie, you will need a 4" by 10" (10 by 25.5 cm) strip. Cut longer ties if you want to make bows instead of knots. Determine the number of ties needed by placing one pair at each end of a curtain panel, one pair in the center, and spacing the remaining pairs of ties at 6" to 8" (15 to 20.5 cm) intervals. Cut ties efficiently with a rotary cutter; cut 4" (10 cm) wide strips as long as possible; then cut the strips into separate ties.

How to Sew a Tie Top Heading

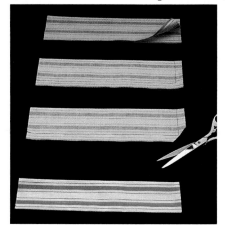

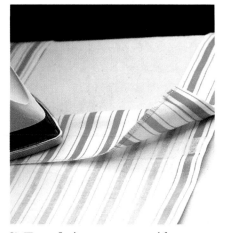

1) Fold strip lengthwise, right sides together, and stitch across one short end and along long edge with ½" (1.3 cm) seam allowance; or overlock. Use continuous stitching. Trim corner, turn right side out, and press.

2) Pin pairs of ties to right side of curtain with raw edges even. Overlock one long edge of facing, or hem with narrow hem. Pin facing strip over ties, with right sides of facing and curtain together. Stitch ½" (1.3 cm) seam at top of facing.

3) Turn facing to wrong side, so ties are free at upper edge. Fold raw edges of facing under ½" (1.3 cm) on each side. Fuse side and lower edges to curtain with fusible web.

Bishop Sleeve Curtains

These elegant pouffed curtains are simply rod pocket curtains with extra length allowed for blousing. The bishop sleeve look is achieved with tiebacks pulling the curtain tight to the window frame. Any number of poufs may be used. Arrange and tie the poufs at a position that is in proportion to the window length and width.

The poufs are balanced on each side of the tieback because the curtain rod extends 6" to 8" (15 to 20.5 cm) on each side of the window. If side space is limited, they may also hang straight on the outer edge, with the pouf draping only to the center of the window.

Tiebacks are tight on this curtain, in contrast to loose-fitting tiebacks on most curtain panels. For a decorative effect, use tasseled tiebacks or floppy bows with long streamers. Or use cord to tie the poufs so tiebacks do not show. As a finishing touch, the soft, flowing look of the bishop sleeve curtains can be repeated with puff or balloon valances (page 80).

✄ Cutting Directions

Cut panels 2 to 2½ times wider than finished width. To finished length, add 12" (30.5 cm) extra for each pouf and 12" (30.5 cm) more to puddle on the floor; add allowance for double top heading and rod pocket. Add 2" (5 cm) for double bottom hem if puddling on floor, or 8" (20.5 cm) for double bottom hem if curtains come to the floor.

YOU WILL NEED

Decorator fabric for curtains.

Tiebacks and cup hooks for each pouf.

Flat curtain rod or Continental® rod.

How to Sew a Bishop Sleeve Curtain

1) Turn under and stitch double 1" (2.5 cm) side hems. Turn under and stitch rod pocket and heading. Stitch double bottom hems.

2) Insert rod; hang and gather panels evenly. Determine location of poufs by tightly bunching the panel with your hands and lifting it to different positions until you find a pleasing proportion.

3) Mark tieback position. Attach cup hook behind pouf to hold tieback. Tissue paper can be tucked into the pouf to improve blousing if fabric does not have as much body as you would like.

Hourglass Curtains

Hourglass curtains take their name from their shape. They are held taut between sash rods at the top and bottom of the window glass, and then pulled in at the center to create the hourglass shape. Use tension rods, instead of sash rods, for mounting inside a window frame.

Because these curtains are held tight to the glass, they are a practical treatment for doors. They also work well on windows where there is not room for a return. They allow sunlight to get in and, for extra airiness, are attractive in lace and sheer fabrics.

You will need to take two length measurements: the length at the center of the curtain and the *adjusted* length at the sides. The adjusted length accommodates the pinching in of the fabric at the center of the window. Estimate 2" (5 cm) extra at the sides for every 12" (30.5 cm).

✂ Cutting Directions

Cut the fabric 2 to 2½ times the width of rod. Cut the length as measured in step 1, right. Add allowance for rod pockets and headings at top and bottom of curtain plus 1" (2.5 cm) to turn under.

YOU WILL NEED

Lightweight decorator fabric for curtains.

Two sash rods or tension rods; mount rods before measuring.

How to Sew an Hourglass Curtain

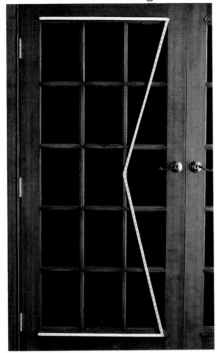

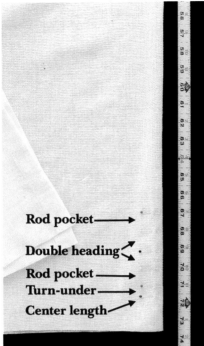

Rod pocket⟶

Double heading

Rod pocket⟶

Turn-under⟶

Center length⟶

1) Measure for side finished length. With a tape measure or string, plan the curve of the hourglass shape on the door or window. The narrowest part of hourglass should be no less than one-third the width of the glass.

2) Turn under and stitch double 1" (2.5 cm) side hems. Fold panel in half lengthwise; on the fold, mark the center finished length, plus rod pocket and heading allowance. Be sure markings are equal at both ends of fabric.

3) Mark a gentle curved line from side length at hemmed edge to center length about 3" (7.5 cm) from center fold. Line should not have any curve at the fold. Cut on marked line at top and bottom.

4) Stitch rod pockets and headings at top and bottom of curtain, easing in excess fullness. Insert sash rods.

5) Mount curtain. With string or tape measure, pull panel into hourglass shape at midpoint and measure for tieback. Add 2" (5 cm) for overlap. For tiebacks, see pages 62 to 64. To sew rosette, see page 65.

Rod-pocket Swags & Cascades

This swagged window treatment is not only easy to sew, but is also easier to install than most swags. Just insert the drapery rod into the rod pockets and adjust the gathers evenly. When a print fabric is used, choose one of the colors in the print as the accent color in the swags.

Swags may be used with or without cascades. Cascades add a more vertical appearance to the window treatment. When swags and cascades are used with underdraperies, make the cascades to match the draperies so they blend in, or make them from an accent color in the swags to contrast with the draperies.

Triple fullness is recommended for this window treatment. At this fullness, each cascade covers about 15" (38 cm) of the window width; each swag covers about 10" to 12" (25.5 to 30.5 cm) of the width. If you are not making cascades for the sides of the window, determine the number of swags you need by dividing the width of the window by 10" (25.5 cm); round up or down, if necessary, to the closest number. If you are making cascades, first subtract 30" (76 cm) from the width of the window; then divide the remaining width by 10" (25.5 cm) to determine the number of swags.

✂ Cutting Directions

To determine the depth of the rod pocket, add 1" (2.5 cm) ease to the width of the drapery rod. The cut length of each swag panel is equal to two times the desired finished length, two times the depth of the rod pocket, two times the depth of the heading, 3" (7.5 cm) for pouffing, and 1" (2.5 cm) for seam allowances.

One fabric width will make three swags. If two fabrics of different widths are being used, cut the wider fabric to the same width as the narrower one. Cut each fabric to the calculated length, and then cut lengthwise into thirds.

The short point of the cascades is equal to the finished length of the swags. The long point should be at least 12" (30.5 cm) longer than the short point, but may be two-thirds the length of the window, sill-length, or apron-length. If used with underdraperies, the long point is usually two-thirds the length of the draperies.

The cut length of the cascades is equal to the finished length at the long point, the depth of the rod pocket, the depth of the heading, and 2" (5 cm) for seam allowances. For each cascade, you will need one cut length of each of the two fabrics.

YOU WILL NEED

Decorator fabrics in two contrasting colors.

Flat drapery rod; projection of rod must be at least 2" (5 cm) more than projection of underdraperies or other undertreatment.

How to Sew Rod-pocket Swags

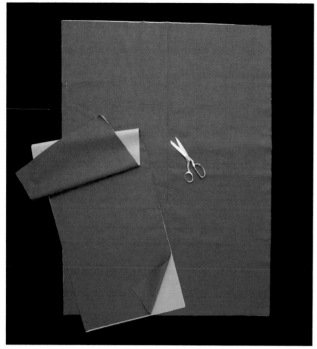

1) **Place** face fabric and lining right sides together. Mark width of fabric into three equal panels; cut.

2) **Stitch** panels of face fabric and lining together around all four sides in ½" (1.3 cm) seam, leaving 6" (15 cm) opening at upper edge for turning; trim corners. Turn right sides out; press.

3) **Measure** combined depth of rod pocket and heading from upper edge of panel; fold and press to lining side at this depth. Measure combined depth of rod pocket and heading from lower edge of panel; fold and press to face-fabric side at this depth.

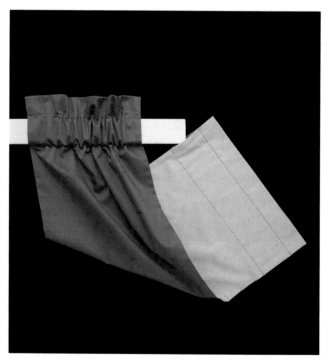

4) **Stitch** rod pockets. Insert drapery rod into rod pocket at upper edge. Then fold panel under, and insert drapery rod into rod pocket at lower edge. Repeat for remaining swag panels.

How to Sew Rod-pocket Cascades

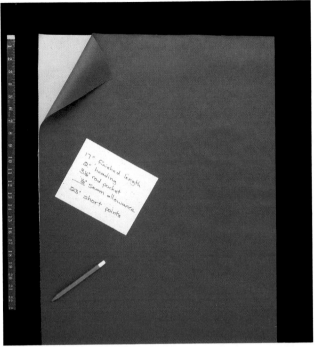

1) **Place** face fabric and lining right sides together. Determine length at short points by adding finished length of swag, depth of heading, depth of rod pocket, and ½" (1.3 cm) seam allowance. On inner sides of cascades, measure this distance from upper edge; mark short points.

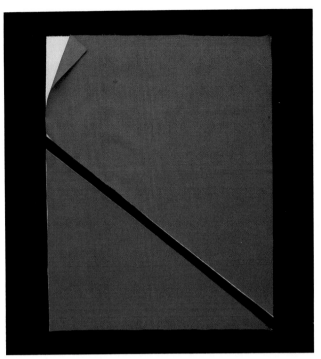

2) **Draw** a line on each cascade from marking for short point to lower edge of outer side, or long point. Cut on marked line.

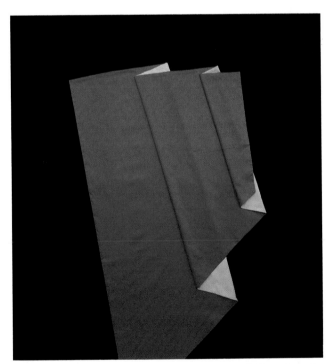

3) **Stitch** panels around all four sides in ½" (1.3 cm) seam, leaving 6" (15 cm) opening at upper edge for turning; trim corners. Turn right sides out; press.

4) **Measure** combined depth of rod pocket and heading from upper edges of cascades; fold and press to lining side at this depth. Stitch rod pockets. Insert drapery rod into rod pockets.

Pleated Draperies

Pleated draperies are easy to sew with pleater tape, which eliminates tedious, complicated measuring.

Pinch pleats are the traditional pleated heading for draperies. Each pinch pleat is actually three small pleats grouped together at regular intervals. Pleater tape for pinch pleats has evenly spaced pockets woven into it; special four-pronged pleater hooks inserted into the pockets draw up the pleats.

Select pleater tape that gives the desired drapery fullness. Some pleater tapes are designed to give an exact double fullness; others allow for more or less than double fullness, depending on how the pockets are used. Determine the drapery fullness (page 45) according to the fabric weight; lightweight fabrics require more fullness than heavy fabrics.

Panel draperies are stationary pleated panels that hang at the sides of the window.

Draw draperies can be closed to cover the entire width of the window. These draperies hang on traverse rods and pull open to one side only (one-way draw) or to both sides (two-way draw).

Before cutting fabric or tape, prepleat the *tape only* using pleater hooks to determine the finished width of the draperies and the pleat position. Pleat tape to the width of the drapery panel and hang it on the rod. Adjust pleats as necessary so the last pleat of the panel is at the corner of the rod return. Do not position pleats on the return or at the center of two-way draperies where panels overlap. Remove pleater hooks and measure tape to determine the finished width of drapery panels, as in steps 1 and 2, opposite.

✂ Cutting Directions

After pleating tape to correct size, cut pleater tape for each panel so that panels have pockets in the same position. Add ½" (1.3 cm) at each end of pleater tape for finishing.

Cut decorator fabric so width is the length of the pleater tape plus 4" (10 cm) to allow for 1" (2.5 cm) double-fold side hems. Seam fabric if necessary, allowing 1" (2.5 cm) for each seam. For length, cut fabric finished length, plus 6½" (16.3 cm) to allow for 3" (7.5 cm) double-fold hem and ½" (1.3 cm) for turning under on upper edge.

YOU WILL NEED

Decorator fabric for draperies.

Pleater tape to match style of heading.

Pleater hooks and end pins.

How to Sew Unlined Pinch-pleated Draperies

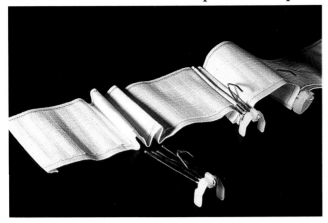

1) Prepleat pleater tape to finished width of drapery panel. Leave space unpleated at one end of tape for overlap and at other end for return.

2) Position the pleater tape on installed traverse rod and adjust pleats if necessary. Fold ends under ½" (1.3 cm). Remove hooks. Cut drapery panels using pleater tape as guide.

3) Turn under double-fold hem on lower edge and double-fold hems on sides; stitch. Mark ½" (1.3 cm) from upper edge on right side of drapery.

4) Pin upper edge of pleater tape, pocket side up, along marked line so that pleater tape overlaps drapery ½" (1.3 cm). Stitch ¼" (6 mm) from edge of pleater tape.

5) Fold pleater tape to inside of drapery so it is even with finished upper edge of drapery; press. Stitch lower edge and both sides of tape, following guideline on tape, if marked.

6) Insert hooks. Push prongs all the way up into pleats. Adjust folds between hooks.

Tiebacks

Jumbo welting tiebacks are a versatile change from traditional straight or tapered tiebacks. They can be braided, twisted, knotted, or shirred to coordinate with drapery and curtain panels. Piped tiebacks with a shirred insert are perfect coordinates with the soft, puffy look of bloused curtains or lightweight tieback panels.

Placing a tieback low gives a visual effect of widening the window; place it high to add height. The most popular positions are approximately one-third or two-thirds of the window height, or at the sill. If cafe curtains are used under the draperies or curtains, the tiebacks are most often held back at the level of the cafe rods.

To determine how long to make tiebacks, measure around the curtain by holding a tape measure loosely at the height you want the tieback. Add 1" (2.5 cm) to the length for seam allowances.

You can also estimate that for a pair of draperies, a tieback is half the rod width, plus 4" (10 cm). It is generally not a good idea to tie back a drapery that is wider than it is long. If a drapery is tied back, it should remain tied back as a stationary panel; wrinkles and folds take several days to fall out.

How to Sew Braided Tiebacks

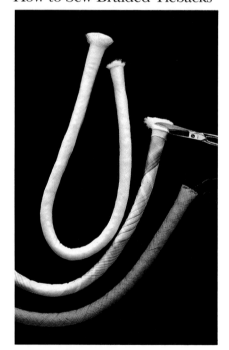

1) Cut cording 3 times the finished length of tieback; cut fabric strips 1½ times the length of tieback. Encase jumbo cording as on page 132, steps 4 to 6. Trim cording out of the ends; turn ends to inside, and slipstitch closed.

2) Overlap the three tubes slightly at one end. Hand-stitch tubes together, and braid. Cut other ends of tubes to desired tieback length; finish as for first end of tieback.

3) Use pin-on ring **(a)** or tack a curtain ring **(b)** in the center of each end. Attach rings to cup hook on the wall.

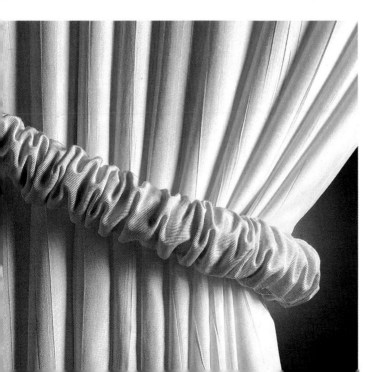

Jumbo Knotted Tieback

Cut cording 2 times the finished length of tieback plus 40" (102 cm) for knot. Cut fabric strips the length of tieback plus 20" (51 cm). Encase cording, page 132, steps 4 to 6. Tie big knot near center. Cut tieback to desired length. Trim cording out of ends. Turn ends to inside; slipstitch closed. Tack curtain ring on each end.

Jumbo Twist Tieback

Cut cording 2 times the finished length of tieback; cut fabric strips the length of tieback plus 1" (2.5 cm). Encase jumbo cording, page 132, steps 4 to 6. Trim cording out of ends. Turn ends to inside; slipstitch closed. Hand-stitch ends of tubes together, and twist. Tack curtain ring on each end.

Shirred Jumbo Welting Tieback

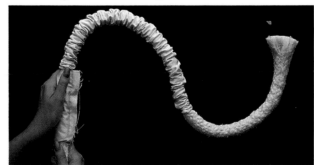

Cut cording 3 times the tieback length. Cut fabric strips 2 times the tieback length and 2" (5 cm) wider than circumference of cording. Fold strip around cording, *right* sides together. Encase cording, bottom of page 132, steps 4 and 6, gathering fabric as tube is turned. Finish ends, catching cording in stitching. Attach rings.

Shirred Insert Tieback

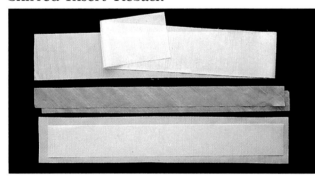

1) Cut insert 2 times finished length plus 2" (5 cm) and finished width plus 1" (2.5 cm). Cut lining 2" (5 cm) longer and 1" (2.5 cm) wider than finished tieback. Cut buckram ¼" (6 mm) narrower than finished size. Cut bias strips for welting (page 205) 2 times the finished length, plus 4" (10 cm) extra for finishing ends.

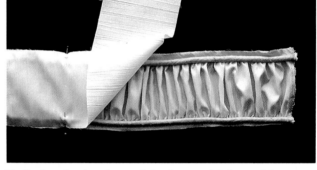

2) Gather both edges of the insert. Make welting as on page 129, steps 1 and 2. Machine-baste welting on right side of shirred strip in ⅜" (1 cm) seam. Pin right side of lining to right side of strip. Stitch ½" (1.3 cm) seam. Turn right side out.

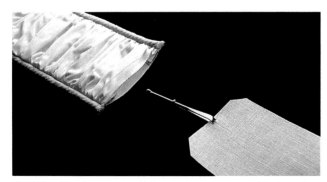

3) Trim buckram to slight point at one end. Attach bodkin to pointed end, and insert buckram between gathered insert and lining.

4) Trim 1" (2.5 cm) of cording out of welting at ends. Turn under a double ½" (1.3 cm) hem at ends, and slipstitch in place. Attach rings in center of tieback.

Fabric Rosettes

Use fabric rosettes as decorative accents at the corners of swags and on tiebacks, valances, and balloon table toppers. They need a fairly crisp fabric such as chintz or moiré to stand up; in a soft fabric they take on a draped look. Rosettes may be cut on either the crosswise grain or on the bias; they have a softer effect when cut on the bias.

The directions that follow are for a 7" (18 cm) rosette. For a smaller rosette, reduce cutting measurements proportionately. The finished rosette is as wide as the original cut strip.

✂ Cutting Directions
Cut fabric strip 7" (18 cm) wide and 72" (183 cm) long for 7" (18 cm) rosette.

How to Sew a Fabric Rosette

1) **Fold** strip in half lengthwise, *wrong* sides together; gather raw edges; stitch across short ends to round the corners. Trim excess fabric at ends.

2) **Roll** one of the rounded ends tightly toward center to make center of rosette.

3) **Continue** rolling loosely toward opposite end, tacking gathers together with needle and thread.

4) **Shape** "petals" with your hands. Hand-tack rosette in place.

Scarf Swags

Scarf swags are an adaptation of the traditional swag window treatment, which consists of a swag draped across the top of the window, and cascades draped at the sides. A scarf swag can look like an elegant, traditional window treatment or can have a more contemporary, unstructured look. Scarf swags are suitable for nearly any size or shape of window, including arch windows.

The scarf swag is created from a long, lined rectangle of fabric, and is folded and draped at the window. The swag can be shaped to form rosettes at the corners of the treatment, using special U-shaped swag holders, or can be draped over tieback holders.

The swag holders or tieback holders may be installed at the outer corners of the window frame or on the wall, positioned up and out from the corners. For arch windows, shown opposite, the brackets can be installed symmetrically or asymmetrically around the arch of the window.

After deciding on the placement of the brackets, determine the length of the cascades at the sides of the window. For good proportion, cascades are often two-thirds the length of the window or end at the window sill. On large windows, they may be floor-length, or even longer, to "puddle" onto the floor. An asymmetrical look can be achieved by making one cascade noticeably longer than the other.

Mediumweight decorator fabric, such as chintz and sateen, is recommended. Avoid heavyweight fabrics, because they do not drape well and may not fit into a swag holder. Select a contrasting lining to accent the folds of the cascades. If a patterned fabric with a one-way design is used, the fabric for one cascade must be turned in the opposite direction and stitched to the swag portion of the treatment.

If the swag holders can be seen from the side view, cover the extensions of the brackets with rod panels for a more finished appearance. The cascade-length panels are placed over the extensions before the brackets are installed.

✄ Cutting Directions

Cut outer and lining fabrics the length calculated, below. The entire width of both fabrics is used; if outer fabric and lining are of two different widths, cut the wider fabric to match the narrower width.

If rod panels are desired for the brackets at the top of the cascades, cut two pieces of fabric for each rod panel, 7" (18 cm) wide by the length of cascade plus 1¾" (4.5 cm) for the rod pocket and the seam allowance. One piece may be cut from the outer fabric and one from the lining, or both pieces may be cut from the outer fabric.

YOU WILL NEED

Decorator fabric and contrasting lining.

Swag holders or tieback holders (page 41).

Drapery hooks, one per rosette; or wire.

How to Calculate Yardage for a Scarf Swag

Drape cord or tape measure across window, between swag holders or tieback holders, to simulate the planned shape of each swag. Add desired length of cascades to this measurement. For swag with rosettes, add 24" (61 cm) for each rosette.

How to Sew a Scarf Swag

1) Place outer fabric and lining right sides together. At one selvage, measure in 18" (46 cm) from each end of fabric; draw a line from these points diagonally to the corners of the opposite selvage. Trim away triangular pieces of fabric at each end.

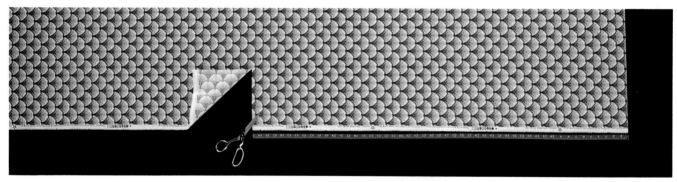

2) Stitch around all four sides in ½" (1.3 cm) seam, leaving 12" (30.5 cm) opening at center for turning. Press seams open. Turn right side out; stitch opening closed. Press edges.

Fabric with one-way design. 1) Determine length of one cascade from lower edge up to tieback holder or swag holder; add 1" (2.5 cm) to this measurement. Measure this distance from one end of fabric; cut across width.

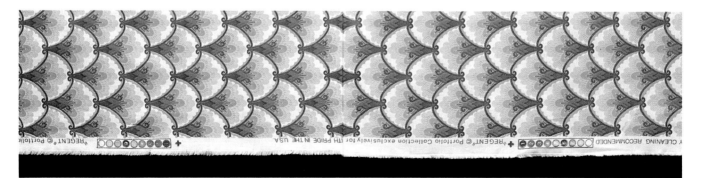

2) Turn fabric so design goes in opposite direction; stitch ½" (1.3 cm) seam. Seam will be concealed in rosette.

How to Sew a Rod Panel

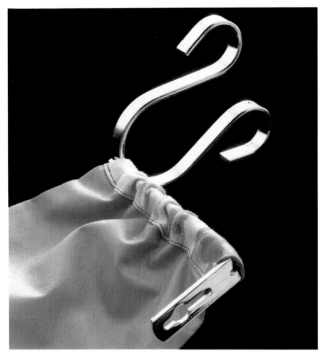

1) Place two rod panel pieces right sides together. Stitch around long sides and lower edge in ½" (1.3 cm) seam. Clip corners; turn right side out, and press. Fold under ¼" (6 mm) at upper edge to wrong side; then fold under 1" (2.5 cm). Stitch near second fold, forming rod pocket.

2) Slide rod pocket over extension of swag holder. Mount bracket onto wall or window frame.

How to Fold and Install a Scarf Swag

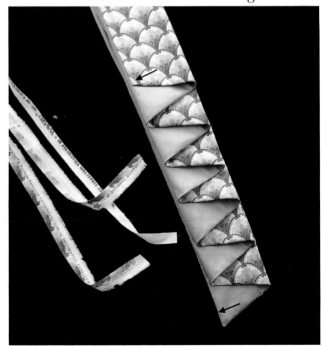

1) Lay scarf swag on long surface, such as floor, with lining side up. Accordion-fold entire width of swag in about 4" (10 cm) folds, beginning at longer side; both edges must face in same direction (arrows).

2) Tie folded swag with remnants of fabric every 18" to 24" (46 to 61 cm). This keeps folds in place, making swag easier to handle during installation.

(Continued on next page)

3) Place swag over bracket extensions, with shorter side facing down and in toward window. Drape folded swag portion the amount planned. If window treatment is to be symmetrical, check to see that cascade lengths are even. Remove ties.

4) Pull gently on lower folds for a deeper swag; pull gently on upper folds, toward brackets, to decrease amount of draping at top of swag. Adjust folds as desired; secure at brackets, using safety pins.

5) Measure down from bracket 24" (61 cm). Fold this 24" (61 cm) portion of fabric in half, forming 12" (30.5 cm) loop, with shorter side facing forward; do not twist swag. Bring fabric through U-portion of bracket, as shown; widen U-portion, if necessary for thickness of fabric. Keep fabric in accordion folds, with shorter side and contrasting folds facing window.

6) Adjust rosette portion so cascades are even in length if window treatment is to be symmetrical. Gently squeeze U-portion of bracket closed at the top as much as possible, to prevent rosette from sliding out of bracket during shaping. Secure top of bracket with a piece of wire or a drapery hook.

7) Pull the inside fold in middle of fabric loop, spreading fabric apart.

8) Form the rosette by continuing to pull out the fabric folds.

9) Tuck top and bottom of rosette back into bracket to round out the rosette, preventing peaks. Secure rosette as necessary with pins.

10) Adjust folds of cascades as necessary to achieve desired drape.

Swags with Side Drapes

This swag is a valance draped across the top of a window, with a fabric drape at the sides. Swags can be draped from post-type drapery holdbacks mounted at or above the corners of a window frame, or they can be draped around decorative finials at the ends of curtain rods.

To simplify the construction of the elegant and graceful lined swag (right), shape a fabric panel to size with two easy window measurements. Measure the width between holdbacks or finials. Measure finished length from top of hardware to point on side of window where you want the drape to end. The cut length of panel equals the width, plus twice the length, plus 1" (2.5 cm) for seam allowances. Line the panel to the edge to eliminate hems and headings; then use shirring tape to gather the fabric for draping. To save cutting time, cut the decorator fabric and lining together.

Save even more time by making a swagged valance or curtain from a fabric with no apparent right or wrong side, such as gauze, handkerchief linen, silk broadcloth, or lace. Drape artfully over a decorative rod. There is no need to line or shirr the panel. To finish edges and ends, fuse or glue hems for a custom look without taking a stitch. Swag can also be tied to finials with separate bows or tasseled cords.

How to Make a No-sew Swag

1) Drape tape measure across window between finials of decorative rod to estimate finished width of swag. Measure finished length. The cut length of panel equals the finished width, plus twice the finished length, plus two hem allowances; allow extra fabric for draping adjustments.

2) Drape fabric over rod to test effect. If fabric panel is too wide, trim side edges for desired effect. Mark hems, and fuse or glue them. Drape finished panel over rod, and adjust fabric into soft folds. Tie cord around folds at corners to hold in place. Knot soft or slippery fabrics around finials to anchor swag.

How to Sew Lined Swag with Side Drape

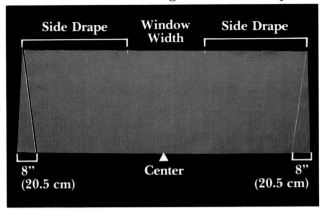

1) **Measure** and mark center and window width. On opposite side, mark 8" (20.5 cm) in from each corner. Layer decorator fabric and lining, and cut diagonally to opposite corner on each side.

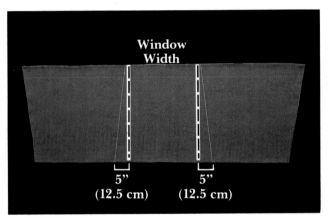

2) **Sew** lining to panel, with right sides together. At center of shorter edge, leave an opening for turning. Trim corners. Turn right side out; press. Fuse or glue opening closed. On lining, mark shorter edge of panel 5" (12.5 cm) out from the width markings.

3) **Position** 2-cord shirring tape on diagonal lines from window width mark on long side to 5" (12.5 cm) mark on short side.

4) **Stitch** shirring tape between each set of marks. Knot cords of tape at shorter edge. Pull up cords to gather swag. Mount on drapery holdbacks and adjust folds.

Tent-flap Curtains

Stylish tent-flap curtains require a minimum amount of fabric and provide a tailored, uncluttered look. Choose two fabrics that complement each other for the outer fabric and the lining. The lining is just as important as the outer fabric.

✂ Cutting Directions

Cut each panel half the width of the mounting board plus return, plus 2" (5 cm) for seam allowances and overlap; cut length as measured from the top of the mounting board to desired finished length, plus the depth of the mounting board and ½" (1.3 cm) for seam allowance. Cut face fabric and lining panels the same size.

YOU WILL NEED

Decorator fabric and lining for curtains.

Mounting board: For outside mount, board should extend at least 1" (2.5 cm) on each side of window frame and be deep enough to clear window by 2" (5 cm). For inside mount, cut 1" × 2" (2.5 × 5 cm) to fit inside window.

Two tieback holders or two wooden blocks.

Two angle irons for mounting.

Heavy-duty stapler, staples.

How to Sew a Tent-flap Curtain

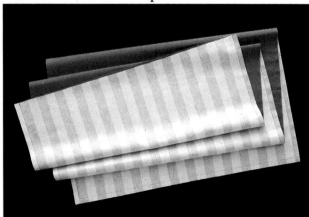

1) Pin face fabric to lining, right sides together, and stitch three sides in ½" (1.3 cm) seam, leaving upper edge open.

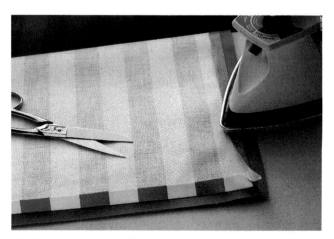

2) Press one seam allowance back to make it easier to turn a crisp, sharp edge. Trim seam allowance across corners. Turn panels right side out, and press.

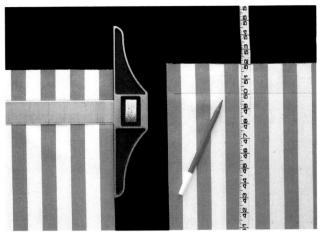

3) Mark finished length across the top of the panels, making sure that both panels are exactly even and that end is at perfect right angle to sides.

4) Align panel length marking with front edge of mounting board. Staple panel to board, starting at return. At corner, make diagonal fold to form a miter. Panels overlap about 1" (2.5 cm) at center.

5) Mount board with angle irons positioned at edge of window frame.

6) Fold the front edges of the panels back to side edges, and adjust opening. Measure to be sure they are even on both sides.

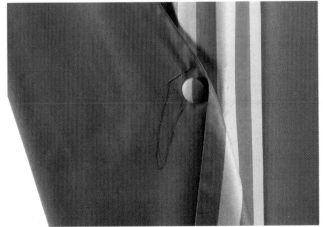

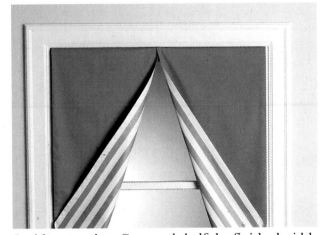

7) Hand-tack two layers together, and finish with decorative or covered button. Or hand-tack ties at front edge and sides. To maintain projection at sides, attach panel to tieback holder or wooden block attached to window frame behind ties.

Inside mounting. Cut panels half the finished width of mounting board, plus 2" (5 cm). Sew as for steps 1 to 3. Mount panels on top of board. Fold flap; tack to side of curtain. At side, sew ring to curtain back; attach to cup hook inside frame.

Roller Shades

Mount roller shades inside the window opening with ¼" (6 mm) or less clearance around the edges to increase the energy efficiency of a window. Roller shades can also be hung on brackets on the frame or wall outside the window. For inside mounting, measure from outside edges of brackets. If you do not want the roller to show, use reverse brackets, and cut the roller to fit.

Select a firmly woven fabric that bonds well. Water-resistant and stain-resistant fabrics that are treated with silicone do not bond.

✂ Cutting Directions

Cut fabric 1" to 2" (2.5 to 5 cm) wider than jamb or bracket measurement, and 12" (30.5 cm) longer than area to be covered top to bottom. Cut fusible backing with same dimensions.

YOU WILL NEED

Fabric and fusible shade backing for shade.

Wooden slat, ¼" (6 mm) shorter than finished width of shade.

Roller to fit window width.

Staple gun with ¼" (6 mm) staples, masking tape or other strong tape and white glue.

Shade pull (optional).

How to Make a Roller Shade

1) **Mark** center at upper and lower edges of fabric and fusible backing. Place the wrong side of the fabric to the resin side of the backing, matching edges and center markings.

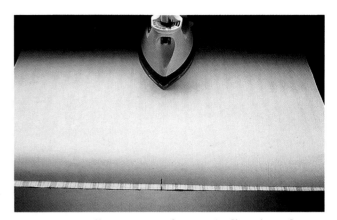

2) **Fuse** according to manufacturer's directions for time and temperature, working from center to outside and from top to bottom. Allow shade to cool before moving so bond is permanently set.

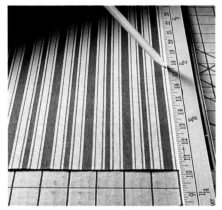

3) **Use** a yardstick to mark cutting lines on sides of shade; distance between cutting lines should be equal to finished width of shade. Use a carpenter's square or cutting board for right angles.

4) **Cut** carefully along cutting lines with smooth, even strokes. To keep edges from raveling, put a small amount of white glue on your finger and draw it along each edge. Let dry completely.

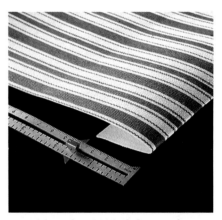

5) **Fold** under 1½" (3.8 cm) along lower edge for a straight hem and slat pocket. Use carpenter's square to check right angles at corners.

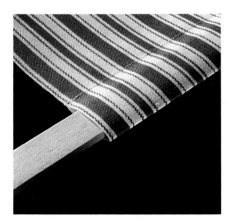

6) **Stitch** 1¼" (3.2 cm) from folded edge, using long stitches to form a pocket for the slat. Press pocket. Insert the slat. Attach shade pull if desired.

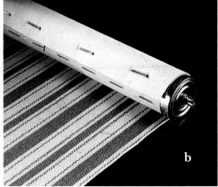

7) **Position** roller under or over top of shade, depending on how shade is to roll. To attach roller under shade, place flat pin to the right (**a**); to attach roller over shade, place round pin to the right (**b**). Make sure wrong side of hem is turned so it will not show when shade is hung. Staple or tape shade to roller.

Top Treatments

Top treatments give curtains, draperies, or shades a custom look that sets the window apart from the ordinary. They may be used alone, to allow the maximum light or view through a window, or with any curtain or drapery to cover an unattractive rod, or simply as a decorative accent. Top treatments are used not only with curtains and draperies, but also with shower curtains, mini-blinds, pleated shades, vertical blinds, and shutters to soften the overall appearance or to coordinate fabric or color within a room.

A top treatment can create optical illusions. It can help to extend the visual height of a window or can make it appear shorter, depending on the style and placement. Valances and cornices can make windows that are at different levels in a room appear uniform. When wall space is limited, a top treatment used by itself can give the window a finished look without a great deal of effort.

Choice of fabric determines the finished look or style of the valance. The same style can be made in moiré or linen; the moiré will be elegant for a tailored look, and the linen will be more casual for a country look. A flat valance (page 80) looks more tailored than one that is gathered, but in a formal fabric, such as moiré, a gathered one can be just as elegant.

Valances are a short version of curtains, draperies, or shades used at the top of a window. A valance may be mounted on a separate curtain rod or on a mounting board inside or outside the window frame (pages 42 and 43). Mounting boards are cut from 1" (2.5 cm) lumber; the depth may be 2" to 5" (5 to 12.5 cm), or more, depending on the return of the underdrapery,

curtain, or shade. Valances may be basic, such as balloon, flat, or puff, or more stylized, such as the stagecoach or handkerchief valance.

Short swags as well as covered poles and finials add to window top interest. A sunburst curtain is used with Palladian windows.

Measuring for a Top Treatment

There are few hard-and-fast rules for top treatments, because they are an excellent opportunity to express creativity. In general, the length of the valance should be in proportion to the total length of the window or window treatment. This length is usually about one-fifth of the window treatment. To add visual height to a room, a top treatment may be mounted at the ceiling, or at least several inches (centimeters) above the window.

For scalloped treatments such as the balloon valance or butterfly swag, the shortest point of the scallop should come 4" (10 cm) below the top of the window glass and cover 6" to 8" (15 to 20.5 cm) of an underdrapery heading.

If a valance is not mounted at the ceiling, allow at least 4" (10 cm) of clearance between the top of the drapery and the valance for the mounting brackets.

For mounting a top treatment over draperies, add 4" (10 cm) to the width, and 2" to 3" (5 to 7.5 cm) to the depth on each side, to allow for clearance at the return. For example, if using a valance with an underdrapery, use a 5½" (14 cm) valance return over a standard 3½" (9 cm) underdrapery return.

Basic Valances

Balloon valance. A balloon valance, above, gives simple sheers or draperies a soft, casual look. This valance, with bottom hem draped into swags, looks complicated but is actually easy to sew. It is a basic rod-pocket curtain, shortened to valance length. Each swag is created with shade tape or by tying cord through plastic rings. The balloon valance can be used on a curtain rod, a cafe pole, or a Continental® rod.

For graceful draping, make balloon valances about 28" (71 cm) long. To determine cut length, add to the finished length allowances for the heading, rod pocket, and double lower hem. To determine cut width, allow triple fullness if using sheer or lightweight fabric, or 2 to 2½ times fullness for medium-weight decorator fabrics; allow for double side hems.

Flat valance. A flat valance, right, takes little fabric and even less sewing time. It is a plain fabric panel with rod pockets for a pair of curtain rods. The simple, tailored style of this valance can complement contemporary or traditional decor. Choose a medium to heavyweight fabric with a crisp, firm hand; or back lightweight fabric with a layer of fusible interfacing. Textured fabrics such as cotton jacquard, raw silk, cotton velvet, and synthetic suede are appropriate as are quilted fabrics and needlework such as trapunto.

To determine cut length, install the rods so the distance between them equals the desired finished length. Most valances are made 12" to 14" (30.5 to 35.5 cm) long, depending on the proportion to window size. To measure, pin a tape measure around the top rod, down, and around the bottom rod. Add 1"

(2.5 cm) for turning under the raw edges. To determine the cut width of a flat valance, measure the length of the curtain rod, including returns. Add 3" (7.5 cm) for side hems.

Puff valance. A puff valance, right, has a light, airy look. It is a natural for sheers and other lightweight fabrics. Combine a puff valance with shades, curtains, or blinds for a layered window treatment, or use it alone as a decorative accent.

This valance is made from a strip of fabric cut large enough to form a self-lining. To determine cut length, double the finished length of the valance; add heading and rod-pocket allowances. To determine cut width, use triple fabric fullness for sheer and lightweight fabric or 2½ times the finished width for mediumweight fabric; add 4" (10 cm) for double side hems.

How to Sew a Balloon Valance

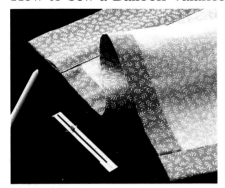
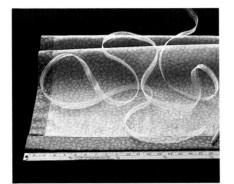
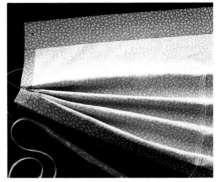

1) Make double side and bottom hems. Turn upper raw edge under ½" (1.3 cm), and press. Fold edge over to form heading and rod pocket; mark stitching lines. Stitch as marked.

2) Mark location for shade tape at lower edge of shade. Swags should hang at even intervals across valance, about 8" to 12" (20.5 to 30.5 cm) apart; if width is double fabric fullness, tapes should be 16" to 24" (40.5 to 61 cm) apart.

3) Cut strips of shade tape 24" (61 cm) long, making sure that the first tack over the cord is at the top of the hem. Stitch tape in place. Pull up cord from both ends, and tie. Tuck cords into swag.

How to Sew a Flat Valance

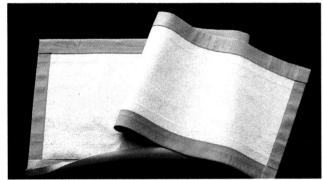

1) Turn under raw edges at sides ½" (1.3 cm). Press. Turn under 1" (2.5 cm), and stitch side hems. Fold fabric to wrong side to form rod pockets on upper and lower edges, turning under raw edges ½" (1.3 cm). Stitch rod pockets.

2) Insert rods through rod pocket at top and bottom to install valance at window. Valance takes shape of rods and has custom upholstered look. For quick trim, fuse grosgrain ribbon over stitching lines.

How to Sew a Puff Valance

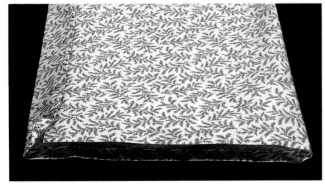

1) Make double side hems. Turn upper raw edge under ½" (1.3 cm), and press. Fold edge over to depth of heading. Bring lower raw edge up, and lap ½" (1.3 cm) under heading. Stitch along folded edge to form heading. Stitch parallel row below folded edge to form rod pocket.

2) Slip rod through rod pocket to install valance. Pull fabric layers apart along length of valance to create puffs. If valance seems limp, stuff with tissue paper or plastic drycleaning bags for fuller look.

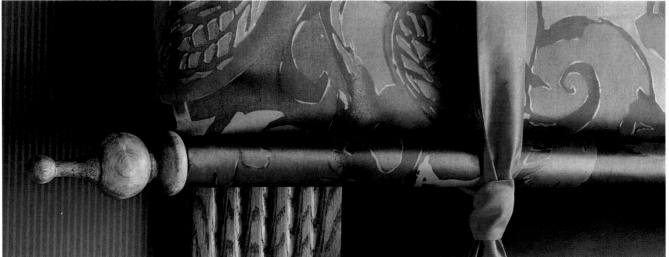

Outside mounted stagecoach valance has side returns; finials may be added at ends of wood pole, if desired.

Stagecoach Valances

This stationary, tailored top treatment features decorative ties and resembles the curtains used in the stagecoaches of the past. The valance may be lined with matching or contrasting fabric. The lining shows when the stagecoach valance is rolled at the lower edge.

A stagecoach valance is attached to a mounting board and is frequently mounted inside the window frame. When an inside mount is used, the finished width of the valance is 1/4" (6 mm) less than the measurement inside the window frame, and the window treatment is attached to a 1" × 1" (2.5 × 2.5 cm) mounting board.

For an outside mount, side returns are added to the valance. The return is the distance from the wall to the front edge of the mounting board. The mounting board can either be mounted at the top of the window frame or on the wall above the window. The finished width of the valance should be at least 2" (5 cm) wider than the outside measurement of the window frame or 2" (5 cm) wider than the width of an undertreatment.

The ties are usually spaced 24" to 36" (61 to 91.5 cm) apart. If they are spaced farther apart, the valance fabric may buckle between the ties. If possible, plan the placement of the ties so they will be aligned with any existing vertical lines in the window.

✂ Cutting Directions

If this treatment is used on a window that is wider than the fabric width, railroad the fabric whenever possible (page 23). If the fabric cannot be railroaded, plan the placement of the seams so they will be concealed under the ties.

For an inside mount, the cut width of the face fabric is equal to the finished width of the valance plus 1" (2.5 cm) for seam allowances. For an outside mount, the cut width of the face fabric is equal to the finished width of the valance plus two times the return plus 1" (2.5 cm) for seam allowances.

The cut length of the face fabric is equal to the finished length plus the width of the mounting board plus 12" (30.5 cm) for a rolled effect at the lower edge plus 1" (2.5 cm) for seam allowances.

Cut the matching or contrasting lining the same size as the face fabric.

Cut two fabric strips for each tie location, with the cut width of each strip two times the finished width of the tie plus 1/2" (1.3 cm) for seam allowances. The finished width of the ties in the photo is 2" (5 cm). The fabric strips may be cut on the crosswise grain, with the cut length of the strips equal to the width of the fabric. Cut fabric to cover the mounting board (page 43).

YOU WILL NEED

Decorator fabric for valance and mounting board.

Matching or contrasting fabric for lining.

Contrasting fabric for ties.

1⅜" (3.5 cm) wood pole, cut to finished width of valance after it is stitched.

Mounting board, cut 1/4" (6 mm) shorter than the finished width of valance after it is stitched. For inside mount, use 1" × 1" (2.5 × 2.5 cm) board. For outside mount, use a board at least 2" (5 cm) wider than projection of window frame or undertreatment.

Heavy-duty stapler; staples.

Angle irons, one for each end and one for every 45" (115 cm) interval across the width of the mounting board; pan-head screws or molly bolts (page 42) for outside mount.

Pan-head screws (page 42) for inside mount.

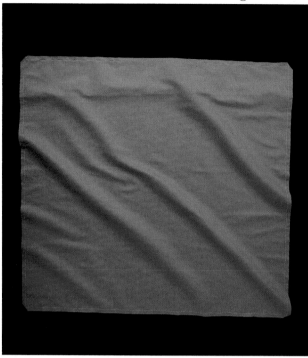

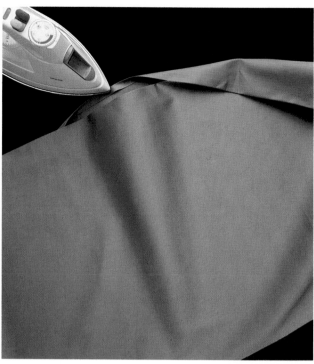

1) Seam fabric widths as necessary. Place face fabric and lining right sides together, matching raw edges. Stitch ½" (1.3 cm) seams around all sides; leave an 8" (20.5 cm) opening at center of upper edge for turning. Trim corners diagonally.

2) Turn valance right side out. Press edges, folding in seam allowances at center opening.

3) Cut two 3" (7.5 cm) circles. Attach to ends of wood pole, using fabric glue or spray adhesive.

4) Hold pole firmly against table; using pencil, draw line on pole where it touches table.

5) Center pole on right side of valance at lower edge; staple in place, aligning lower edge of valance to marked line on pole.

6) Roll up valance to desired finished length. Anchor pole in place with pins.

7) Fold fabric strips for ties in half lengthwise, right sides together. Stitch long edge and one short end, using ¼" (6 mm) seam allowance. Trim diagonally across corners, turn tie right side out, and press. Two ties are used at each placement.

8) Mark desired placement of ties at upper edge of valance. Staple valance to covered mounting board (page 43), aligning upper edge of valance to back edge of board. Do not place staples at markings for ties.

(Continued on next page)

How to Sew an Inside-mounted Stagecoach Valance (continued)

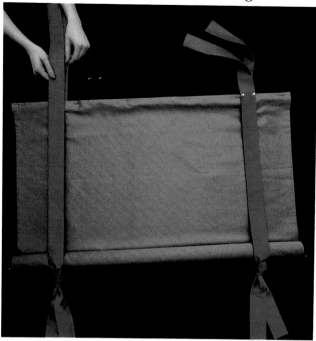

9) Sandwich valance between two ties at placement marks; tack in place, using map tacks Tie finished ends; adjust length of ties from upper edge, for desired effect, making sure all ties are the same length. Staple ties to board. Trim excess ties at top.

10) Mount valance by screwing board inside window frame, using #8 gauge 1½" (3.8 cm) pan-head screws. Predrill the holes, using ⅛" (3 mm) drill bit.

How to Sew an Outside-mounted Stagecoach Valance

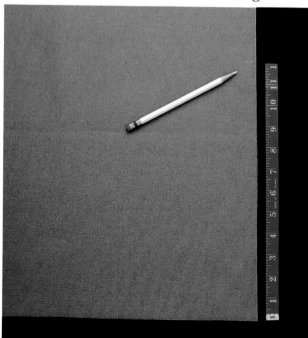

1) Seam fabric widths as necessary. Fold face fabric in half lengthwise, right sides together. At sides, mark a line 12½" (31.8 cm) from lower edge; this is the amount needed for rolled effect plus seam allowance.

2) Draw line in from side at marked line, the amount of one return. Draw line, parallel to side, down to lower edge; cut out section through both layers. The cut width at lower edge should now be the finished width of valance plus 1" (2.5 cm). Repeat for lining.

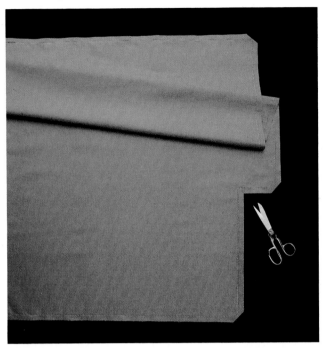

3) Place face fabric and lining right sides together, matching raw edges. Stitch ½" (1.3 cm) seams around all sides; leave an 8" (20.5 cm) opening at center of upper edge for turning. Clip and trim corners.

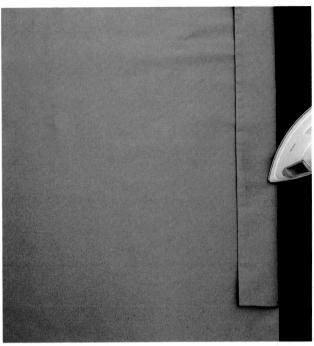

4) Turn valance right side out. Press edges, folding in seam allowances at center opening. Press returns lightly. Complete steps 3 to 7 on pages 84 and 85.

5) Mark desired placement of ties at upper edge of valance. Staple valance to covered mounting board (page 43), aligning upper edge of valance to back edge of board and centering upper edge on board, with returns extending at ends of board. Do not place staples at markings for ties.

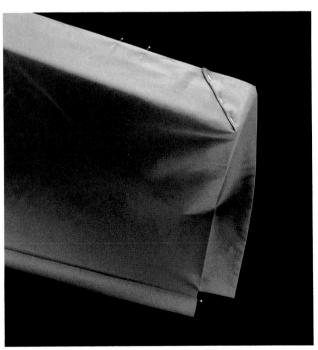

6) Miter corners of returns; staple in place. Finish valance with ties, as in step 9, opposite. Mount as on pages 42 and 43.

Handkerchief Valances

This easy, tailored valance features a 3" (7.5 cm) band at the lower edge, which is simply an extension of the contrasting lining. The valance can be used alone or over another window treatment, such as blinds or underdraperies. It works well for small windows, without being overpowering, but this banded styling is also attractive on larger windows.

A handkerchief valance should be mounted as an outside mount (pages 42 and 43). The board can either be mounted at the top of the window frame or on the wall above the window. The finished width of the valance should be at least 2" (5 cm) wider than the outside measurement of the window frame or undertreatment; the finished width does not include the fabric drop at the sides of the valance.

✂ Cutting Directions

The cut width of the outer fabric is equal to the length of the mounting board plus two times the finished length of the valance plus 1" (2.5 cm) for seam allowances. The fabric may be railroaded if the design is not directional (page 23). Fabric that cannot be railroaded will require piecing if the cut width of the valance is wider than the fabric width; when the fabric is pieced, add the necessary extra width for seam allowances. To determine the cut length of the outer fabric, add the width of the mounting board to the desired finished length of the valance; then

subtract 2" (5 cm) from this measurement to allow for seam allowances and for a 3" (7.5 cm) contrasting band at the lower edge.

Cut the contrasting lining the same width as the outer fabric. To determine the cut length of the lining, add the width of the mounting board to the desired finished length of the valance; then add 4" (10 cm) to this measurement to allow for seam allowances and for a 3" (7.5 cm) contrasting band at the lower edge.

Cut fabric to cover the mounting board (page 43).

YOU WILL NEED

Decorator fabric in two contrasting colors for outer fabric and lining.

Mounting board, cut to the desired finished width of valance. Mounting board must be at least 2" (5 cm) wider than projection of window frame or undertreatment.

Angle irons, one for each end and one for every 45" (115 cm) interval across the width of the mounting board.

Heavy-duty stapler; staples.

Pan-head screws or molly bolts (page 42).

How to Sew a Handkerchief Valance

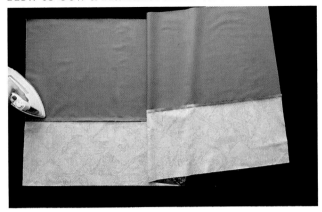

1) Seam fabric widths, if necessary. Place outer fabric and lining right sides together, matching the lower edges; stitch ½" (1.3 cm) seam. Press seam toward outer fabric.

2) Place outer fabric and lining right sides together, matching upper edges. Stitch ½" (1.3 cm) seams at sides and upper edge; leave an 8" (20.5 cm) opening at center of upper edge for turning. Trim corners diagonally. Press seam allowances open at edges.

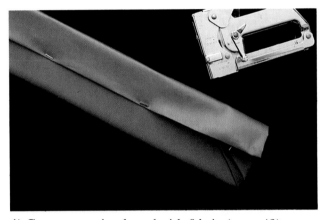

3) Turn valance right side out. Press edges, folding in seam allowances at center opening.

4) Cover mounting board with fabric (page 43); staple fabric in place at 4" (10 cm) intervals, folding under raw edges.

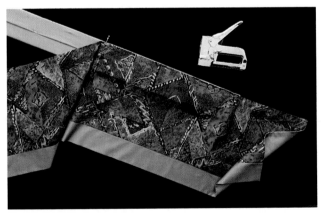

5) Mark center of mounting board; mark center of valance at upper edge. Place valance, right side up, on mounting board, aligning upper edge of valance to back edge of board; match center markings. Near back edge, staple valance to board at center. Working from center to sides, staple valance to board at 4" (10 cm) intervals, with one staple close to each end.

6) Screw angle irons to bottom of mounting board, positioning one at each end and spacing them at 45" (115 cm) intervals. Install valance on window frame or wall (pages 42 and 43). Adjust the drape at ends of valance.

Rod-sleeve Valances

Make quick and easy rod-sleeve valances by simply shirring fabric over a wide curtain rod. Tapered headings are added to the basic plain rod sleeve to create many different styles. This ruffled top treatment works well over shirred draperies for a feminine look, but may also be used with tailored blinds or pleated shades. The headings may be made from fabric that either matches or contrasts with the fabric for the rod sleeves.

For a dramatic top treatment, two or more drapery rods, covered with plain or tapered-heading rod sleeves, can be grouped together. When two rods are mounted next to each other, there is a small space between the rods, due to the mounting brackets. To fill in any space between the rods and prevent a light gap, a 1/2" (1.3 cm) ruffle is added to one of the rod sleeves and tucked behind the rods when the top treatment is mounted. For best results in preventing a light gap between the rods, add the ruffle to the lower edge of the upper rod sleeve.

✄ Cutting Directions

For either a plain rod sleeve or a rod sleeve with one heading, the cut length of the sleeve is equal to twice the width of the drapery rod plus 1" (2.5 cm) for ease and 1" (2.5 cm) for seam allowances. To add

The tapered heading at the top of this rod sleeve adds height above the window frame.

The heading can form a ruffle at the bottom of the rod sleeve by turning the top treatment upside down. A second drapery rod with a plain rod sleeve is used for a more pronounced effect.

a ½" (1.3 cm) ruffle between closely mounted rods, add an extra 1" (2.5 cm) to the cut length. The cut width of the rod sleeve is equal to three times the length of the drapery rod.

If you are making a rod sleeve with two headings, cut separate sections for the front and back of the sleeve, with the cut length of each equal to the width of the rod plus 1" (2.5 cm) for ease and 1" (2.5 cm) for seam allowances. If desired, the back of the rod sleeve may be cut from lining fabric. For each front and back, the cut width is equal to three times the length of the rod.

The cut length of a tapered heading is equal to twice the finished length of the heading plus 1" (2.5 cm) for seam allowances. The cut width of the heading is the same as the cut width of the rod sleeve. Tapered headings may be from matching or contrasting fabric.

YOU WILL NEED

Decorator fabric; one or two colors may be used.

Wide curtain rods, one for each rod sleeve.

Contemporary metal pole sets, if desired, for multiple-rod treatments.

Tapered headings are used at both the top and bottom of this rod sleeve for a different look.

Multiple drapery rods are used together to create a dramatic top treatment. In the treatment shown here, wide curtain rods are covered with rod sleeves and the contemporary metal pole sets are left uncovered.

How to Sew a Plain Rod Sleeve

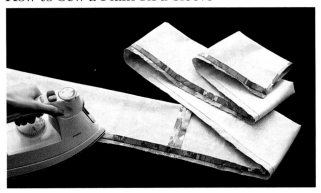

1) Seam fabric widths together. Press seams open. Stitch double ¼" (6 mm) side hems. Fold rod sleeve in half lengthwise, with right sides together and raw edges even. Stitch ½" (1.3 cm) seam; press open.

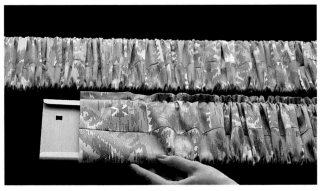

2) Turn rod sleeve right side out; press so seam is centered on back of sleeve. If ruffle is required to prevent a light gap on multiple-rod treatment (page 90), stitch ½" (1.3 cm) from folded edge. Insert drapery rod, gathering fabric evenly.

How to Sew a Rod Sleeve with One Heading

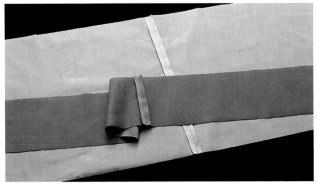

1) Seam fabric widths together for rod sleeve and heading. Press seams open.

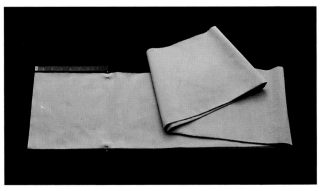

2) Fold heading in half lengthwise, *wrong* sides together; press foldline. Then fold in half crosswise; measure from ends a distance equal to twice the depth of return, and pin-mark. For example, for 4" (10 cm) return, pin-mark 8" (20.5 cm) from ends.

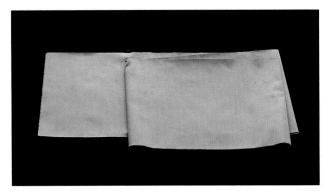

3) Determine one-third the distance from pin mark at return to crosswise foldline; measure this distance from crosswise foldline, and pin-mark. This is where tapering will begin.

4) Measure from lengthwise fold at return pin mark to desired height of heading plus ½" (1.3 cm) seam allowance; mark with pencil. For example, for 4" (10 cm) heading at return, mark 4½" (11.5 cm) from lengthwise fold.

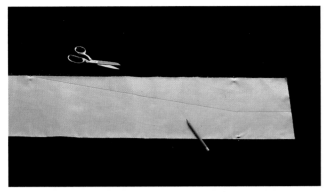

5) Draw straight line parallel to lengthwise fold, from ends of heading to pencil mark at return. Draw straight line at an angle from pencil mark at return to pin mark in center portion. Cut on marked lines.

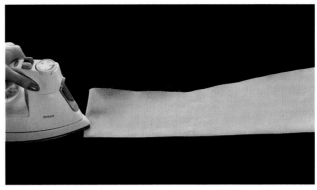

6) Fold heading lengthwise, right sides together; stitch ½" (1.3 cm) seams at ends. Turn heading right sides out; press.

7) Stitch double ¼" (6 mm) side hems on rod sleeve. Fold rod sleeve in half lengthwise, right sides together; sandwich heading in between, matching raw edges. Pin layers together, easing in seam allowances of heading, as necessary, so fabric lies flat. Stitch ½" (1.3 cm) seam.

8) Turn right side out; press. If a ruffle is required to prevent a light gap on multiple-rod treatment (page 90), stitch ½" (1.3 cm) from folded edge. Insert drapery rod, gathering fabric evenly.

How to Sew a Rod Sleeve with Two Headings

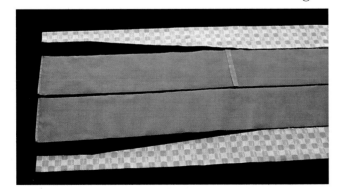

1) Seam fabric widths together for headings and front and back of rod sleeve. Press seams open. Make two headings as in steps 2 to 6, opposite. Stitch double ¼" (6 mm) side hems in front and back of rod sleeve.

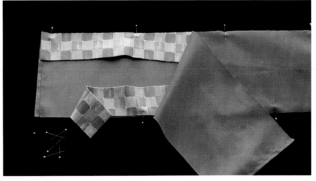

2) Place front and back of rod sleeve right sides together; sandwich headings in between, matching raw edges. Pin layers together, easing in seam allowances of headings, as necessary, so fabric lies flat. Stitch ½" (1.3 cm) seams. Turn right side out; press. Insert drapery rod, gathering fabric evenly.

Butterfly Swags

Butterfly swags have a soft, informal look. The edge of the valance is trimmed with a matching ruffle, and for easy construction, the swag is gathered with two-cord shirring tape.

Butterfly swags are attached to a mounting board. Determine the finished width of an inside-mounted or outside-mounted valance as for a stagecoach valance (page 83). When an outside mount is used, the sides of the mounting board will show, because the valance does not wrap around the sides. To make the board less noticeable, cover it with fabric that matches the valance. For good proportion, the center swagged portion is usually two-thirds or three-fourths the finished width.

✂ Cutting Directions

If this treatment is used on a window that is wider than the fabric width, railroad the fabric whenever possible, to avoid seaming. If the fabric cannot be railroaded, place the seams so they will be aligned with the shirring tape and concealed in the gathers.

Cut the decorator fabric and the lining the same size. The cut width of the fabrics is equal to the finished width of the valance plus 1" (2.5 cm) for the seam allowances minus twice the finished width of the ruffle. When the fabric is railroaded, the full width of the fabric is used for the cut length. Otherwise, the cut length of the fabric is 45" to 54" (115 to 137 cm),

giving a 15" to 18" (38 to 46 cm) drop length at the center of the swag.

For a 2½" (6.5 cm) self-lined ruffle, cut fabric strips 6" (15 cm) wide. To calculate the total cut length of the strips, multiply the distance around the sides and lower edge of the valance by two for double fullness, or by three for triple fullness. Piece the fabric strips together, as necessary.

Cut two pieces of shirring tape, with the length of each piece equal to the cut length of the valance minus the width of the mounting board.

YOU WILL NEED

Decorator fabric for valance and ruffle.

Lining fabric.

Two-cord shirring tape.

Mounting board, cut as for stagecoach valance (page 83).

Heavy-duty stapler; staples.

Angle irons; pan-head screws or molly bolts (page 42) for outside mount.

Pan-head screws (page 42) for inside mount.

How to Sew a Butterfly Swag

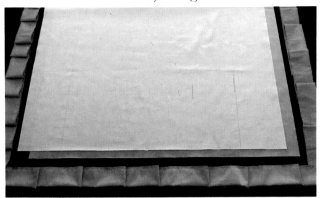

1) **Seam** the fabric widths together if fabric is not railroaded. Mark vertical placement lines for shirring tape on right side of lining. Fold pieced ruffle strip in half lengthwise, *wrong* sides together; press. Stitch gathering stitches by zigzagging over a cord, as on page 169, step 9.

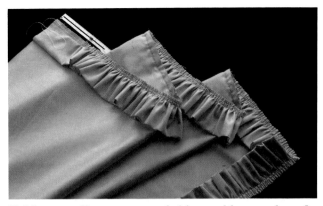

2) **Measure** distance around sides and lower edge of valance; divide into fourths, and pin-mark. Divide ruffle strip into fourths, and pin-mark. Pin ruffle to right side of valance, matching pin marks. Pull up gathering threads to fit; leave ruffle strip flat at upper edge for a distance equal to width of mounting board. Stitch a scant ½" (1.3 cm) from raw edges.

3) **Place** the lining and valance fabrics right sides together, matching raw edges; pin. Stitch around sides and lower edge of valance in ½" (1.3 cm) seam. Trim corners diagonally. Turn valance right side out; press. Finish upper edge.

4) **Fold** under ¼" (6 mm) on both ends of shirring tape pieces. Pin tape in place, starting at lower edge and centering it over marked lines on lining; tape will not reach upper edge. Stitch three rows of stitching on tape through all layers of fabric; stitch center row of stitching first, then along outer edges.

5) **Knot** cords at upper end of tape. Pull cords from lower end, gathering fabric to desired length. Check to see that both shirred tapes are the same length; knot ends, and conceal cords behind valance.

6) **Cover** the mounting board with matching fabric (page 43). Staple valance to board. Mount valance (pages 42 and 43).

Sunburst Curtains

A sunburst curtain dresses a Palladian window while diffusing the light. Designed to perfectly outline the arch shape, this sheer rod-pocket curtain is custom-fitted for your window.

Flexible plastic tubing, which shapes easily to curve around the window opening, is inserted into the rod pocket at the upper edge. Drapery cord, inserted into the opposite casing, holds the gathers at the center. A large rosette (pages 138 and 139) is used to finish the treatment.

Trace the shape of the inside window frame onto paper to make a pattern. Fitting adjustments can be made on the curtain, using the pattern, before it is installed.

✂ Cutting Directions

The cut width of the fabric is equal to one and one-half to two times the measurement of the curved line on the pattern, depending on the fullness desired. Railroad the fabric whenever possible to prevent seams (page 23).

To determine the cut length of the fabric, divide the length of the lower straight line on the pattern by two; then add 4½" (11.5 cm). This allows for a double ½" (1.3 cm) heading and a double 1" (2.5 cm) rod pocket at the outer edge, a double ½" (1.3 cm) casing at the center, and ½" (1.3 cm) for ease.

YOU WILL NEED

Sheer drapery fabric for curtain and rosette.

⅜" (1 cm) flexible plastic tubing (page 41), cut to fit curve at inside edge of window frame.

Sockets for ⅜" (1 cm) round rodding.

1" (2.5 cm) cup hooks; one for every 8" to 10" (20.5 to 25.5 cm) around curve of window, plus one for center of sunburst.

Nylon drapery cord; binder clips or clamps.

How to Sew and Install a Sunburst Curtain

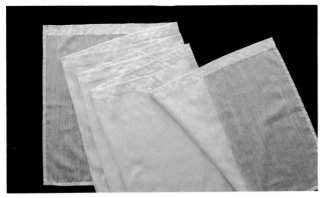

1) Seam fabric widths, if necessary. Press under ½" (1.3 cm) twice at sides; stitch to make double-fold hems. Press under 1½" (3.8 cm) twice at upper edge; stitch rod pocket close to first fold, then 1" (2.5 cm) away. Press under and stitch double ½" (1.3 cm) rod pocket on lower edge.

2) Tie safety pin to one end of drapery cord; thread through casing at lower edge. Pull up cord as tightly as possible, and tie ends together; trim excess cord. This becomes center of sunburst.

3) Insert plastic tubing into casing at upper edge, gathering fabric. Pin or tape paper pattern to heavy cardboard or foam core board. Aligning heading of curtain to marked arc on pattern, clamp ends of tubing to cardboard; distribute gathers evenly and pin heading in place. Clamp center at lower edge.

4) Pull curtain taut toward center to remove slack, using double strand of thread. Cover center with a small half-circle of matching fabric, if necessary for neater appearance on outside of window treatment. Make rosette (pages 138 and 139); hand-stitch to center.

5) Screw sockets at ends of bottom window frame. Screw cup hooks into window frame at 8" to 10" (20.5 to 25.5 cm) intervals around arch, with hook openings facing into the room; position all cup hooks the same distance from edge of window frame. Screw one cup hook at center of bottom window frame.

6) Insert ends of tubing into sockets. Snap tubing into cup hooks around inside curve of window. Hook center of sunburst into cup hook at center of bottom window frame. It may be necessary to trim tubing to fit around window.

Covered Poles & Finials

Fabric-covered drapery poles and ball finials add a designer touch to scarf swags and other window treatments. Use unfinished wood poles and finials. The poles may be covered with either shirred or flat fabric.

A smooth covered rod is used to support the scarf swag shown at right. Twisted welting, draped with the swag, is also used to embellish the coordinating covered finial. A shirred covered rod is featured with rod-pocket curtains and covered finials with ruffles (inset, right).

✂ Cutting Directions

The cut length of the rod sleeve is equal to the rod circumference plus 1½" (3.8 cm) for 1⅜" (3.5 cm) diameter wood poles, or the circumference plus 1¾" (4.5 cm) for 2" (5 cm) wood poles.

For a flat rod sleeve, the cut width of the rod sleeve is equal to the length of the wood pole. For a shirred rod sleeve, the cut width is two or three times the length of the wood pole.

Cut the fabric circles for the finials as on page 100 or 101.

YOU WILL NEED

Decorator fabric.

Wood pole set with ball finials.

Brackets designed to be used with Cirmosa® rods.

Cord, braid, or ribbon trim for finials.

Fabric glue.

Tacks; or heavy-duty stapler and staples.

How to Make a Smooth Covered Pole

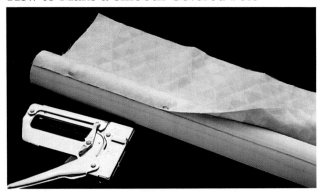

1) Mark line on wood pole, as in step 4, page 84. Staple or tack one edge of fabric to pole, aligning raw edge with marked line.

2) Wrap fabric snugly around pole. Fold under raw edge; staple or tack in place. Apply glue around end of pole so rod sleeve will adhere. Allow glue to dry.

How to Make a Shirred Covered Pole

Sew plain rod sleeve as on page 92, except do not stitch side hems. Insert drapery rod, gathering fabric evenly. Apply glue around end of wood pole, so rod sleeve will adhere. Allow glue to dry.

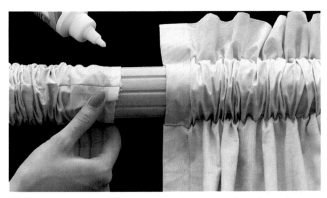

Alternate method for rod-pocket curtain. Sew plain rod sleeve for exposed portion of wood pole only, as on page 92, except do not stitch side hems. Insert drapery rod, gathering fabric evenly. Apply glue to pole at ends of rod sleeve; allow to dry. Curtain covers remainder of pole.

How to Make a Covered Finial

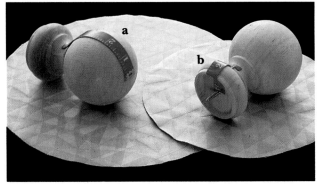

1) Measure ball portion of finial from top of finial to neck **(a);** cut one fabric circle for each finial, with a radius 1" (2.5 cm) longer than measurement. Measure the crown portion of finial from neck to base **(b);** cut one fabric circle for each finial, with radius 1" (2.5 cm) longer than measurement.

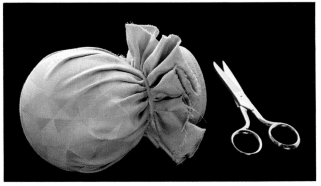

2) Center ball of finial on first fabric circle; wrap fabric around ball to neck of finial. Secure fabric at neck with rubber band, adjusting fullness evenly; trim to within ½" (1.3 cm) of rubber band.

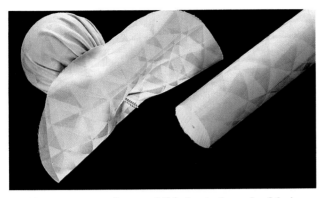

3) Pierce center of second fabric circle; twist fabric over screw. Attach finial to wood pole.

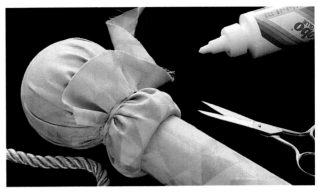

4) Apply bead of glue around neck. Wrap second circle to neck, securing with second rubber band and adjusting gathers evenly; allow glue to dry. Trim fabric close to rubber band. Cover rubber band with cord, braid, or ribbon trim.

How to Make a Covered Finial with a Ruffle

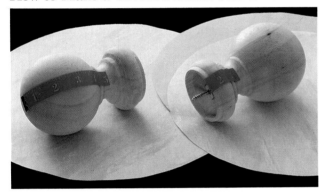

1) Measure ball of finial and cut one fabric circle for each finial, as in step 1 for covered finial, opposite. Measure crown of finial as in step 1; cut two fabric circles for each finial, with radius of each circle equal to measurement plus depth of ruffle plus ½" (1.3 cm).

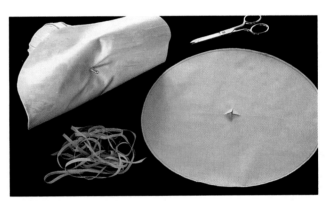

2) Place fabric circles for crown right sides together. Stitch in ¼" (6 mm) seam; trim to ⅛" (3 mm). Slash 1" (2.5 cm) "X" through one layer of fabric at center. Turn right side out through slash; press. Finish as in steps 2 to 4 for covered finial, opposite, but do not trim ruffle.

How to Install a Covered Pole with Finials

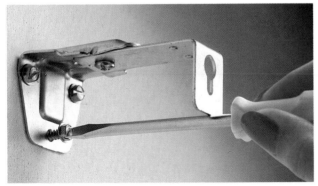

1) Attach brackets to the wall or window frame, using molly bolts (page 40) or pan-head screws (page 42).

2) Attach screws to covered rod, positioning them same distance apart as keyhole openings on brackets. Hang covered rod on brackets.

Bathroom
Decorating

Basic Shower Curtains

A shower curtain is one of the simplest curtains to sew. Valances and tiebacks can be used with the standard shower curtain. Because of its size, the shower curtain is a good place to use bold colors and prints. The instructions for sewing a shower curtain can also be used for cafe curtains or straight curtains hung with rings or hooks on decorative poles.

✄ Cutting Directions

Measure the distance from the bottom of the shower rod to the desired length. Add 10" (25.5 cm) for upper and lower hems. Measure the width of the area to be covered by the curtain and add 4" (10 cm) for side hems. Standard shower curtain liners are 72" × 72" (183 × 183 cm), so the curtain should be cut 76" (193 cm) wide if using a standard liner. Seam fabric together as needed, using French seams.

YOU WILL NEED

Decorator fabric for shower curtain.

Fusible interfacing.

Plastic shower curtain liner.

Eyelets or grommets (not necessary if buttonholes are used), equal to number of holes in plastic liner.

Shower curtain hooks, equal to number of eyelets or buttonholes.

The fabric curtain and plastic liner can hang together on the same rings or hooks, or separately on a shower rod and a spring tension rod. When they hang together, the shower curtain and the liner should be the same width.

How to Sew a Shower Curtain

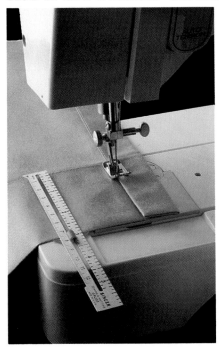

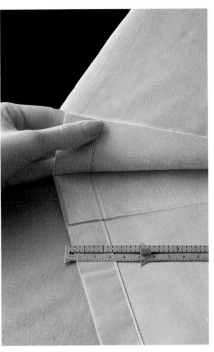

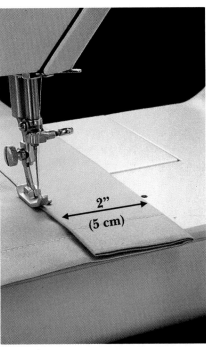

1) Turn under and stitch a 3" (7.5 cm) double-fold hem on lower edge of curtain. Turn under and stitch 1" (2.5 cm) double-fold hem on each side of the curtain.

2) Press under 2" (5 cm) double-fold hem at upper edge of curtain. Open out fold and fuse a 2" (5 cm) strip of fusible interfacing along foldline. Fold again to form a double-fold hem.

3) Edgestitch upper hem in place. Or apply fusible web, following the manufacturer's directions. Fusing adds more stability to upper edge of curtain.

4) Mark positions for eyelets, grommets or buttonholes across upper hem, using the plastic liner as the guide for spacing holes. Position liner ¼" (6 mm) down from upper edge of curtain.

5a) Fasten eyelets securely using eyelet set and hammer or eyelet pliers. If using eyelet set, work on a piece of scrap wood or a hard surface that will not be damaged when pounding eyelets.

5b) Make vertical buttonholes, ¼" to ½" (6 mm to 1.3 cm) long. To prevent buttonholes from raveling, apply liquid fray preventer to cut edges. Insert rings or hooks.

Shower Curtains & Valances

A simple shower curtain can instantly change and refresh a bathroom. Use the shower curtain as a bold splash of color. Coordinate window treatments, towels, and other accessories with your new shower curtain.

The shower curtain pictured , used with a plastic liner, is especially easy to sew because it does not require grommets or eyelets in the heading. Instead, use a drapery folding or pleating tape, and insert metal shower curtain hooks in the loops that are woven right into the tape. These self-styling drapery tapes can also be used for valances and attached to a flat tension rod with standard drapery hooks.

A valance is a special finishing touch on a shower curtain. It helps to enclose the space and coordinate the room. Most of the valance top treatments used for windows are appropriate shower curtain headings as well. The cloud, pouf, and smocked valances are soft, light treatments; the straight lines of pleated and flat valances are more tailored.

Trim a shower curtain with lace, eyelet, ruffling, or grosgrain or satin ribbon.

✂ Cutting Directions

Cut two 81" (206 cm) lengths of fabric (extra fabric will be needed for matching prints); stitch lengths together. Cut shower curtain 6" (15 cm) wider and 9" (23 cm) longer than vinyl liner.

Cut valance width 2½ times the length of rod, and the desired length plus 6½" (16.3 cm) for heading and hems. Seam together as necessary for desired width. Cut smocking tape the cut width of the valance, plus a little extra for aligning and finishing ends.

YOU WILL NEED

Shower curtain fabric, 4½ yd. (4.15 m) for standard liner; extra needed for matching prints.

Drapery folding tape, 2⅛ yd. (1.95 m) for shower curtain; smocking tape for valance, 2½ times the length of the rod.

Vinyl shower curtain liner, 70" × 72" (178 × 183 cm); 12 metal shower curtain rings; flat tension rod for valance.

Drapery hooks.

How to Sew a Shower Curtain

1) Turn under and stitch double 1" (2.5 cm) side hems. At bottom edge, make a double 3" (7.5 cm) hem. At top, press under 1" (2.5 cm). Do not stitch.

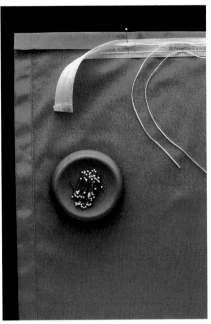

2) Remove pull-cords from folding tape. You will use hook loops only. With loop side facing you and toward the top, pin tape on wrong side of fabric ½" (1.3 cm) from upper edge. Turn under raw edge at ends of tape; stitch in place.

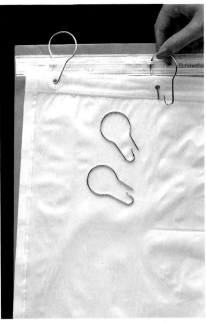

3) Insert shower curtain rings into holes of vinyl liner and into hook loops of folding tape. Hang on shower curtain rod.

How to Sew a Smocked Shower Curtain Valance

1) Stitch double 1" (2.5 cm) side hems; stitch double 2" (5 cm) bottom hem; turn upper edge under 2½" (6.5 cm), and press.

2) Pin smocking tape ½" (1.3 cm) from upper folded edge with loops on top. Turn under 1" (2.5 cm) of tape at each end, and lift out strings. Stitch both sides of tape.

3) Knot strings securely to prevent them from being pulled out. Pull up strings to smock, adjusting fullness to fit rod. Insert drapery hooks every 3" to 4" (7.5 to 10 cm). Mount flat tension rod; hang valance from rod.

Shower Curtain Ideas

Puff valance. Make valance (page 80). Mount valance on tension rod. The valance may be mounted at ceiling or just above shower curtain rod.

Eyelet-trimmed curtain. Stitch flat eyelet to curtain in ½" (1.3 cm) seam. Press. Turn under seam allowance; stitch narrow hem.

Box-pleated valance. To make this box-pleated valance, use self-styling tape. Attach separate rod pocket, and cover stitching line with satin or grosgrain ribbon. Mount valance on tension rod.

Balloon valance. Make valance (page 80). Make two shower curtain panels (page 106) to tie back at sides. Mount curtain panels on shower curtain rod with plastic liner. Mount valance on separate tension rod above shower curtain.

How to Sew a Sink or Vanity Skirt

1) Turn under and stitch double 1" (2.5 cm) hem on bottom edge. Turn under double 1" (2.5 cm) hem on center front edges. For 2-piece skirt, stitch narrow hem on back edges.

2) Press under 1" (2.5 cm) on upper edge of panels. Turn under raw edges on ends of shirring tape; pull out shirring cords. Place tape, right side up, over raw edge, with upper edge of tape ¼" (6 mm) from fold. Stitch both sides of tape.

3) Tie cords at both ends of shirring tape. From wrong side of skirt, pull up cords in shirring tape to the finished width. Knot cords; wrap and tuck under skirt. Adjust the gathers evenly.

Sink & Vanity Skirts

For covering up an outdated sink or bringing more fabric coordination into the bathroom, the sink skirt is a perennial favorite. It conceals the plumbing and provides a hidden storage area.

Vanity skirts are sewn the same way as the sink skirt. They can transform an unsightly table into a charming bedroom or bath accessory.

Self-styling shirring tapes, available in a variety of styles, make the sewing quick and easy and add a dimensional interest to the top of the skirt. For a more traditional approach, gather the upper edge (page 30). Attach the skirt to the sink or vanity with hook and loop tape so the skirt can easily be removed for laundering or a quick change. To make the skirt washable, hand-sew the tape in place.

If the sink skirt is attached on the outside porcelain, make two side panels; each panel of the skirt will extend from the center front to the wall. If the skirt is attached underneath the apron of the sink, it can be made in one piece with a center front opening.

✁ Cutting Directions

To finished length, add 3" (7.5 cm) for a double 1" (2.5 cm) bottom hem and 1" (2.5 cm) to turn under at the top. To determine cut width, measure the distance around the sink or vanity where the skirt will be attached; multiply by 2½ times the fullness. Add 4" (10 cm) for front opening hems.

Cut the number of panels as figured above, and seam together for width as needed. If necessary to seam extra widths, place seams toward back.

YOU WILL NEED

Decorator fabric for skirt.

Shirring tape the cut width of the upper edge of the flat panels before gathering.

Adhesive-backed hook and loop tape to go around the sink or vanity.

4) Finger press loop side of self-adhesive hook and loop tape to the wrong side of the skirt, over the shirring tape.

5) Attach the hook side of self-adhesive tape to the outside of the sink or vanity table. Attach skirt to tape.

Alternative mounting. To hang skirt under apron of sink, attach loop side of tape on right side of skirt ½" (1.3 cm) from upper edge; adhere the hook side of tape to underside of the sink. Attach skirt.

Embellished Towels

Perk up the bath with designer touches added to inexpensive, plain towels. Laces, ribbons, or monograms can be added to coordinate with bedroom sheets and trims, window treatments, and shower curtains.

Preshrink or steam-shrink woven ribbon trims, particularly all-cotton trims; polyester laces will not need preshrinking. Mark trimming placement on towel with water-soluble marking pen.

When applying trims to terry towels, loosen the tension and use a long stitch length. Ease the trimming slightly as you stitch; when the towel is folded on the rack, the trim will lie smooth.

Lace and ribbon. Trim towels with prefinished lace beading (**1**), lace edging (**2**), or galloon lace (**3**). For lace beading, insert ribbon into beading, position beading on towel, and straight-stitch upper edge. For lace edging, position so lower edge of lace covers towel fringe or hem. Cover upper edge of lace with ribbon trim; straight-stitch along both edges of ribbon. For galloon lace, position trim on towel, and straight-stitch near edges of lace.

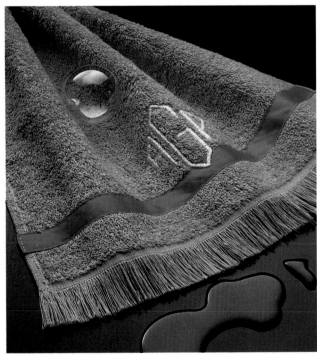

Machine monogram. On electronic sewing machine, insert monogram cassette and program desired lettering. Cover monogram area with dissolvable plastic film protector to prevent snagging terry loops. Stitch; tear away plastic film. Laundering dissolves any remaining film.

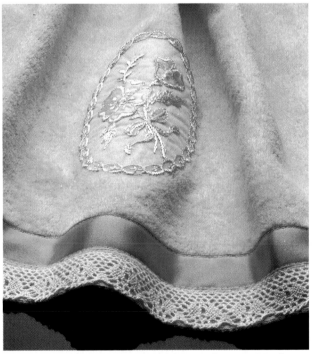

Lace motif. Cut single motif from Cluny or Venice lace, or use purchased appliqué. Fusible web may be used to hold appliqué in place; stitch with narrow zigzag. Coordinating trims may be stitched at lower edge of towel.

Pillows

Pillows

Pillows can add softness and texture to a room for a decorative finishing touch. Instructions for several pillow designs, from pillows with rosettes to pillows with knotted jumbo welting, are included on the following pages.

For most pillows, cut the pillow top and back 1" (2.5 cm) wider and longer than the finished size of the pillow. If using a pillow form, cut the fabric 1" (2.5 cm) wider and longer than the form. To prevent dog-eared corners on square or rectangular pillows, taper the corners of the fabric, opposite.

A zipper closure can be added to make it easier to clean the pillow cover. An invisible zipper can be inserted along one side for an inconspicuous closure; use the special zipper foot designed for applying invisible zippers.

If the pillow has welting, it may be easier to add a seam and insert the zipper on the pillow back. To make a zippered pillow cover that has a back seam, cut the pillow front 1" (2.5 cm) wider and longer than the finished size of the pillow, or 1" (2.5 cm) wider and longer than the pillow form. Cut one pillow back piece the width of the pillow front and 3¾" (9.5 cm) long; cut another piece, the width of the pillow front and 2¼" (6 cm) shorter than the length of the pillow front.

When the pillow cover is completed, insert a pillow form, or fill the cover with polyester fiberfill or quilt batting. Push fiberfill or batting into the corners and along the sides as necessary to fill out the pillow. Even when a pillow form is used, you may want to add fiberfill or batting to the corners and sides.

How to Prevent Dog-eared Corners

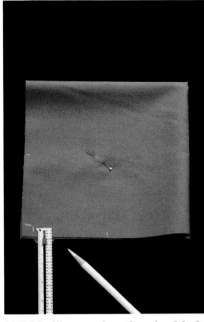

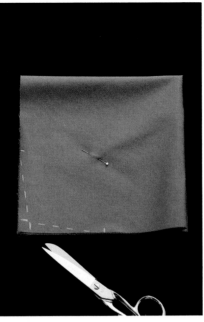

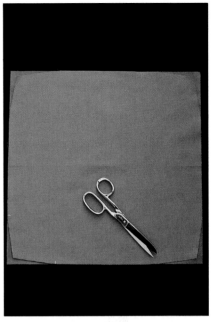

1) Fold pillow top into fourths. Mark a point halfway between corner and fold on each open side. At corner, mark a point ½" (1.3 cm) from each raw edge.

2) Mark lines, tapering from raw edges at center marks to mark at corner. Cut on marked lines.

3) Use pillow top as pattern for cutting pillow back so all corners are tapered. For zippered pillow cover, below, corners may be tapered on pillow back after the zipper is inserted.

How to Sew a Pillow with a Back Zipper

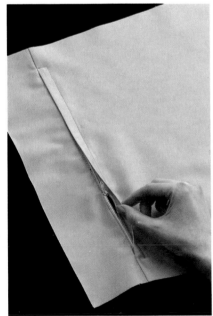

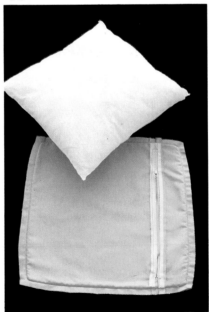

1) Cut pillow pieces, opposite. Stitch pillow back pieces together in ¾" (2 cm) seam, basting in zipper area. Apply zipper that is about 2" (5 cm) shorter than the finished width of the pillow. To prevent dog-eared corners, taper corners of pillow front and back, above.

2) Apply welting (pages 120 to 123) to pillow front, if desired. Pin pillow front to pillow back, right sides together; stitch ½" (1.3 cm) seam. Turn right side out.

3) Stuff pillow cover by inserting pillow form. Push polyester fiberfill or quilt batting into corners of the pillow and along sides as necessary to fill out pillow.

Twin-needle Stitched Pillows

Twin-needle stitching is done using a twin needle, two needle threads, and a single bobbin thread. The bobbin thread draws the fabric up between the rows of stitching to form a decorative raised design or a pintuck. Twin-needle pintucks take up so little fabric that it is usually not necessary to allow extra fabric for the project. Synthetic suede makes an elegant yet easy pillow for this project. Keep the design simple with straight or slightly curved design lines. Make a square pillow (page 116) and add twin-needle stitching to pillow top before sewing pillow together.

Twin needles vary in size and are numbered according to the distance in millimeters between the needles and by the size of the needles. For example, a 2.0/80 twin needle has two size 80 needles, spaced 2 mm apart. When pintucks are sewn using twin needles, they are always even in width, because the two rows of stitching are exactly parallel.

A special-purpose presser foot or an open-toe foot is used for twin-needle stitching. A pintuck foot is used for sewing multiple rows of twin-needle pintucks. The grooves on the underside of the pintuck foot keep the pintucks the same distance apart. Consult your sewing machine dealer about the pintuck feet available for your machine; there may be more than one size available to accommodate different weights of fabric. Use a larger-grooved foot for pintucks in bulkier fabrics such as synthetic suede. Choose the twin-needle size that most closely corresponds to the spacing of the grooves.

A more distinct raised appearance may be achieved in several ways. You can use a heavier thread in the bobbin to increase the tension on the underside. Or you can use cording to emphasize the raised design and to prevent puckering. Select the filler cord according to the size of the grooves in the pintuck foot. Buttonhole twist, pearl cotton, or gimp may be used.

How to Sew Multiple Rows of Twin-needle Pintucks

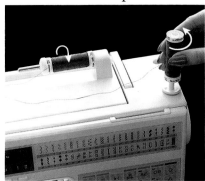

1) Place two spools of thread on machine so they unwind in opposite directions, to prevent tangling. Tighten needle thread tension, as necessary. Attach pintuck presser foot.

2) Mark placement line for first pintuck on right side of fabric. Stitch, guiding one needle along marked line.

3) Continue stitching rows, guiding previous tuck under one of the channels in pintuck foot; spacing between tucks depends on channel used. Stitch all pintucks in same direction to prevent distortion.

How to Sew Corded Twin-needle Stitching

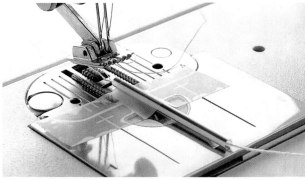

1) Thread machine and adjust tension as in step 1, above. Cut 2" (5 cm) length of drinking or cocktail straw. Tape straw to sewing machine bed directly in front of needle hole and ⅛" (3 mm) in front of presser foot. Thread end of cord through straw.

2) Place ball or spool of cord in lap. Stitch, placing cord under fabric and guiding fabric along marked design lines; cord automatically fills pintuck during stitching. For multiple rows of corded pintucks, use pintuck foot, and stitch as in step 3, above.

How to Turn Corners Using a Twin Needle

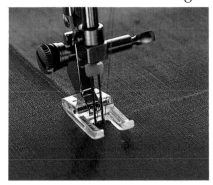

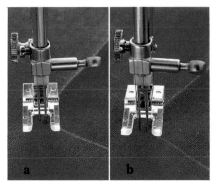

1) Thread machine and adjust the tension as in step 1, above. Using open-toe presser foot, stitch to corner; cord stitches, if desired, as above.

2) Raise presser foot, leaving needles down; turn fabric at a 45° angle, or halfway around corner **(a).** Lower presser foot. Take one stitch, turning flywheel by hand, taking care that inner needle stitches in place **(b).**

3) Leave needles down and raise presser foot. Turn fabric again to complete the corner. Lower the presser foot and continue stitching.

Welting

Many decorator pillows have welting to emphasize the edges. You can make welting by covering cording with fabric strips (opposite), or make gathered welting (pages 122 and 123). Or use purchased twisted welting (pages 124 and 125).

To make welting, cut fabric strips on the bias for greater flexibility around curved edges and corners. The bias strips do not have to be cut on the true bias. Strips that are cut at an angle less than 45 degrees provide the necessary flexibility but require less yardage. For economical use of fabric, the strips may be cut on the crosswise grain instead of the bias, but the welting may not be as smooth and may appear wrinkled.

The width of the fabric strips depends on the size of the cording. To determine how wide to cut the strips, wrap a piece of fabric around the cording. Pin it together, encasing the cording. Measure this distance and add 1" (2.5 cm) for seam allowances. Cut fabric strips to this width.

Cording, which comes on large spools, may have a tendency to curl or twist even after it is uncoiled from the spool. When sewing the welting, take care to smooth out the cording, removing any twists, to prevent the finished welting from appearing twisted.

How to Make and Attach Welting

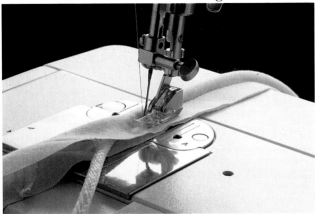

1) **Cut** fabric strips, opposite; seam strips together as necessary for desired length. Fold fabric strip around cording, wrong sides together, matching raw edges. Using a zipper foot, machine-baste close to cording; smooth cording as you sew, removing twists.

2) **Stitch** welting to right side of fabric over previous stitches, matching raw edges and starting 2" (5 cm) from end of welting; clip and ease welting at corners, or ease welting at curves.

3) **Stop** stitching 2" (5 cm) from point where ends of welting will meet. Cut off one end of welting so it overlaps the other end by 1" (2.5 cm).

4) **Remove** stitching from one end of welting, and trim ends of cording so they just meet.

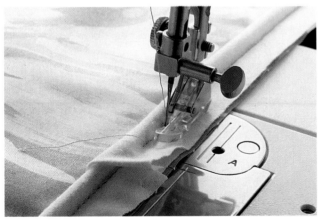

5) **Fold** under ½" (1.3 cm) of fabric on overlapping end of welting. Lap it around the other end; finish stitching welting to pillow front.

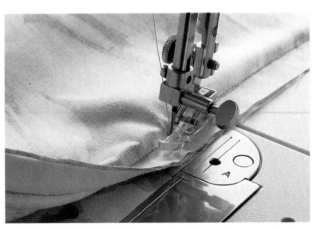

6) **Stitch** pillow back to pillow front, right sides together, using zipper foot; stitch inside previous stitching line, crowding stitches against welting. Leave opening on one side for turning, if pillow cover is not zippered.

Gathered Welting

Gathered welting is used for a shirred border on a pillow and adds textural interest. For a dramatic, bold effect, jumbo cording is used.

Cut a length of jumbo cording about 10" (25.5 cm) longer than the distance to be welted. Cut fabric strips for the gathered welting on the straight of grain. The width of the fabric strips depends on the size of the jumbo cording. To determine how wide to cut the strips, wrap a piece of fabric around the cording, and pin it together, encasing the cording. Measure this distance, and add 2" (5 cm) to allow for ease and seam allowances; cut straight-grain fabric strips to this width. The combined length of the strips should be two or three times the length of the cording to allow for the fullness of the gathers.

How to Make and Apply Gathered Welting

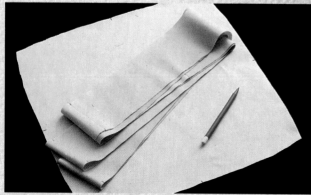

1) Stitch fabric strips together into a continuous circle. Divide fabric strip and outer edge of pillow into fourths; mark with water-soluble marking pen.

2) Fold strip around cording, wrong sides together, matching raw edges; secure cording to strip 4" (10 cm) from end, using safety pin. Using zipper foot, stitch about 10" to 12" (25.5 to 30.5 cm), stitching 3/8" (1 cm) from edge. Stop stitching, leaving needle in fabric.

3) Pull cording gently and push fabric strip back to end of cording until fabric behind needle is tightly gathered. Stitch 10" to 12" (25.5 to 30.5 cm) at a time, leaving 6" (15 cm) opening if welting has double fullness, or 9" (23 cm) opening if welting has triple fullness.

4) Pin gathered welting to right side of pillow front, matching raw edges and pin marks; distribute gathers evenly. Stitch ½" (1.3 cm) from raw edge, using zipper foot, leaving 3" (7.5 cm) unstitched at opening in gathered welting; ease welting at curves and corners. A tool, such as a seam ripper, is helpful for guiding the gathers.

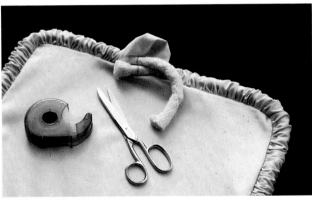

5) Turn welting into finished position. Adjust cording at corners for a smooth fit around pillow. Mark a line on each end of cording so marked lines just meet. At marked lines, wrap ends of cording with transparent tape. Cut off excess cording on marked lines.

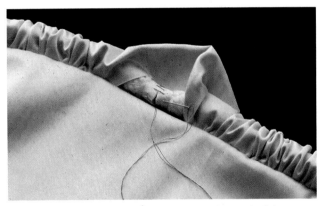

6) Hand-stitch ends of cording together, stitching through tape.

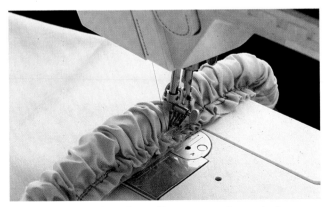

7) Fold fabric around cording at opening; stitch gathering threads at opening, and pull threads to gather remaining welting. Distribute gathers evenly. Stitch welting to fabric.

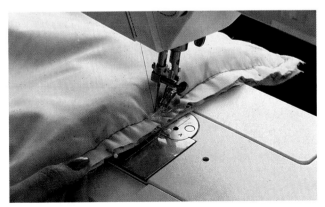

8) Stitch pillow back to pillow front, right sides together, using zipper foot; stitch inside previous stitching line. Leave opening on one side for turning, if pillow cover is not zippered.

Twisted Welting

Twisted welting, a decorative alternative to fabric-covered welting, has an attached tape, or lip, that can be stitched into the seams. Rayon welting, which has a shiny appearance, is more difficult to handle than cotton welting.

From the right side of the welting, the inner edge of the tape is not visible. For easier stitching and a more finished appearance on the front of the pillow, the welting is applied to the pillow back, right sides up. The ends of the welting can be twisted together to join them inconspicuously.

How to Attach Twisted Welting to a Pillow

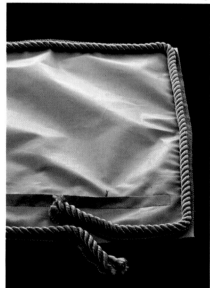

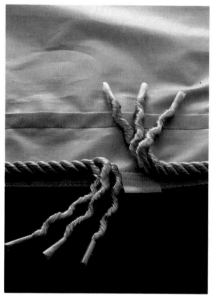

1) Stitch twisted welting to pillow back, using zipper foot, with right sides up and edge of welting tape aligned to raw edge of fabric. Leave 1½" (3.8 cm) unstitched between ends; leave 3" (7.5 cm) tails.

2) Remove stitching from welting tape on tails. Separate cords; wrap transparent tape around ends to prevent raveling. Trim welting tape to 1" (2.5 cm) from stitching; overlap ends and secure with transparent tape. Arrange cords so those at right turn up and those at left turn down.

3) Insert cords at right end under welting tape, twisting and pulling them down until welting is returned to its original shape. Secure in place, using transparent tape or pins.

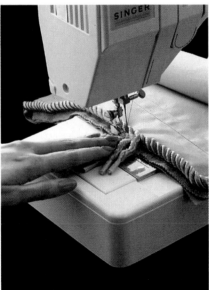

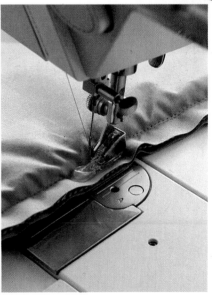

4) Twist and pull cords at left end over cords at right end until the twisted ends look like continuous twisted welting; check both sides of welting.

5) Position zipper foot on left side of needle; this will allow you to stitch in the direction of the twists. Machine-baste through all layers to secure welting at seamline, or cords may be hand-basted in place, if desired.

6) Place pillow back on pillow front, right sides together. Stitch as close to welting as possible, using zipper foot. If pillow cover is not zippered, leave an opening on one side for turning. With pillow front facing up, stitch again, crowding stitches closer to welting.

Butterfly Pillows

This plump pillow trimmed with twisted welting has
a dimensional effect. The butterfly pillow consists of
two pillows, one square and one rectangular, tied
together tightly at the center. The twisted welting is
applied to the pillow back, for easier stitching and a
more finished appearance on the front of the pillow.
Fabric-covered welting can be substituted for the
twisted welting, if desired. When fabric-covered
welting is used, it is applied to the pillow front
(pages 120 and 121).

✂ Cutting Directions
Cut two 15" × 19" (38 × 48.5 cm) rectangles, two
15" (38 cm) squares, and two 2" (5 cm) squares of
decorator fabric.

YOU WILL NEED

1 yd. (0.95 m) decorator fabric.

4¼ yd. (3.9 m) twisted welting; or two colors of
twisted welting, 2⅛ yd. (1.95 m) each.

One rectangular pillow form, 14" × 18" (35.5 ×
46 cm).

One square pillow form, 14" (35.5 cm).

How to Sew a Butterfly Pillow

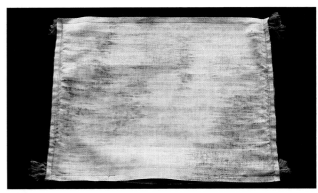

1) Pin 15" (38 cm) lengths of twisted welting to fabric, right sides up, along 15" (38 cm) sides of rectangular pillow back and two opposite sides of square pillow back. Remove the stitching from welting tape for 1" (2.5 cm) at ends. Untwist each end slightly, and curve cording into seam allowance; pin. Machine-baste welting in place, using zipper foot.

2) Pin rectangles, right sides together. With pillow back facing up, stitch around pillow, stitching as close as possible to welting on sides and stitching ½" (1.3 cm) seam on upper and lower edges; leave 8" (20.5 cm) opening at center of lower edge for turning.

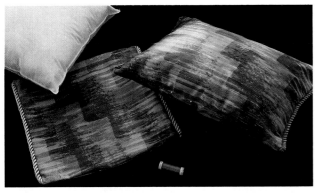

3) Repeat step 2 for square pillow. Insert pillow forms; slipstitch openings closed.

4) Remove welting tape from remaining welting. With square pillow centered over rectangular pillow, wrap welting tape around pillows twice, cinching them tightly; tie at bottom of pillows. Tuck ends of welting tape between pillows.

5) Cut remaining welting in half if using one color. Machine-stitch cords together at one end to right side of 2" (5 cm) fabric square, stitching ¼" (6 mm) from raw edge of fabric. Trim ends of welting. Fold square down and fold in all edges, enclosing ends of welting; hand-stitch. Twist welting tightly. Apply fabric square to other end.

6) Wrap welting around pillows twice. Tuck ends between pillows or under twisted welting.

Shirred Pillows

Shirred cording or boxing strips give pillows a formal look.

✂ Cutting Directions

For shirred box pillow, cut pillow front and back 1" (2.5 cm) larger than finished pillow. Cut boxing strip 1" (2.5 cm) wider than depth of form and two to three times longer than distance around form.

For shirred corded pillow, cut pillow front and back 1" (2.5 cm) larger than finished pillow. For cording, cut fabric strips on the crosswise grain, wide enough to cover cord plus 1" (2.5 cm) for seam. The combined length of the strips should be two to three times the distance around pillow.

YOU WILL NEED

Decorator fabric for pillow front and back and for cording or boxing strips.

Cord (twisted white cotton or polyester cable, if making shirred cording). Cut 3" (7.5 cm) longer than distance around pillow.

Gathering cord (string, crochet cotton or dental floss).

Pillow form wrapped in polyester batting, or liner.

How to Make a Shirred Box Pillow

1) Join short ends of boxing strip with ½" (1.3 cm) seam. Prepare raw edges for gathering by zigzagging over cord (page 30) or by stitching two rows of bastestitching. Fold strip into fourths and mark both edges of folds with ⅜" (1 cm) clips.

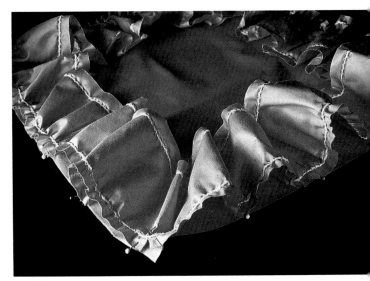

2) Pin boxing strip to pillow front, right sides together, raw edges even, matching clips on boxing strip to pillow corners. Pull up the gathering cord to fit each side of the pillow.

How to Make Shirred Cording

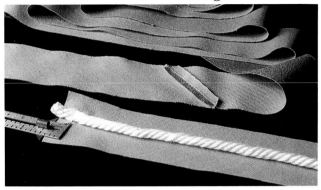

1) Join ends of cording strips using ¼" (6 mm) seams. Press the seams open. Stitch one end of the cord to the wrong side of the cording strip, ⅜" (1 cm) from the end of the strip.

2) Fold cording strip around cord, wrong sides together, matching raw edges. Using zipper foot, machine-baste for 6" (15 cm), close to but not crowding cord. Stop stitching with needle in fabric.

3) Raise presser foot. While gently pulling cord, push cording strip back to end of cord until fabric behind needle is tightly shirred. Continue stitching in 6" (15 cm) intervals until all cording is shirred.

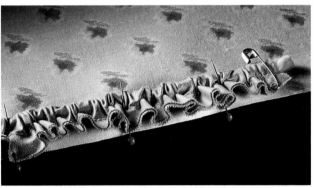

4) Insert pin through strip and cord at each end to secure cord. Distribute gathers evenly. Attach shirred cording to pillow front and join ends of cord as on page 121, steps 4 and 5.

3) Distribute gathers evenly. Stitch all four sides inside gathering row, shortening stiches for 1" (2.5 cm) on each side of corner. Take one or two stitches diagonally across each corner.

4) Pin the lower edge of the boxing strip to pillow back. Repeat steps 2 and 3, except stitch only three sides, leaving one side open to insert the pillow form.

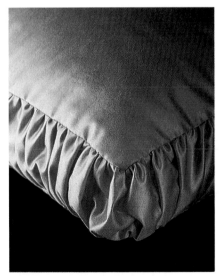

5) Finish as for pillow without welting (page 117), inserting a pillow form wrapped in polyester batting.

Knotted-corner Pillows

On the knotted-corner pillow, jumbo welting forms pretzel-like knots and creates a border. Smaller versions of these pillows can accent sofas and chairs; larger ones can serve as comfortable floor cushions.

For creative detailing and easier sewing, the covered welting is pulled through self-fabric sleeves on all sides of the pillow. It is helpful to wrap the ends of the cording with masking tape to prevent the ends from fraying while you are handling the cording.

✂ Cutting Directions

Cut the pillow front and pillow back 1" (2.5 cm) longer and wider than the pillow form. Measure the height of the pillow form. Measure in from the corners of the pillow front and pillow back a distance equal to one-half the height of the pillow; mark with notches.

Measure the circumference of the jumbo cording loosely. Cut four fabric sleeves for the sides of the pillow, with the width of each sleeve equal to the circumference plus 1" (2.5 cm), and the length of each sleeve equal to the distance between the notches plus 2" (5 cm). If textured fabric is used, the fabric sleeves may need to be cut about ⅜" (1 cm) wider, so the fabric-covered cording can be pulled through the sleeve more easily.

Cut fabric strips to cover the jumbo cording, with the width of the strips equal to the width of the fabric sleeves and with the combined length of the strips equal to the length of the jumbo cording.

YOU WILL NEED

1¼ yd. (1.15 m) decorator fabric, for 20" (51 cm) pillow.

Jumbo cording, the length equal to the distance around the pillow plus about 60" (152.5 cm); each knot takes up 12" to 15" (30.5 to 38 cm), depending on the size of the cording.

Fusible web.

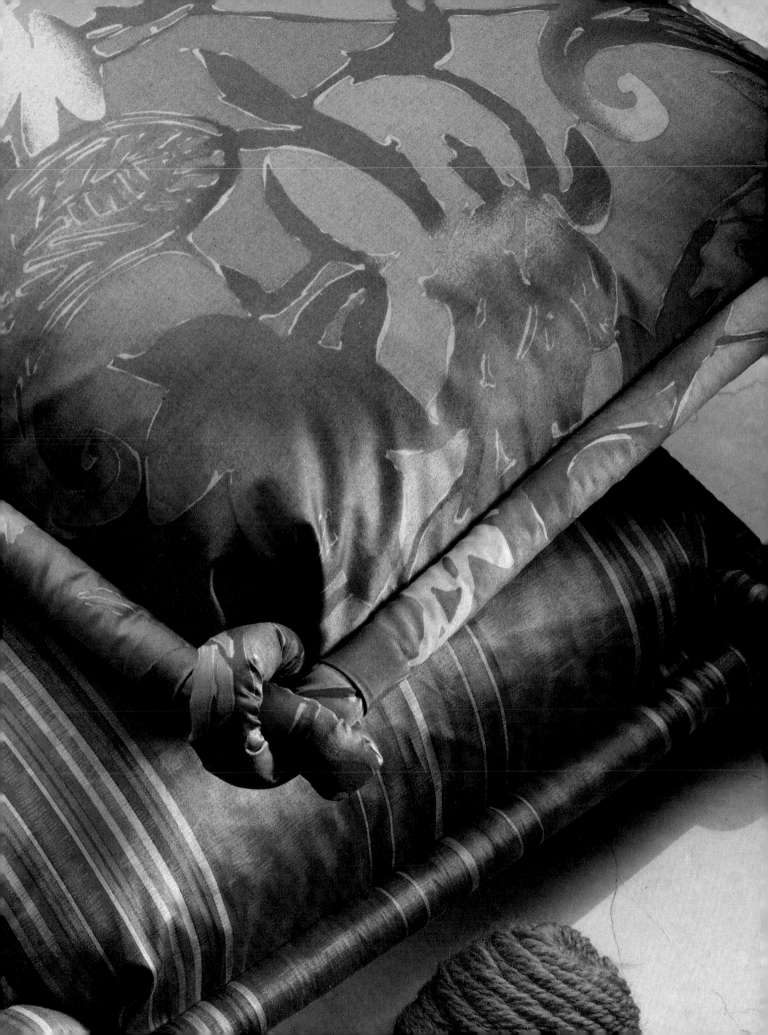

How to Sew a Knotted-corner Pillow

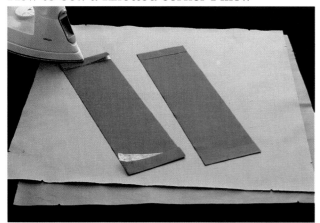

1) Mark notches on pillow front and pillow back, as on page 130. Press under 1" (2.5 cm) on short ends of fabric sleeves; fuse in place, using fusible web.

2) Fold fabric sleeves in half lengthwise, wrong sides together; pin to pillow front between the notches, matching raw edges. Baste strips in place on seamline.

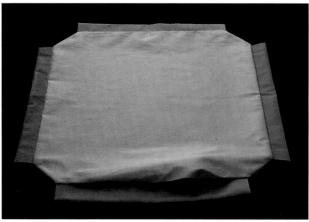

3) Pin pillow front to pillow back, right sides together. Stitch ½" (1.3 cm) seam on sides of pillow, stitching diagonally across corners between notches; leave an opening on one side for turning. Trim excess fabric at corners. Turn pillow cover right side out.

4) Fold fabric strip in half lengthwise, right sides together; stitch ½" (1.3 cm) seam. Turn right side out, using large safety pin or bodkin.

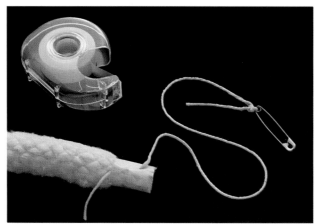

5) Cut piece of string the length of one side of pillow. Tie string around end of cording. Secure string to cording by wrapping it with tape. Attach safety pin or bodkin to end of string.

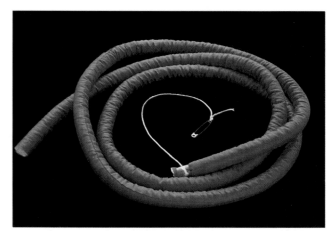

6) Pull cording through fabric strip to make welting. Tie string around end of welting; secure string to welting by wrapping it with tape.

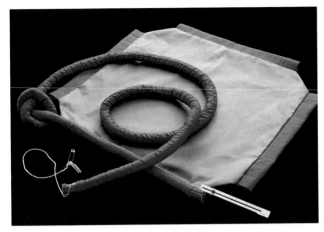

7) Pull welting through fabric sleeve on pillow, leaving 1" (2.5 cm) tail at beginning. Tie overhand knot at end of sleeve.

8) Pull welting through next sleeve; tie another overhand knot. Repeat with remaining sleeves.

9) Insert pillow form, as on page 117; pin opening closed. Adjust all knots to same size. Turn seam on welting inward at knots.

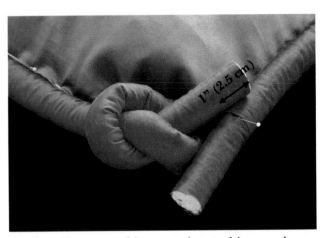

10) Cut off excess welting at end, so welting overlaps first sleeve 1" (2.5 cm), arrow. Mark welting at beginning of first sleeve.

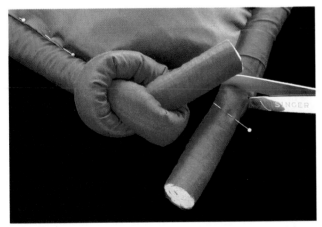

11) Pull end of welting out of first sleeve. Cut welting 1" (2.5 cm) beyond mark.

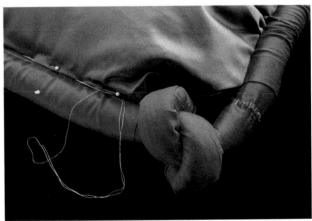

12) Whipstitch ends of welting together. Slide ends back into sleeve. Slipstitch opening on pillow closed.

Sunburst Pillows

Framed with a ruffle and welting, this half-circle pillow can be made in any size and is an interesting accent on sofas and beds. The pillow shown is made from a pattern 18" (46 cm) across and 11½" (29.3 cm) high and has a 3" (7.5 cm) finished ruffle. When twisted welting is used, it is applied to the pillow back over the ruffle, for easier stitching and a more finished appearance on the front of the pillow. When fabric-covered welting is used, it is applied to the pillow front.

✂ Cutting Directions

Cut the pillow front and pillow back, using the pattern, opposite. For the ruffle, cut fabric strips two times the finished width of the ruffle plus 1" (2.5 cm) for seam allowances. For triple fullness, the combined length of the fabric strips is equal to three times the measurement along the curved edge of the pattern.

YOU WILL NEED

¾ yd. (0.7 m) decorator fabric, for pillow shown.

1½ yd. (1.4 m) twisted welting with welting tape or lip; or fabric-covered welting (pages 120 and 121).

Polyester fiberfill.

How to Make the Pattern for a Sunburst Pillow

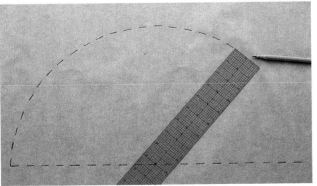

1) Draw a dotted line on paper equal to the desired diameter of circle. Using straightedge and pencil, mark half circle, measuring a distance equal to the radius from midpoint of dotted line.

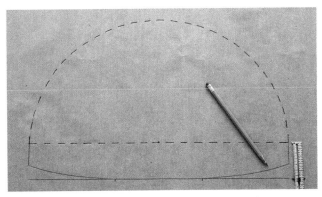

2) Extend lines straight down at sides for 1½" (3.8 cm). Draw line 2½"(6.5 cm) away from dotted line; divide into thirds, and mark. Draw slightly curved line between side and one-third markings. Cut on marked lines to complete pattern piece.

How to Sew a Sunburst Pillow

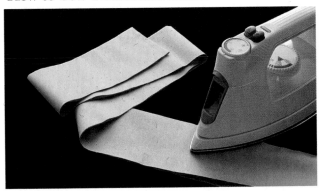

1) Stitch fabric strips together for ruffle in ¼" (6 mm) seams, right sides together. Fold pieced strip in half lengthwise, right sides together; stitch across ends in ¼" (6 mm) seam. Turn right side out; press. Stitch two rows of gathering threads on strip, ½" (1.3 cm) and ¼" (6 mm) from raw edge; or zigzag over cord as on page 169, step 9.

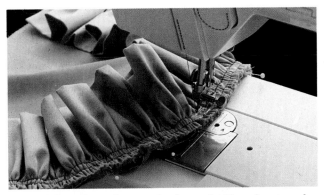

2) Divide strip and curved edges of pillow front and back into fourths; pin-mark. Place strip on curved edge of pillow back, right sides together, matching raw edges and pin marks; pull gathering threads to fit. Machine-baste ruffle, leaving pin marks in place.

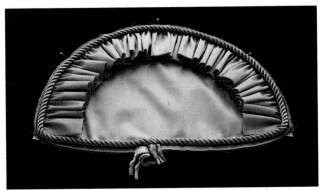

3) Machine-baste twisted welting around pillow back, over ruffle, and join ends as on pages 124 and 125. Or machine-baste fabric-covered welting around pillow front and join ends as on page 121.

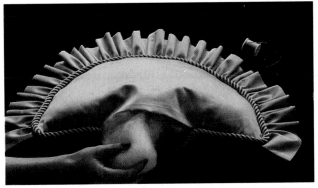

4) Pin pillow front to pillow back, right sides together, matching the pin marks. Stitch, using a zipper foot, crowding stitches against welting; leave 8" (20.5 cm) opening at bottom for turning. Stuff pillow with fiberfill, pushing it firmly into corners of pillow and along sides. Slipstitch opening closed.

Reversible Rosette Pillows

Perfect for the bedroom, a rosette pillow is simply a circular pillow cover tied around a pillow form. The pillow cover is lined to finish off the edges and to make it reversible. Select lightweight fabrics so the pillow cover can be gathered up tightly at the center; avoid fabrics that are stiff.

Twisted welting or fabric-covered welting is applied to the outer edge of the pillow cover. The welting defines the edge and helps the rosette stand out.

✂ Cutting Directions

For a 12" (30.5 cm) pillow, cut one 30" (76 cm) circle from the outer fabric and one from the lining. For a 14" (35.5 cm) pillow, cut 35" (89 cm) circles, or for a 16" (40.5 cm) pillow, cut 40" (102 cm) circles. To make it easier to mark and cut the circles, cut a square of each fabric, 1" (2.5 cm) larger than the diameter of the circle; then follow step 1, opposite.

Also cut a fabric strip, 2" × 18" (5 × 46 cm), to tie around the center of the pillow.

If fabric-covered welting is desired for the outer edge, cut bias fabric strips, with the combined length of the strips equal to the circumference of the circle. To estimate the length needed, multiply the diameter by three and one-half. The width of the bias strips depends on the size of the cording (page 120). For a 12" (30.5 cm) pillow, ⁵⁄₃₂" cording works well; for a larger pillow, use ⁸⁄₃₂" cording.

YOU WILL NEED

Decorator fabrics for outer fabric and lining.

Twisted welting with welting tape or lip; or cording and fabric for fabric-covered welting.

Circular pillow form.

How to Sew a Reversible Rosette Pillow

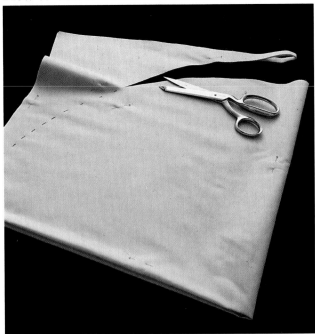

1) Fold fabric square into fourths, right sides together. Using straightedge and pencil, mark one-quarter of the circle on fabric, measuring a distance equal to the radius from the folded center of fabric. Cut on marked line through all layers; notch raw edge at foldlines. Use as pattern for cutting and notching remaining fabric circle.

2) Apply twisted welting to outer edge of one fabric circle, as on pages 124 and 125. Or make fabric-covered welting and apply to outer edge, as on page 121. Pin fabric circles, right sides together, matching notches; stitch close to welting, using zipper foot and leaving 6" (15 cm) opening for turning.

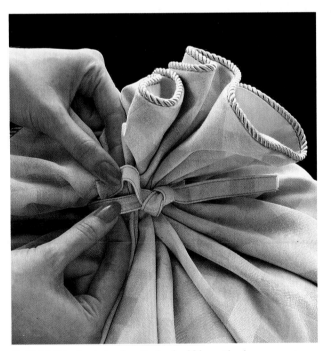

3) Turn pillow cover right side out; press. Slipstitch opening closed. Center pillow form on pillow cover; draw up fabric around pillow form, securing with rubber band. Adjust folds, arranging welting for desired effect.

4) Fold fabric strip for tie in half lengthwise, wrong sides together; press. Fold raw edges to center and press. Refold, and edgestitch on both long edges. Tie around bunched fabric, concealing rubber band and cinching in pillow cover tightly. Cut ends to desired length; tuck ends under tie to conceal them.

Sash Pillows

Sash pillows coordinate well with scarf swag window treatments and may have either a rosette or a tie at the center of the sash. The rosette can also be used at the center of the sunburst window treatment for an arch, or Palladian, window (pages 96 and 97).

✄ Cutting Directions

Cut two 17" (43 cm) squares of fabric for the pillow body and one 23" (58.5 cm) square for the sash. Cut bias strips for cording from contrasting fabric, with the total length of the strips equal to 2 yd. (1.85 m); piece the strips together as necessary. The width of the bias strips depends on the size of the cording (page 120).

For a pillow with a rosette, also cut one 25" (63.5 cm) circle for the rosette from contrasting fabric. To make

it easier to mark and cut the circle, cut a 26" (66 cm) square of fabric; then follow step 1 on page 137.

For a pillow with a tie, also cut one 5" × 6" (12.5 × 15 cm) rectangle for the tie from contrasting fabric.

YOU WILL NEED

½ yd. (0.5 m) decorator fabric for pillow body.

1½ yd. (1.4 m) contrasting decorator fabric for pillow with rosette, to make rosette, sash, and bias cording.

¾ yd. (0.7 m) contrasting decorator fabric for pillow with tie, to make tie, sash, and bias cording.

2 yd. (1.85 m) cording.

Pillow form, 16" (40.5 cm).

How to Make a Rosette

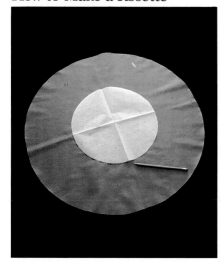

1) Mark center of rosette circle on right side of fabric, using a pencil. Make paper pattern of circle with 12" (30.5 cm) diameter; mark center. Match centers of fabric and paper circles; trace outline of paper circle onto right side of fabric.

2) Finish outer edge of circle, using zigzag or overlock stitch. Hand-baste on marked lines of small circle, using ½" (1.3 cm) running stitches. Pull basting stitches tight; secure threads. Hand-baste around outer edge and pull basting stitches tight; secure stitches, but do not cut thread tails.

3) Position eraser end of pencil on marked center of rosette. Push the center of smaller pouf through the opening at center of larger pouf; secure fabric on wrong side. Do not cut thread tails.

How to Sew a Sash Pillow with a Rosette

1) **Fold** 23" (58.5 cm) fabric square in half, right sides together. Stitch long edges together; press seam open. Turn tube right side out; center seam on underside of tube. Fold tube in half, matching raw edges. Press fold; do not press lengthwise edges.

2) **Open** out sash; hand-baste on pressed foldline. Pull basting stitches tight to cinch the sash at center.

3) **Lay** sash diagonally across pillow top, right sides up, pinning seams of sash at corners of pillow top. Trim excess sash fabric.

4) **Make** welting and apply to pillow top, as on page 205.

5) **Place** the pillow back on pillow front, right sides together. Stitch around all sides of pillow close to cording, using zipper foot; leave an opening on one side for turning.

6) **Turn** pillow right side out. Insert pillow form. Hand-stitch rosette to sash over basting stitches. Slipstitch opening of pillow closed

How to Sew a Sash Pillow with a Tie

1) **Complete** steps 1 to 5, opposite. Fold 5" × 6" (12.5 × 15 cm) rectangle of fabric in half lengthwise, right sides together. Stitch ½" (1.3 cm) seam along 6" (15 cm) side; turn right side out. Press flat, with seam centered on underside of tie.

2) **Turn** pillow right side out. Insert pillow form. Fold in one end of tie. Wrap tie around center of the sash, tucking raw edge into folded end; slipstitch in place. Turn tie so seam is under sash. Slipstitch opening of pillow closed.

Reversible Rolled Bolsters

The reversible rolled bolster is edged with welting for dimension and appeal. This soft pillow is actually a fabric cover and batting rolled together for easy construction. The bolster is lined to finish off the edges and to make it reversible. The ends of the bolster are tied with bows.

The striped fabric in the pillow above has been railroaded (page 23) so the stripes encircle the bolster. Extra yardage is needed for railroading.

✂ Cutting Directions

For pillow body, cut one 18" × 45" (46 × 115 cm) rectangle of decorative fabric and one of lining. For welting, cut bias fabric strips with combined length of strips equal to 3¼ yd. (3 m). The width of the bias strips depends on the size of the cording (page 204). For ties, cut two 1½" × 28" (3.8 × 71 cm) fabric strips.

Cut as many 12" × 30" (30.5 × 76 cm) rectangles of batting as necessary for 2" to 3" (5 to 7.5 cm) thickness.

YOU WILL NEED

½ **yd. (0.5 m) decorator fabric** for pillow body, or 1¼ yd. (1.15 m) if fabric is to be railroaded.

½ **yd. (0.5 m) contrasting fabric** for lining.

¾ **yd. (0.7 m) matching or contrasting fabric** for ties and welting.

3¼ **yd. (3 m) cording.**

Quilt batting.

How to Sew a Rolled Bolster

1) Round corners at one short end of rectangle. Make welting as on page 205. Machine-baste welting on right side of one fabric piece to long sides and rounded end, matching raw edges and stitching over previous stitches; ease cording at corners and leave at least 3" (7.5 cm) of welting at ends.

2) Remove stitching from ends of welting. Trim cords ½" (1.3 cm) from raw edges of pillow fabric. Fold excess fabric strip back over welting, then diagonally, as shown. Pin, and stitch in place.

3) Pin fabric pieces, right sides together. Stitch on all sides, stitching as close as possible to welting; leave 6" (15 cm) opening at the end without welting. Notch out rounded corners to remove excess fullness. Turn right side out; press. Stitch opening closed.

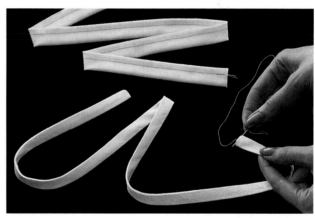

4) Fold each tie in half lengthwise, right sides together; stitch ¼" (6 mm) seam on long edge. Turn ties right side out, using loop turner; tuck in and slipstitch ends.

5) Center batting on finished rectangle. Roll fabric up to batting, starting from the end without welting.

6) Continue rolling fabric and batting together loosely. Tie ends tightly. Shape welting at ends for spiral effect.

Quick Pillows

Four Timesaving Pillows

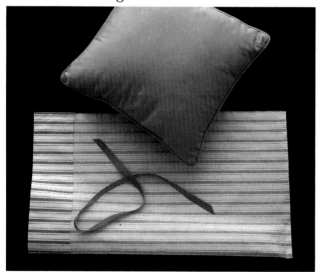

Sack pillow. Cut a 30" (76 cm) square. Turn under a deep hem on one side and fuse or stitch in place. Fold in half with right sides together and stitch raw edges together. Turn right side out. Insert pillow and tie a ribbon around open end.

Tie-on cover. Overlock the edge of large lace or decorator fabric square, or hem with narrow hem. Or make reversible slipcover by using two fabrics back to back. Tack ribbon tie or decorative cord at each corner. Lay pillow diagonally on slipcover, and fold corners over pillow. Tie closed.

Wrapped neckroll. Cut large fabric rectangle. Overlock raw edges, or hem with narrow hem. Wrap around foam bolster form or rolled quilt batt. Roll up excess fabric at each end, and tack. Tie ribbon or cord around rolled fabric.

Slip-on cover. Overlock one edge of both pillow cover sections, or hem with narrow hem. With right sides together, stitch remaining three sides in ½" (1.3 cm) seam. Clip corners. Turn right side out. Tack ribbon ties to open side. Insert fabric-covered pillow, and tie ribbons into bows.

Basic Comforter Cover

Change the look of a bed with a covered comforter. It can replace a top sheet and blanket, and the removable cover of the comforter makes laundering easy. Sew your own comforter, or use a purchased one of down or of polyester batting.

Choose a washable, lightweight, firmly woven fabric for the cover. Sheets are good fabric choices because they do not require piecing. Seam decorator fabrics together by using a full fabric width in the center of the cover, with partial widths along the sides.

Leave a 36" (91.5 cm) opening in the back of the cover for inserting the comforter. Place the opening about 16" (40.5 cm) from the lower edge on the inside of the cover so it will not show at the ends. Use snap tape, hook and loop tape, a zipper or buttons for closure.

✂ Cutting Directions

Cut the front of the cover 1" (2.5 cm) larger than the comforter. Cut the back of the cover according to the closure method you choose. For button closures, add 5½" (14 cm) to back length. For a snap tape, hook and loop or zipper closure, add 1½" (3.8 cm) to back length.

Cut four small fabric strips for tabs, each about 2" (5 cm) square.

YOU WILL NEED

Decorator fabric or sheets for cover, and small amount of extra fabric for tabs.

Snap tape, hook and loop tape, zipper or buttons.

Gripper snaps to hold comforter in place.

How to Sew a Comforter Cover

1) Press under 16" (40.5 cm) across the lower edge of the back, right sides together. If using tapes or zipper, snip the fold to mark ends of closure. Stitch ¾" (2 cm) from the fold; backstitch at snips and bastestitch across the closure area. Cut on fold; press seam open.

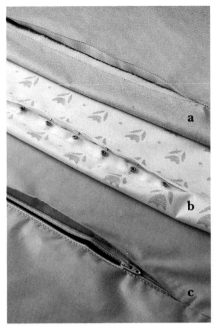

2a) Insert hook and loop tape (**a**), snap tape (**b**), or zipper (**c**) according to instructions for zipper closure (page 151).

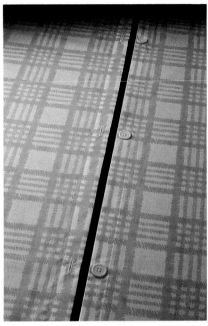

2b) Cut back apart on 16" (40.5 cm) fold line for button closure. Press under ¼" (6 mm) then 1" (2.5 cm) hem on each edge; stitch. On hem of shorter piece, make buttonholes 10" to 12" (25.5 to 30.5 cm) apart; attach buttons opposite buttonholes.

3) Pin cover front to cover back, right sides together. For button closure, pin the shorter piece first, lapping the longer piece over it.

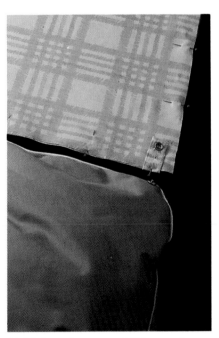

4) Make tabs, page 207, step 1. Attach socket side of snaps to tabs, and ball sides to corners of the comforter. Pin a tab at each corner of the cover, edges even.

5) Stitch front and back of cover together with ½" (1.3 cm) seam. Diagonally trim bulk from corners. Turn cover right side out. Insert comforter; snap cover to comforter at corners.

Welted Comforter Cover

Comforter covers can protect a new comforter or change the look of an existing one. Less bulky to handle than a full-size bedspread, a comforter cover is as easy to sew as a pillow sham. For a complete bed set, make the comforter cover, bed skirt, and pillow shams to coordinate.

The drop length of the comforter cover must be long enough to extend beyond the upper edge of the bed skirt and cover any blankets. The drop length is usually about 3" (7.5 cm) longer than the depth of the mattress. Purchased comforters may vary in drop length from 9" to 14" (23 to 35.5 cm). If the drop length is too short, jumbo welting or a ruffle can be added to the comforter cover.

To determine how many widths of fabric are needed, divide the total width of the comforter cover by the fabric width; round off to the next highest number. Most comforter covers require two fabric widths. Multiply the number of widths by the length of the comforter cover for the amount of fabric needed. Divide by 36" (100 cm) to determine the number of yards (meters).

✄ Cutting Directions

Determine the finished size of the comforter cover by measuring the size of the comforter. The finished

comforter cover may be the same size as the comforter, or, for a snug fit on a down comforter, the comforter cover may be up to 2" (5 cm) shorter and narrower than the comforter.

The cut size of the comforter front is 1" (2.5 cm) wider and longer than the finished size. When more than one fabric width is required, cut one full width for the center panel of the comforter cover and two equal, partial-width panels for each side; add an extra ½" (1.3 cm) seam allowance to each panel for seaming them together. Cut the comforter back the same width as the comforter front, and 1½" (3.8 cm) shorter than the front. Cut a zipper strip 3½" (9 cm) wide and the same length as the cut width of the comforter back.

Cut fabric strips for plain jumbo welting (page 120), gathered jumbo welting (page 122), or ruffle (page 134).

YOU WILL NEED

Decorator fabric.

Two zippers, each 22" (56 cm) long.

Welting or ruffle, optional.

How to Sew a Comforter Cover

1) Overlock or zigzag upper edge of zipper strip and lower edge of comforter back. Press the finished edge of zipper strip under ½" (1.3 cm) and the finished edge of back under 1" (2.5 cm).

2) Place closed zippers face down on seam allowance of comforter back, with zipper tabs meeting in center and with edges of zipper tapes on fold. Using zipper foot, stitch along one side of zippers.

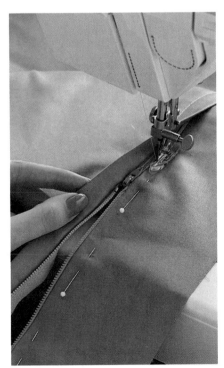

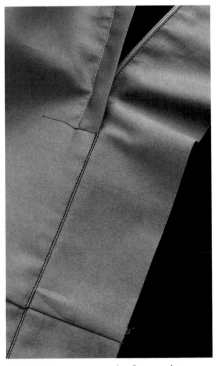

3) Turn right side up. Pin pressed edge of zipper strip along edge of zipper teeth; stitch close to pressed edge. Backstitch at ends of zippers.

4) Stitch across end of one zipper; then topstitch through all layers to stitch seam from zipper to side of comforter cover. Repeat at other end of zipper. Open zippers. (Contrasting thread was used to show detail.)

5) Apply welting, if desired, and stitch comforter front to comforter back as for pillows (page 121). Turn comforter cover right side out; insert comforter.

Ideas for Comforter Covers

Make a comforter cover to coordinate with pillow shams and other room accessories. Because the construction of comforter covers is similar to that of pillow covers, most pillow designs can be adapted to make coordinating comforter covers.

Twisted welting and a coordinating ruffle have been added to this comforter cover, using the same basic construction as the sunburst pillow (page 134). The ruffle and the twisted welting are applied to the sides and the lower edge of the comforter back after the zipper is inserted; the upper edge is not ruffled.

Bows or rosettes can be tied at the corners of a comforter cover for an added detail that coordinates with bow picture hangers (page 230) or sash pillows (page 138).

Knotted jumbo welting is added to this comforter cover to coordinate with the knotted-corner pillows (page 130). The jumbo welting is inserted into the fabric sleeves on three sides of the comforter cover; the upper edge of the comforter cover does not have welting.

Comforter

Comforters have the look of quilts but do not require time-consuming and intricate hand-quilting. They should reach just below the mattress line and be used with dust ruffles or bed skirts.

Comforters are made from three layers: a backing or lining, a bonded polyester batting for warmth and body, and a top layer of decorator fabric.

Because the bulk of the comforter makes machine-quilting difficult to manage, it should be hand-tufted. Tufting, or hand-tied yarn, holds the layers together and emphasizes the appealing puffiness. Place tufts 6" to 10" (15 to 25.5 cm) apart; the design of the fabric may dictate their placement.

✂ Cutting Directions

Cut and seam fabric for comforter top equal to finished size. Cut lining 8" (20.5 cm) larger than finished size for self-binding edge. Or cut lining same as top; finish edge with wide bias binding strips as for quilted placemats (page 217).

YOU WILL NEED

Decorator fabric for comforter.

Lining for comforter.

Bonded polyester batting, proper size for bed width and cut to finished size of comforter.

Yarn, pearl cotton or embroidery floss for tufting, washable if comforter will be laundered.

How to Sew and Tuft a Comforter

1) Place lining face down on flat surface. Leaving 4" (10 cm) border, place batting on lining, then decorator fabric, right side up, edges even with batting.

2) Pin three layers together. Hand-baste layers together with long stitches in parallel rows 8" to 10" (20.5 to 25.5 cm) apart, so layers do not slip.

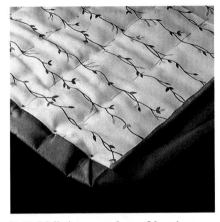

3) Fold lining to edge of batting. Fold corners diagonally, then fold lining again over front of comforter to form 2" (5 cm) border. Pin in place. Slipstitch binding to comforter along folded edge.

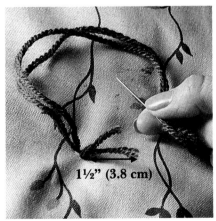

4) Mark positions for tufts. Thread a large needle with double strand of yarn. Working from right side of comforter, make a ¼" (6 mm) stitch through all layers. Leave 1½" (3.8 cm) tail of yarn.

1½" (3.8 cm)

5) Hold all four strands of yarn in one hand, close to comforter. Bring needle behind four strands and over two strands to form loop.

6) Draw needle through loop. Pull ends to secure knot. Clip ends of yarn to ¾" (2 cm).

Circular Ruffle Bed Skirt

The circular ruffle bed skirt has soft draping. Its simple style complements a tailored decor, but also works well for a room that is elaborately decorated, without detracting from other furnishings.

The circular ruffle bed skirt is easy to sew and requires less time than most bed skirts, because there are no gathers or pleats. To prevent the bed skirt from shifting out of position, the upper edge of the skirt is attached to a fitted sheet. If the bed does not have a footboard, the bed skirt is attached as one continuous strip. For a bed with a footboard, a split-corner bed skirt can be attached to the sheet in three sections.

✂ Cutting Directions

Determine the number of circular pieces required, as indicated in the chart, opposite. To make it easier to cut the circles, cut fabric squares the size of the circle diameter; then cut the circular pieces, opposite.

The calculations given in the chart are based on a 15½" (39.3 cm) cut length. This gives an adequate amount of ruffling for any cut length up to at least 15½" (39.3 cm); you may have excess ruffling, which can easily be cut off during construction. The actual length of ruffling per circle is equal to the circumference of the inner circle minus 1" (2.5 cm) for seams and side hems.

YOU WILL NEED

Decorator fabric, in the yardage amount indicated in the chart, opposite.

Fitted sheet.

How to Cut Circles

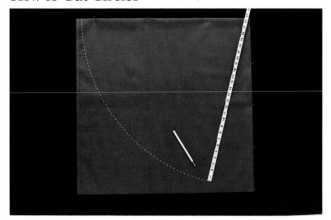

1) Fold the fabric square in half lengthwise, then crosswise, right sides together. Using straightedge and pencil, mark an arc on fabric, measuring from the folded center of fabric, a distance equal to the radius. Cut on marked line through all layers.

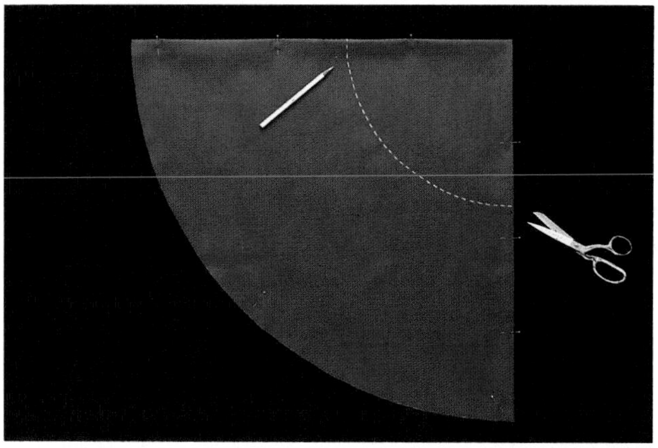

2) Add 1" (2.5 cm) to the drop length of bed skirt; measure and mark this distance away from arc. Draw second arc at this distance. Cut on marked line through all layers. Circumference of inner circle minus 1" (2.5 cm) determines length of ruffling per circle.

How to Cut Half-circles

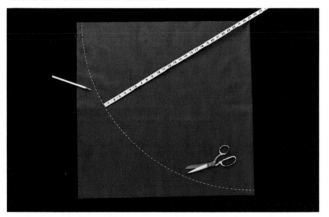

1) Cut rectangle across the width of fabric, with short sides equal to one-half the width of the fabric. Fold fabric in half, matching short sides. Using straightedge and pencil, mark an arc on fabric, measuring from the lengthwise fold, a distance equal to the radius. Cut on marked line through both layers.

2) Add 1" (2.5 cm) to the drop length of bed skirt; measure and mark this distance away from arc. Draw second arc at this distance. Cut on marked line through both layers.

Determining the Circular Pieces Needed

Diameter of Circles	Ruffling Length per Circle	Twin		Full		Queen		King	
		Circles Needed	Yardage Needed	Circles Needed	Yardage Needed	Circles Needed	Yardage Needed	Circles Needed	Yardage Needed
45" (115 cm)	47" (120 cm)	4	5 yd. (4.6 m)	4½	5⅝ yd. (5.15 m)	5	6¼ yd. (5.75 m)	5½	6⅞ yd. (6.3 m)
48" (122 cm)	58" (147 cm)	3½	4⅔ yd. (4.33 m)	3½	4⅔ yd. (4.33 m)	4	5⅓ yd. (4.92 m)	4½	6 yd. (5.5 m)
54" (137 cm)	76" (193 cm)	2½	3¾ yd. (3.45 m)	3	4½ yd. (4.15 m)	3	4½ yd. (4.15 m)	3½	5¼ yd. (4.8 m)
60" (153 cm)	95" (242 cm)	2	3⅓ yd. (3.07 m)	2½	4¼ yd. (3.9 m)	2½	4¼ yd. (3.9 m)	3	5 yd. (4.6 m)

How to Sew a Circular Ruffle Bed Skirt

1) Cut circles for bed skirt (pages 156 and 157). Slash each piece from outer to inner edges on crosswise grain. Staystitch ½" (1.3 cm) from inner edge.

2) Stitch circles together in a long strip, right sides together; finish seam allowances. Clip up to the staystitching at 2" (5 cm) intervals; space the clips evenly so bed skirt will hang in even folds.

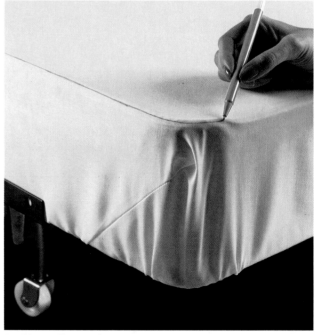

3) Machine-stitch ¼" (6 mm) from hem edge. Turn edge to wrong side on stitching line; press fold. Stitch close to fold. Trim excess fabric close to stitching. Turn hem edge to wrong side a scant ¼" (6 mm), enclosing raw edge. Edgestitch.

4) Place fitted sheet over box spring; mark sheet along upper edge of box spring, using water-soluble marking pen or chalk.

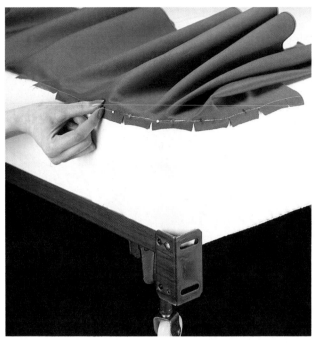

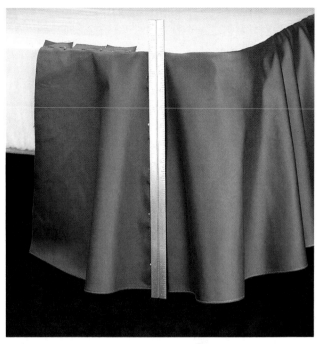

5) Lay circular ruffle on top of box spring; pin ruffle to sheet, right sides together, matching staystitching to marked line. Ruffle may extend around corners at head of bed, if desired; extend raw edge ½" (1.3 cm) beyond desired endpoint to allow for side hem.

6) Mark side hems at head of bed perpendicular to floor, allowing ½" (1.3 cm) for double ¼" (6 mm) hem.

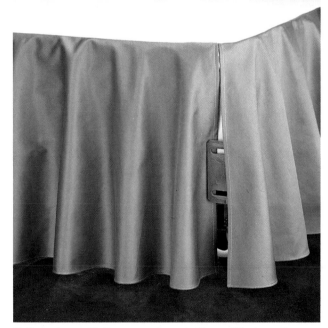

7) Remove fitted sheet and ruffle from bed. Cut off any excess ruffle at sides; stitch side hems. Stitch ruffle to fitted sheet, stitching just beyond staystitching.

Split corners. Follow steps 1 to 4. Cut ruffle into three sections, each section long enough to fit on one side of the bed plus 1" (2.5 cm) for side hems. Lay section for foot of bed on top of box spring; pin to sheet, right sides together, matching staystitching to marked line. Mark side hems at corner, as in step 6. Pin side sections to sheet, overlapping hem allowances at corners. Complete bed skirt, as in steps 6 and 7.

Envelope Pillow Shams

These pillow shams open like an envelope, making it easy to insert pillows; the flap closes with hook and loop tape. Edged in plain or gathered jumbo welting, these pillows can be either traditional or contemporary. Make envelope pillow shams for any size bed pillow.

✂ Cutting Directions

Cut one rectangle of fabric for the pillow back/flap. The cut width is equal to the pillow width plus 1" (2.5 cm) for seam allowances; cut length is equal to one and two-thirds of the pillow length plus 1" (2.5 cm) for seam allowances.

Cut one rectangle of fabric for the pillow front. The cut width is equal to the pillow width plus 1" (2.5 cm) for seam allowances; cut length is equal to the pillow length plus 2" (5 cm) for seam and hem allowances.

Cut one rectangle of fabric for the flap facing. The cut width is equal to the pillow width plus 1" (2.5 cm)

for seam allowances; cut length is equal to two-thirds of the pillow length plus 5" (12.5 cm) for overlap.

Cut fabric strips for plain jumbo welting (page 120) or gathered jumbo welting (page 122).

YOU WILL NEED

Decorator fabric for pillow.

Decorator fabric for welting. Allow up to ½ yd. (0.5 m) for plain jumbo welting, 1 yd. (0.95 m) for double-fullness gathered jumbo welting, or 1½ yd. (1.4 m) for triple-fullness gathered jumbo welting. Exact yardage depends on width of fabric, sizes of cording and pillow, and fullness of welting.

Jumbo cording, equal to the distance around the pillow back/flap.

1" (2.5 cm) hook and loop tape for closure.

How to Sew an Envelope Sham

1) **Fold** the pillow back/flap and flap facing in half lengthwise; mark end of flap 4" (10 cm) from fold for bed pillow or 3" (7.5 cm) from fold for accent pillow. Mark two-thirds the length of pillow on the edge opposite fold. Draw diagonal line between marks; cut on marked line. Round corners of flap and lower edges of pillow front and pillow back/flap.

2) **Press** under ½" (1.3 cm) twice on one crosswise edge of pillow front and on long crosswise edge of flap facing; stitch to make double-fold hems. Stitch loop side of hook and loop tape to flap facing, centered about 1" (2.5 cm) from short edge. Staystitch bias edges of flap and flap facing.

3) **Place** pillow front over pillow back/flap, right sides together, matching raw edges. Place flap facing over flap portion of pillow back/flap, right sides together, matching raw edges. Pin pillow front and flap facing together in lapped area; stitch a rectangle 2" × ½" (5 × 1.3 cm) at ends of overlap.

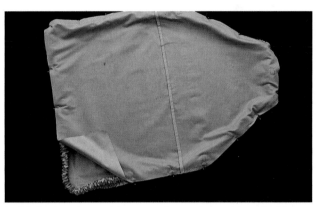

4) **Make** jumbo welting; apply to right side of pillow back/flap. Follow steps 1 to 7 on pages 122 and 123 for gathered welting, or steps 1 to 5 on page 121 for plain welting. Place pillow front/flap facing on pillow back/flap, right sides together; pin.

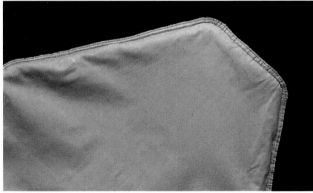

5) **Stitch** around pillow sham through all layers, using zipper foot; stitch inside previous stitching line. Finish seam allowances, using overlock stitch on serger or zigzag stitch on conventional machine.

6) **Turn** sham right side out; insert pillow. Pin hook side of hook and loop tape in position, under flap, on pillow front. Remove pillow and stitch tape in place.

Tuck-pleated Bed Skirt

A fitted lining holds the tuck-pleated bed skirt in place. Although the skirt gives an upholstered look, the four corners are split to fit over the bed frame, then held together with short strips of hook and loop tape. The tape is attached to grosgrain ribbon that is sewn into the seam.

✂ Cutting Directions

If using a sheet or a fabric that lends itself to tearing, tear along the lengthwise grain to obtain strips the desired drop plus 1" (2.5 cm) for seam allowances; join strips together to make one strip 2 times the width and 4 times the length of bed, plus 40" (102 cm) for extensions at head of the bed.

For deck, cut flat sheet 1" (2.5 cm) wider and 1" (2.5 cm) longer than box spring.

Cut lining the same drop as the skirt; cut two pieces the length of box spring, and one piece the width of box spring; cut two extensions to wrap around the head of the bed 11" (28 cm) long.

Cut welting strips 1½" (3.8 cm) wide, and 2 times the length plus 2 times the width of the deck. Cut ⁵⁄₃₂" cording the same length as welting strips.

Cut 8 pieces of grosgrain and 8 pieces of hook and loop tape 2" (5 cm) long.

YOU WILL NEED

Decorator fabric or sheet for bed skirt on three sides of bed plus extensions.

Flat sheets for deck and lining.

Grosgrain ribbon, 1½" (3.8 cm) wide.

Hook and loop tape.

⁵⁄₃₂" cording for welting.

How to Sew a Tuck-pleated Bed Skirt

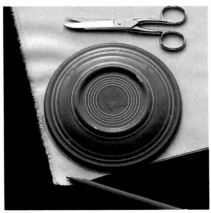

1) Fold deck in half lengthwise, then crosswise so all four cut or torn corners are together. Using a saucer for a guide, cut through all layers to curve corners gently.

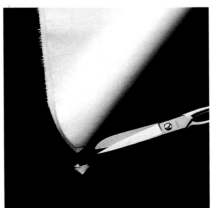

2) Fold curved corners in half to determine centers; mark fold with ¼" (6 mm) clip through all layers.

3) Tuck-pleat skirt ⅜" (1 cm) from upper and lower edges, using ruffler attachment set at 2 to 1 fullness; keep right side of fabric up.

162

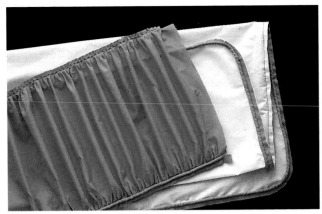

4) Make welting, page 205; machine-baste welting ⅜" (1 cm) from lower edge of pleated skirt and around deck edge. Steam press lightly to flatten tucks.

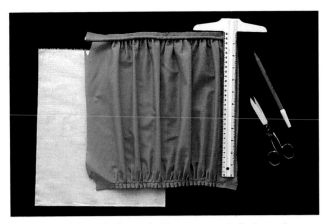

5) Cut lengths of pleated skirt to match lining pieces. Release a few pleats if necessary to flatten skirt for 1" (2.5 cm) at each end. Square and trim ends to match lining.

6) Cut ½" (1.3 cm) of cording out of ends of welting. Fold welting back on itself, and pin to square and finish ends.

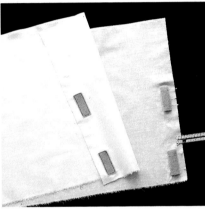

7) Attach loop side of hook and loop tape to ends of long lining pieces; sew one strip ½" (1.3 cm) from raw edge and ½" (1.3 cm) from bottom, and second strip ½" (1.3 cm) from raw edge and in center of side.

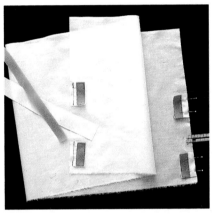

8) Stitch hook side of hook and loop tape on grosgrain strips, ½" (1.3 cm) from edge. Stitch strips on remaining pieces of skirt, matching the tapes that were stitched in step 7.

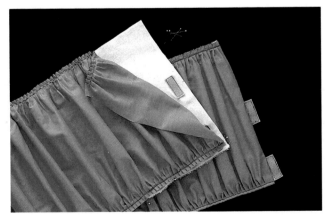

9) Stitch lower and side edges of skirt to lining, right sides together. Turn skirt right side out, and machine-baste top edges of skirt to lining ⅜" (1 cm) from edge. Do not trim grosgrain ribbon.

10) Stitch upper edge of skirt sections to deck edges, right sides together. Skirt sections with tape extensions underlap adjacent section ¼" (6 mm) at corners. Serge or zigzag raw edges together.

How to Sew a Tuck-pleated Pillow Sham

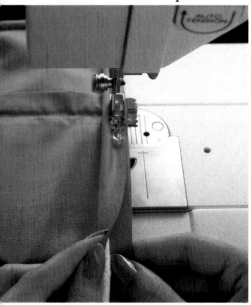

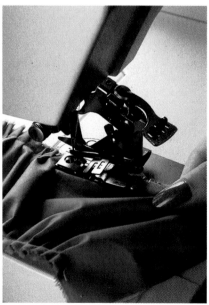

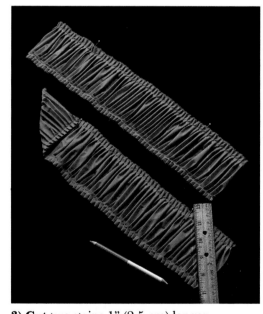

1) Insert zipper in back of sham, following instructions for zipper insertion in comforter (page 151). Cover cording and machine-baste to right side of back in ⅜" (1 cm) seam; join ends of welting (page 121).

2) Tuck-pleat the border strip, ⅜" (1 cm) from both edges, using ruffler attachment at 2 to 1 ratio. Keep fabric same side up when pleating. Steam press finished strip lightly to flatten tucks.

3) Cut two strips 1" (2.5 cm) longer than finished sham length, and two strips 1" (2.5 cm) longer than finished sham width. On wrong side of short strips, fold corner back; mark width of strip with pin. Unfold; mark stitching angle from pin to corner.

Tuck-pleated Pillow Shams

The mitered, tuck-pleated border on this sham is a narrow version of the tuck-pleated bed skirt. The finished sham should be the same size as the pillow.

The technique for mitering a border around a pillow is also used for attaching a mitered trim (page 32).

✄ Cutting Directions

Cut the back 1" (2.5 cm) wider and 1½" (3.8 cm) shorter than the finished size. Cut a back zipper strip the same width as the back and 3½" (9 cm) wide. Cut the center of the front 4" (10 cm) narrower and shorter than finished sham; cut border strips 3½" (9 cm) wide and 4 times the length and width of the sham, plus extra for seaming strips.

For welting, cut strips 1½" (3.8 cm) wide and 2 times the length and 2 times the width of sham, plus extra for seaming.

YOU WILL NEED

Decorator fabric or sheets for sham.

Contrasting border fabric.

5/32" cording for welting.

Zipper, 22" (56 cm) long.

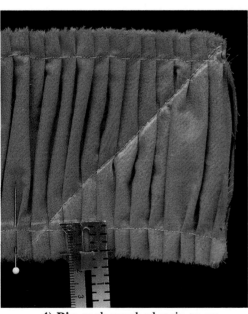

4) Pin each marked strip to an unmarked strip, and stitch from corner to ½" (1.3 cm) from raw edge; backstitch. Trim seams to ¼" (6 mm), and press open.

5) Pin inner edges of border to sham front; stitch one side at a time, backstitching (arrow) at both ends of seam.

6) Pin front to back, right sides together; stitch ½" (1.3 cm) from edge on all four sides. To finish, overlock or zigzag raw edges. Turn to right side; insert pillow.

Swag Bed Skirt

The swag bed skirt has soft drapes of fabric that are layered over a gathered underskirt. This treatment complements swag window treatments and works well for bedrooms with romantic, feminine styling. To show off the bed skirt to its best advantage, select a duvet cover with a drop length that is only 1" to 2" (2.5 to 5 cm) below the mattress.

For easier draping of the swags, two-cord shirring tape is used. For a more finished look, matching or contrasting straps are added to cover the shirring tape. The entire bed skirt is attached to a fitted sheet, which prevents the skirt from shifting out of position.

For a bed with a footboard, a split-corner underskirt can be sewn by attaching three sections to the fitted sheet. For this style, the three sections are hemmed at both sides, and the sections are butted together at the corner. If the bed does not have a footboard, the underskirt is sewn in one continuous strip.

✂ Cutting Directions

Determine the number of swags you will need for the bed skirt, according to the chart, opposite. The size of the swags will vary, depending on the size of the bed. Also, the swags will be a slightly different size on the foot of the bed than on the sides, but this difference is unnoticeable.

Cut a rectangle of fabric for each swag; railroad the fabric to avoid seaming, or piece the rectangles, as necessary. Cut the rectangles 27" (68.5 cm) long and 5" (12.5 cm) wider than the distance between the markings on page 168. If you are using a patterned fabric with large motifs, you may want to center a motif on each rectangle.

Cut 3" × 11" (7.5 × 28 cm) straps from matching or contrasting fabric. You will need one strap for each swag plus one extra strap.

For a bed without a footboard, the cut width of the gathered underskirt is two and one-half to three times the distance around the sides and foot of the bed; the fabric may be railroaded or fabric widths may be pieced together, as necessary. The cut length of the underskirt is equal to the distance from the top of the box spring to the floor plus 2" (5 cm). This allows for the hem and seam allowances and for ½" (1.3 cm) clearance at the floor.

For a bed with a footboard, make a split-corner underskirt. The cut width for each of the two side sections is two and one-half to three times the length of the bed, and the cut width for the foot section is two and one-half to three times the width of the bed. The cut length of the sections is equal to the distance from the top of the box spring to the floor plus 2" (5 cm).

YOU WILL NEED

Decorator fabric.

Fitted sheet.

Two-cord shirring tape, 23½" (59.8 cm) for each swag plus an extra 23½" (59.8 cm).

Determining the Number of Swags Needed

No. of Swags	Twin	Full	Queen	King
At foot	1	2	2	3
Each side	2	3	3	3
Total swags	5	8	8	9

How to Sew a Swag Bed Skirt

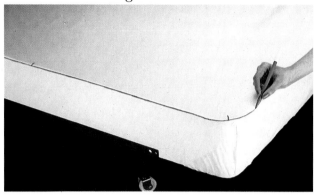

1) Place fitted sheet over box spring; mark sheet along upper edge of box spring, using water-soluble marking pen or chalk. Mark corners at upper edge of box spring on sheet at center of curve. Divide each side of bed into equal parts according to the number of swags.

2) Fold each rectangle in half crosswise; measure and mark 2" (5 cm) in from corner along upper edge. Draw line diagonally to opposite corner. Cut on marked line through both layers.

3) Press and stitch 1" (2.5 cm) double-fold hem at lower edge of each swag piece. Stitch swag pieces together; press seams open. Press under ½" (1.3 cm) at the sides.

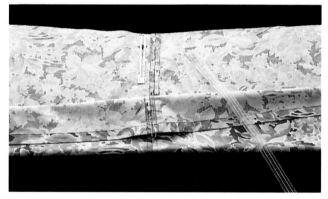

4) Fold under ½" (1.3 cm) on both ends of shirring tape. Center tape over one seam on wrong side, starting above hem; pin in place. Stitch three rows of stitching on tape; stitch along center first, then along outer edges. Repeat for remaining seams and at sides.

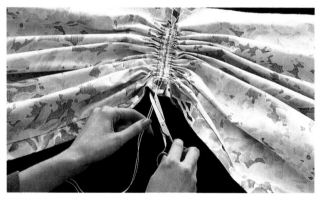

5) Knot cords at upper end of tape. Pull cords from lower end, gathering fabric as tightly as possible; knot ends securely. Trim tails.

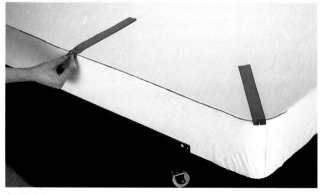

6) Fold strap pieces in half lengthwise, right sides together; stitch ¼" (6 mm) seam. Turn straps right side out; press. Pin straps to fitted sheet, centering them over markings; extend ½" (1.3 cm) at end of each strap beyond marked line, as shown.

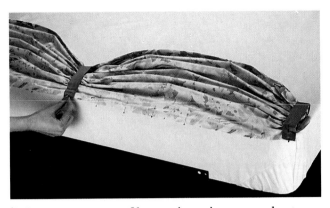

7) Lay swags on top of box spring; pin upper edge to sheet, right sides together, extending ½" (1.3 cm) seam allowance beyond marked line. Wrap straps around swags; pin in place, matching ends. If desired, remove sheet from bed and machine-baste upper edge of swags in place, stitching scant ½" (1.3 cm) from raw edge.

8) Seam underskirt panels together; for bed without footboard, stitch panels in one continuous strip, or for bed with footboard, stitch panels in three sections. Finish seam allowances. Press and stitch 1" (2.5 cm) double-fold hem at lower edge of underskirt. Stitch ½" (1.3 cm) double-fold side hems.

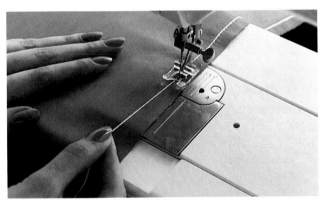

9) Zigzag over a cord at upper edge of underskirt, within seam allowance, just beyond seamline. Zigzag over second cord ¼" (6 mm) from first cord, if desired, for more control when adjusting gathers.

10) Divide marked line on fitted sheet and upper edge of underskirt into fourths or eighths. Lay underskirt, right side down, over swags; match and pin together at markings. Pull on gathering cords, and gather underskirt evenly to fit; pin.

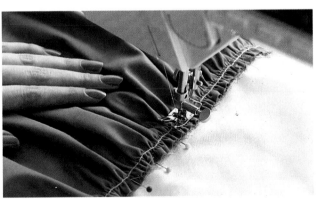

11) Remove bed skirt and sheet from bed. Stitch bed skirt to sheet, stitching ½" (1.3 cm) from raw edge.

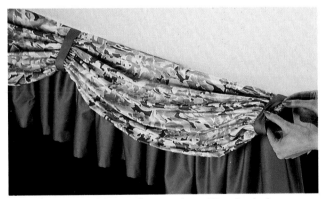

12) Place bed skirt on box spring. Hand-stitch straps to swags at head of bed. Arrange folds of swags.

How to Sew a Reverse Sham Bedcover

1) Fold face fabric and lining in half lengthwise. To round the corners at the foot of the cover and the top of the sham, line up corners evenly and use a saucer to mark curve. Cut on marked line.

2) Fold the bias strip in half lengthwise, wrong sides together; press. Stitch strip to curved sides on right side of cover and sham sections, stitching a scant ½" (1.3 cm) from edge. Ease strip around curves so it lies smooth when turned.

3) Pin lining to face fabric on both sections, right sides together in ½" (1.3 cm) seam; stitch around cover, leaving upper edge open. Trim corners, and turn both sections right side out.

Reverse Sham Bedcover

The reverse sham bedcover is an all-in-one cover for bed and pillows. It has an extra-deep flap at the top to fold back over the bed pillows, making the bed especially quick and easy to make.

The reverse sham technique can be adapted for comforters or full-size bedspreads. It also works as a sheet-weight bedcover for summer sleeping.

For a tailored feeling, without the look of separate pillow shams, add the sham extension to a comforter cover. Follow the instructions for a comforter cover (pages 150 to 153), leaving the upper edge open. Make the sham, and attach it as shown, below.

For versatility, use coordinating fabrics or sheets for the face and the lining and make the cover reversible. The edges are finished with a flat bias trim. If using a striped fabric, as shown here, the stripes may be mitered on the sham section for a decorative effect.

✂ Cutting Directions

Seam panels together as necessary for width. For the cover, cut the face fabric and lining the width of the bed, plus 2 times the drop plus 1" (2.5 cm) seam allowance; cut the length the length of bed plus one drop, plus 1" (2.5 cm) for seam allowance.

For the sham, cut the face fabric and lining 28" (71 cm) deep and the same width as the cut width of the cover. This size is suitable for an average 20" (51 cm) pillow. For larger or smaller pillows, loosely measure over the curve of the pillow and add 1" (2.5 cm) for seam allowance. Cut sham in same direction as cover, matching stripes or motifs, unless stripes are mitered for decorative effect.

For trim, cut 2" (5 cm) bias strips of contrasting fabric 2 times the finished length plus 2 times the finished width, plus extra for seam allowances.

YOU WILL NEED

Decorator fabric and lining for bedcover.
Contrasting fabric for bias trim.

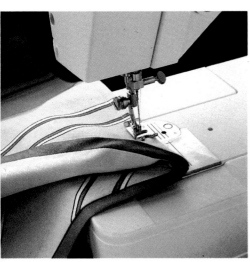

4) Bastestitch raw edges together across open ends of cover and sham. To stitch concealed French seam, match *wrong* side of sham to *right* side of cover. Stitch ¼" (6 mm) seam; press. Trim, turn, press, and stitch ⅜" (1 cm) from fold.

4a) Alternative seam. Match *right* side of sham to *wrong* side of cover, and stitch ½" (1.3 cm) seam; trim. Finish seam with zigzag or overlock stitch, or apply tricot bias binding.

5) Place cover on bed with pillows on top of cover. Fold reverse sham back over pillows. Seam is inside when sham is turned back.

Daybed Dust Skirt & Tufted Cover

This tailored daybed set combines a fitted, tufted cover with a gathered dust skirt. The daybed cover is shaped at the corners to fit smoothly around the frame of the bed.

Most daybed frames have rims on either two or four sides to keep the mattress from shifting; other frames have no rims. Make adjustments accordingly so the dust skirt hangs from the top of the frame or rim, is open at the corners, and hangs evenly ¼" (6 mm) from the floor. For some daybed frames, it may be necessary to attach the dust skirt 1½" to 2" (3.8 to 5 cm) from the corners of the deck, so the gathers will not bunch at the corners. The drop of the cover will overlap the skirt to conceal the frame at the corners.

✂ Cutting Directions (Cover)

Cut center panel 60" (150 cm) long from full width of fabric. Divide another width in half for the side panels; join side panels to center panel, matching design at seams. Trim excess fabric from each side panel so width measures 96" (244 cm).

Cut and seam lining 1" (2.5 cm) longer and 1" (2.5 cm) wider than top.

Cut strips of fabric for welting. Join ends to make a strip 9 yds. (8.25 m) long.

✂ Cutting Directions (Deck & Skirt)

Cut dust skirt deck the length and width of the frame plus 1" (2.5 cm) for seam allowances. For daybeds with rims, cut a strip of decorator fabric for each rim the height of the rim plus 1" (2.5 cm) for seam allowances, and the length or width of the frame plus 2" (5 cm) for hem allowances.

Cut two skirt sections each 2 times the length of the deck plus 2" (5 cm) for hems. Cut two skirt sections each 2 times the width of deck plus 2" (5 cm) for hem. To determine skirt length, measure as in step 1, opposite.

YOU WILL NEED

For dust skirt, 6¼ yd. (5.75 m) of 54" (140 cm) decorator fabric and one twin flat sheet for deck.

For cover top and lining, 3⅜ yd. (3.10 m) of 54" (140 cm) fabric, plus extra for matching and welting.

Extra lofty polyester batting, 60" × 96" (150 × 244 cm).

Cording, 9 yd. (8.25 m).

Narrow ribbon for ties, 18 yd. (17.5 m) of ⅛" (3 mm) ribbon; crewel needle; about 13 dozen safety pins.

How to Sew a Daybed Dust Skirt

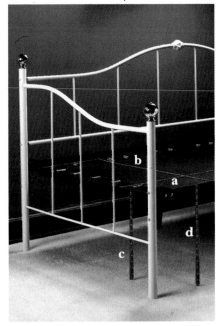

1) Measure frame to determine finished length **(a)** and width **(b)**. To determine skirt length, measure from frame **(c)** to floor and add 2½" (6.5 cm). For sides with rims, measure from top of rim **(d)** to floor and add 2½" (6.5 cm).

2) Press under and stitch double 1" (2.5 cm) hem on lower edge of each skirt section. Gather upper edge, using any method on page 30. For sides with rims, match skirt section to fabric strip, right sides together; stitch ½" (1.3 cm) seam. On all skirt sections, press under and stitch double ½" (1.3 cm) side hems.

3a) For bed without rims. Pin skirt sections to sides of deck, right sides together, with edges of ruffle meeting at each corner. Stitch ½" (1.3 cm) seam. Finish seams with zigzag or overlock stitch.

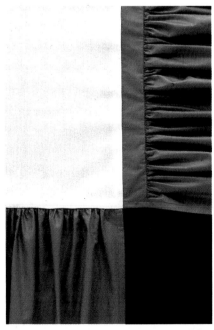

3b) For bed with two rims. For sides that do not have rims, attach to deck as in step 3a. For sides that have rims, stitch strips to edges of deck in ½" (1.3 cm) seam.

3c) For bed with four rims. Stitch strips to edges of deck, right sides together, in ½" (1.3 cm) seam; finish seams with zigzag or overlock stitch.

4) Place dust skirt over frame of daybed, adjusting ruffles so the deck seam is on the upper edge of rim or even with the edge of the frame. Replace mattress on frame.

How to Sew a Tufted Daybed Cover

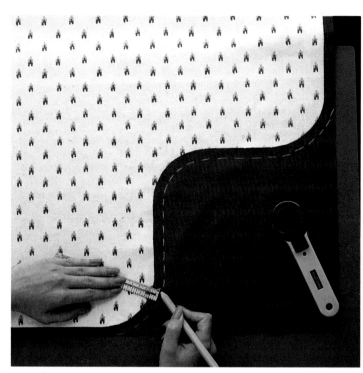

1) Fold top in half lengthwise, then crosswise, with right sides together and corners matching. Draw a 9½" (24 cm) square at matched corner. (This is the corner *without* any folds.) Using a saucer as a pattern, draw three curves as shown. Cut on curved line.

2) Place top over lining so ½" (1.3 cm) seam allowance extends beyond top at straight edges. Following curved corners on top, add ½" (1.3 cm) seam allowance and trim lining corners. Trim polyester batting to match lining.

5) Place lining, *wrong* side up, on large, flat surface. Place batting on lining; place top, *right* side up, on batting. Pin through all layers at each tufting location.

6) Thread needle with ribbon. At each tuft marker, insert needle from right side through all layers. Pull through bottom layer, leaving 4" (10 cm) tail at top for tying. Bring needle to the top ¼" (6 mm) away. Cut ribbon, leaving 4" (10 cm) tail; tie a square knot.

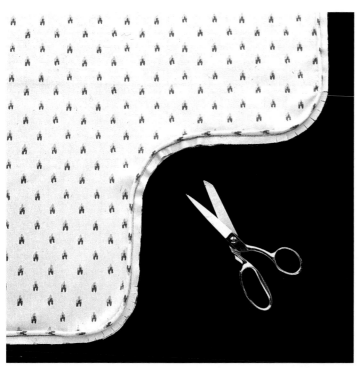

3) Cut and sew welting strips (page 121, steps 1 and 2). Stitch welting to cover top in ½" (1.3 cm) seam, raw edges even. Clip seam allowances on inner curves; be careful not to stretch welting on outer curves.

4) Fold top in half lengthwise, then crosswise, to mark center. Mark tufting locations on right side of top, beginning at center and spacing tufts about 6" (15 cm) apart. Or use the fabric design to space tufts evenly.

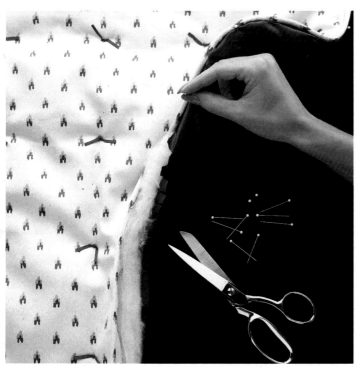

7) Clip lining seam allowances on curves. Turn under ½" (1.3 cm) on outer edges of top and lining layers, enclosing seams. Pin so folded edge of lining butts welting.

8) Slipstitch lining to welting seam by hand. Or edgestitch by machine, using zipper foot; stitch from lining side close to welting.

Padded Headboard

As a finishing touch, a fabric headboard can be coordinated with the bedcover. This is a custom project requiring simple upholstery techniques.

Make a paper pattern template to determine the size and shape of the headboard that will be appropriate to the size of the bed. The headboard should be cut as wide as the bed frame plus allowance for bedding, and 20" to 24" (51 to 61 cm) high plus approximately 20" (51 cm) for legs. Tack the headboard template on the wall behind the bed to check the size and shape. Adjust as necessary.

A shirred border frames the gentle curve of the headboard shown here. Determine the width of the border, approximately 4" (10 cm), and mark template for inner curve.

✂ Cutting Directions
Cut decorator fabric 5" to 6" (12.5 to 15 cm) larger than inner curved section. Cut shirring strip 3 times the measurement of the outer curve and 6" (15 cm) wider than width of shirred border.

For legs, cut fabric the length of leg plus 1" (2.5 cm), and twice the width plus 3" (7.5 cm).

For double welting, cut 3" (7.5 cm) bias strips the length of inner curve, plus extra for finishing.

Use the paper headboard template to cut lining for back of headboard.

YOU WILL NEED

Decorator fabric for front of headboard, for shirred border, and for legs.

Lining for back.

Polyester batting to pad shirred border.

⁵⁄₃₂" cording, 2 times the measurement of inner curve.

½" (1.3 cm) plywood, cut to shape; 2" (5 cm) foam to cover headboard; staple gun with ½" (1.3 cm) heavy-duty staples; cardboard stripping the length of inner curve; foam adhesive; white glue.

How to Make a Padded Headboard

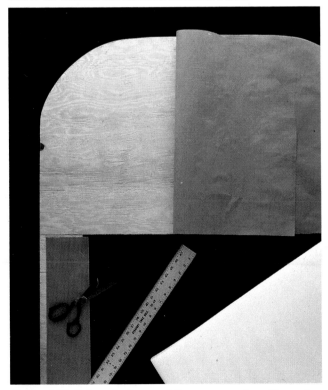

1) Cut ½" (1.3 cm) plywood from paper headboard template. Mark template for inner curved section 4" (10 cm) smaller than outer curve.

2) Cut 2" (5 cm) foam even with lower edge and 1" (2.5 cm) larger than headboard curve. Glue to headboard using foam adhesive. To soften edge, pull excess foam to back and staple to edge of plywood.

(Continued on next page)

How to Make a Padded Headboard (continued)

3) Mark inner curve on foam. Staple cardboard stripping on marked line to establish smooth curve. If staples do not penetrate plywood easily, use hammer to tap them in place.

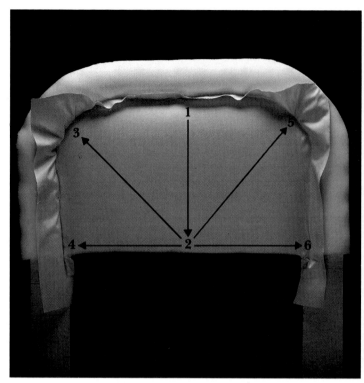

4) Place decorator fabric, right side up, over inner section. Starting at center, smooth fabric taut over foam and staple to cardboard stripping in order shown; then staple every 2" (5 cm). At bottom edge, fold fabric to back; staple. Trim excess fabric.

7) Staple shirring strip to back, easing fabric evenly around curve and forming small tucks as you staple. Keep shirred area an even width on the front.

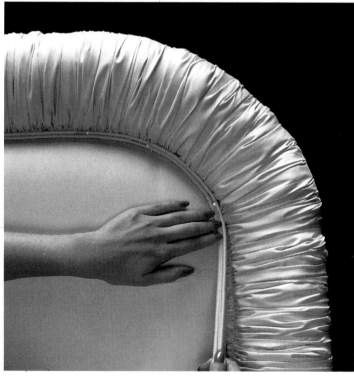

8) Glue double welting (page 33) over stapled area to cover raw edges, stretching welting as you attach it. Secure with pins to hold in place until glue dries.

178

5) Zigzag over cord to gather one long edge of shirring strip. Divide curve and shirring strip into quarters, and mark. Working from right side, staple gathered edge of shirring to curve, matching marks and adjusting gathers evenly.

6) Pad border lightly with polyester batting to puff and shape curve. Pull shirred strip to the back.

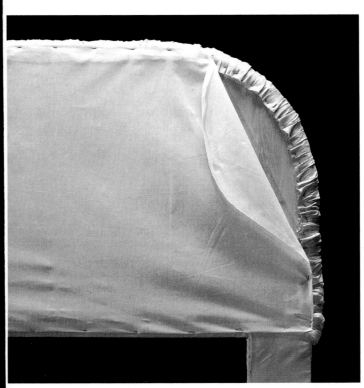

9) Staple or glue fabric to legs. Press edges of lining under ½" (1.3 cm). Finish back by stapling lining fabric over raw edges.

10) Drill holes in headboard to match screws in bed frame. Attach headboard to frame.

Slipcovers

Slipcovers

Slipcovers are removable covers, positioned over the existing fabric of the furniture. They can extend the life of a piece of furniture and update the decor at the same time. You can even change the look in a room from season to season by changing slipcovers. Because the pattern is developed when the first slipcover is made for the piece of furniture, a second slipcover can be made in less time.

A frequent concern about a slipcover is whether it will stay in place. To help secure the slipcover, an attached fabric strip, concealed under the skirt, is pinned to the existing fabric. Also, polyurethane foam pieces are tucked along the sides of the deck to provide a tight fit.

Sewing slipcovers is an alternative to upholstering. However, upholstering is required when the furniture needs structural repair, such as springing. It is easier to sew slipcovers for furniture that is fairly square, with straight lines, than it is for furniture with more details. Furniture with exposed wood usually requires upholstering, but furniture with wood strips on the arm can be slipcovered if the arms are first wrapped with upholstery batting. Recliners should be upholstered because of the movable parts.

Furniture with a concave back design, such as a channel back or barrel back, is difficult to slipcover, and the slipcover may not fit well. For best results, a concave back should be wrapped or covered in a thick upholstery batting before it is slipcovered. Furniture with a tufted back or button back can be slipcovered, but the tufting and buttons are eliminated in the slipcover. The back is wrapped with upholstery batting to fill it out for a smooth-fitting slipcover.

Selecting the Slipcover Fabric

Decorator fabrics are recommended for slipcovers. Heavy upholstery fabrics should be avoided, because they are difficult to sew on most home sewing machines and do not shape easily around curves. Regardless of the fabric selection, dry cleaning is recommended instead of washing to keep the slipcover looking its best.

It may be necessary to underline the slipcover if the fabric on the furniture is heavily textured and the slipcover fabric is smooth, or if the fabric on the furniture is dark or bright and the slipcover fabric is light-colored.

For faster and easier sewing, select a fabric that does not require matching, such as solid-colored fabrics or all-over prints. Striped fabrics require matching in one direction, and plaids require matching in both directions. Many print fabrics have a 27" (68.5 cm) pattern repeat, which fits perfectly on most cushions.

The amount of fabric required depends on the size of the furniture, pattern pieces, fabric width, and pattern repeat. Depending on how close together the pattern pieces can be cut, there may be a lot of scraps. Frequently these scraps can be used for room accessories, such as pillows and bow picture hangers.

As a general rule, a chair requires about 7 to 8 yd. (6.4 to 7.35 m); a love seat, 10 to 12 yd. (9.15 to 11 m); and a sofa, 16 to 20 yd. (14.7 to 19.4 m). These amounts include matching welting and a skirt with pleats at the corners. Allow additional fabric for cushions and ruffled or box-pleated skirts. Each cushion requires 1 to 1½ yd. (0.95 to 1.4 m) of fabric. For a ruffled or box-pleated skirt, allow 1 yd. (0.95 m) extra for a chair, 2 to 3 yd. (1.85 to 2.75 m) for a love seat, and 4 yd. (3.7 m) for a sofa.

YOU WILL NEED

Muslin for pin-fitting the pieces.

Decorator fabric.

Cording for welting; select soft, pliable cording with a cotton core.

Zippers; one for chairs, two for sofas and love seats. The length of each zipper is 1" to 2" (2.5 to 5 cm) shorter than the length of the vertical seam at the side of the outside back. Additional zippers are needed for cushions (page 198).

Upholstery batting, if necessary, to pad the existing furniture.

Polyurethane foam, 2" (5 cm) strips, to insert at sides and back of deck.

T-pins, tacks, or heavy-duty stapler and staples, for securing tacking strip to furniture.

Pin-fitting

The easiest way to make a slipcover pattern is by pin-fitting muslin on the chair or sofa. Before you start, look carefully at the furniture. Usually the seams in the slipcover will be in the same locations as the seams on the existing cover, but you may be able to add or eliminate some details, provided it will not affect the fit of the slipcover. For example, if the existing cushions are wrap-style, you may want to slipcover them as box cushions with welting. Or a chair with a pleated front arm may be slipcovered with a separate front arm piece.

The style of the skirt can also be changed. You may want to gather a skirt all the way around the furniture, allowing double fullness. Or you may want bunched gathers at the corners of a chair, or at the corners and center front of a sofa. For a more tailored look, the skirt may have box pleats instead of gathers.

A chair with rolled arms and loose back and seat cushions is used in the instructions that follow. This example includes the details that are common to most furniture. Although your furniture style may be somewhat different, use these basic steps as a guide.

How to Pin-fit the Pattern for the Inside Back and Outside Back

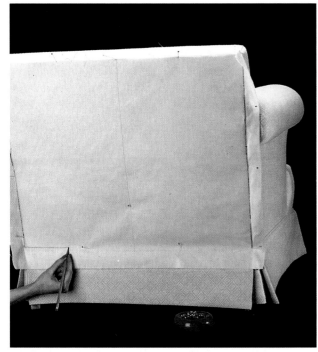

1) Remove cushions. Measure outside back of chair or sofa between seamlines; cut muslin 3" to 4" (7.5 to 10 cm) larger than measurements. Mark center line on outside back piece, following lengthwise grain. Pin to chair, smoothing fabric; mark seamlines.

2) Measure inside back between seamlines; cut muslin 15" (38 cm) wider and about 10" (25.5 cm) longer than measurements. This allows for 6" (15 cm) at the lower edge to tuck into the deck and hold the slipcover in place. Mark center line on inside back piece, following lengthwise grain.

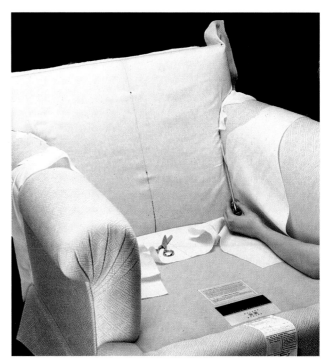

3) Pin outside back and inside back together along top of chair or sofa, matching center lines. Fold out excess fabric on inside back piece at upper corner, forming a dart. Pin muslin snugly, but do not pull fabric tight.

4) Trim excess fabric on sides of inside back to 2" (5 cm); clip along arms as necessary for smooth curve. Push about ½" (1.3 cm) of fabric into crevices on sides and lower edge of inside back; mark seamlines by pushing pencil into crevices.

185

How to Pin-fit the Pattern for a Pleated Arm

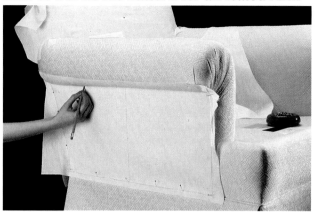

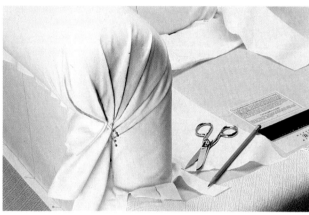

1) Measure outside arm between seamlines; cut muslin 3" (7.5 cm) larger than measurements. Mark lengthwise grainline on muslin. Pin outside arm in place, with grainline perpendicular to floor and with lower edge extending ½" (1.3 cm) beyond seamline at upper edge of skirt. Smooth fabric upward; pin. Pin outside arm to outside back. Mark seamlines.

2) Measure inside arm from deck to seamline at upper edge of outside arm, and from inside back to front of arm; cut muslin about 9" (23 cm) larger than measurements. Mark lengthwise grainline on muslin. Pin inside arm piece in place, with 7" (18 cm) extending at inside back and grainline straight across arm, smoothing fabric up and around arm.

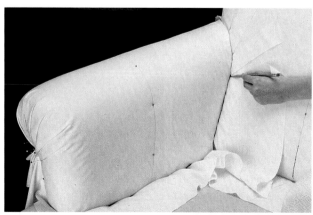

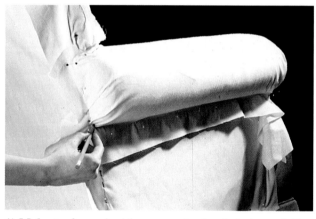

3) Pin inside arm to outside arm at front; clip and trim fabric at front lower edge as necessary for smooth fit. Pleat out fabric for rolled arm to duplicate pleats in existing fabric. Mark radiating foldlines of pleats.

4) Make tucks on inside arm at back of chair, to fold out excess fabric; clip inside arm as necessary for smooth fit. Mark seamline at beginning and end of tucks on inside arm and outside back.

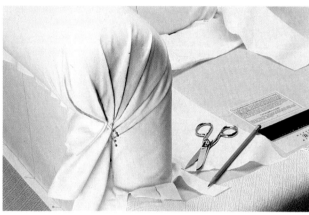

5) Mark inside arm and inside back with large dots, about halfway up the arm. Push about ½" (1.3 cm) of fabric on inside arm into crevices at deck and back.

6) Mark all seamlines on muslin, smoothing the fabric as you go.

How to Pin-fit the Pattern for an Arm with a Front Section

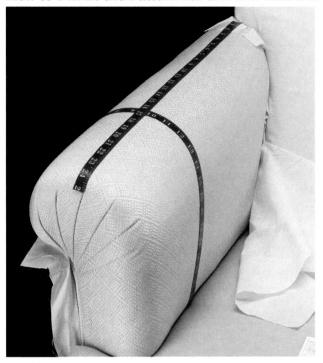

1) Follow step 1, opposite, for outside arm. Measure inside arm from deck to seamline at upper edge of outside arm, and from inside back to front edge of arm; cut muslin about 9" (23 cm) larger than these measurements. Mark lengthwise grainline on muslin.

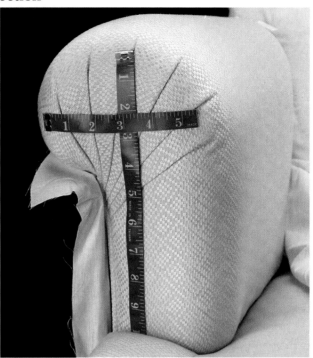

2) Measure front of the arm; cut muslin 2" to 3" (5 to 7.5 cm) larger than measurements. Mark lengthwise grainline on muslin.

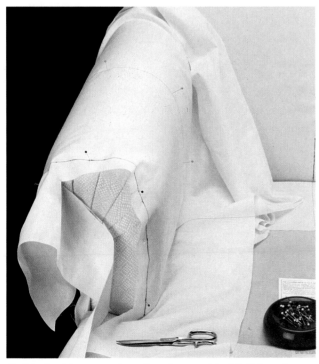

3) Pin inside arm piece in place, with 7" (18 cm) extending at inside back and grainline straight across arm, smoothing fabric up and around arm. Mark seamline at front edge of arm; trim away excess fabric not needed for seam allowances.

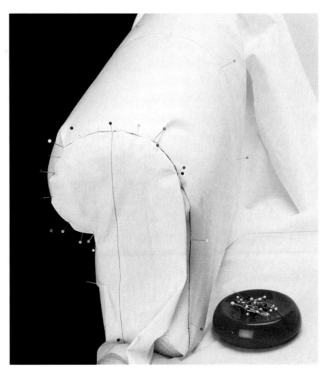

4) Pin front arm piece in place. Fold out excess fabric on inside arm as necessary to fit front arm piece, making two pleats. Mark seamline for curve of arm, following existing seamline on chair. Complete pattern as in steps 4, 5, and 6, opposite.

How to Pin-fit the Pattern for the Deck

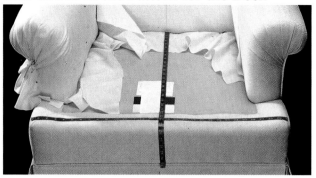

1) **Measure** width at front of deck; measure length of deck, down front of chair to skirt seam; cut muslin 15" (38 cm) wider and 9" (23 cm) longer than the measurements. Mark center line on muslin, following grainline. Mark seamline on muslin at front edge on straight of grain, ½" (1.3 cm) from raw edge.

2) **Pin** marked line on muslin to welting of skirt seam, with center line centered on skirt; this positions muslin on straight of grain. Smooth muslin over front edge and deck, and match center lines of deck and back.

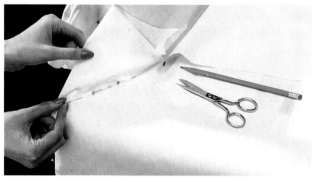

3) **Mark** deck and inside arm pieces with large dots, at point where deck meets front of inside arm. For furniture with T-cushion, clip excess deck fabric to dot. Fold out excess fabric on deck at front corner, forming a dart; pin and mark.

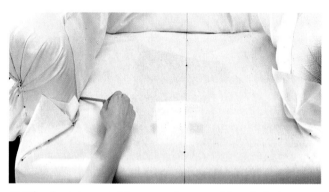

4) **Pin** deck to outside arm piece at side of chair; mark seamline. Do not fit deck snug. Push about ½" (1.3 cm) of fabric into crevices at sides and back of deck; mark seamlines by pushing pencil into crevices.

How to Pin-fit the Skirt

1) **Measure** for skirt around sides, front, and back to determine cut width of skirt; allow for gathers or pleats. Plan seam placement, based on width of fabric and size of furniture, so seams are concealed in gathers or pleats whenever possible; plan a seam at back corner where zipper will be inserted. Cut number of fabric widths needed; cut muslin pieces 1" (2.5 cm) longer than length of skirt.

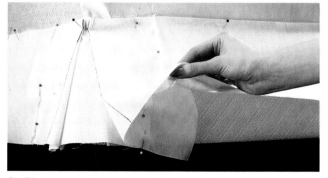

2) **Place** raw edge of muslin just below lower edge of skirt; pin at upper edge of skirt, keeping muslin straight and even. Pin seams as you come to them; pin out fullness for pleats or gathers. Pin vertical tucks in skirt, pinning ⅛" (3 mm) tuck near back corner on each side of chair and ¼" (6 mm) tuck near each corner on back of chair; tucks will be released in step 3, opposite, adding ease to skirt. Mark seams and placement of pleats or gathers.

How to Prepare the Pattern for Cutting

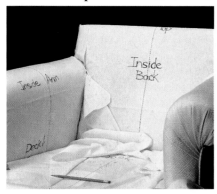

1) Mark upper edge of all muslin pieces; label pieces. Check that all seamlines, darts, gathers, and pleats are marked. Mark dots at intersecting seams; label.

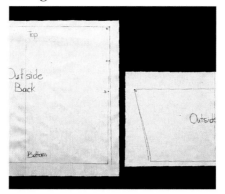

2) Remove muslin. Add ¼" (6 mm) ease to back edge of outside arm at lower corner. Add ½" (1.3 cm) ease to sides of outside back at lower corners. Taper to marked seamlines at upper corners.

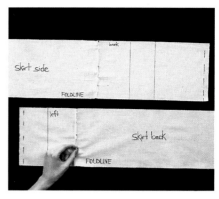

3) Remove the pinned tucks near back corners of skirt pieces. Mark "foldline" at lower edge of muslin for self-lined skirt.

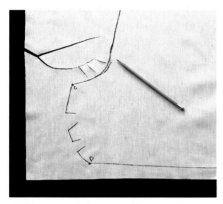

4) True straight seamlines, using straightedge; true curved seamlines, drawing smooth curves. Do not mark seamlines in pleated areas.

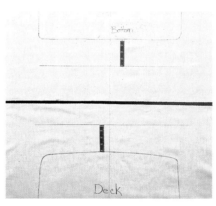

5) Add 4" (10 cm) to lower edge of inside back and back edge of deck.

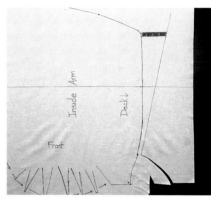

6) Mark the lower edge of inside arm from a point 4" (10 cm) away from seamline at back edge to ½" (1.3 cm) from large dot at front edge; repeat for sides of deck.

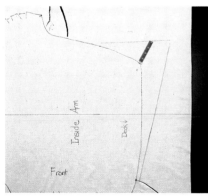

7) Mark back edge of inside arm from a point 4" (10 cm) away from seamline at the lower edge to ½" (1.3 cm) from large dot; repeat for sides of inside back.

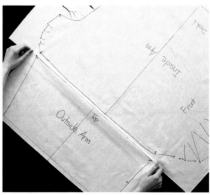

8) Check lengths of seamlines for adjoining seams; adjust as necessary to ensure that seamlines match.

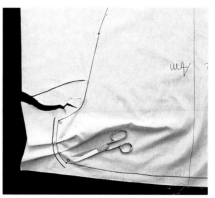

9) Fold pleats on marked lines. Mark seamlines in pleated area; add ½" (1.3 cm) seam allowances. Trim on cutting line through all layers of pleats. Add ½" (1.3 cm) seam allowances to any remaining seams. Cut pieces on marked lines.

189

Laying Out & Cutting the Fabric

Whenever possible, lay out all the pattern pieces on the fabric before you start to cut. This allows you to rearrange the pieces as necessary to make the best use of the fabric. For boxed cushions, follow the cutting directions on pages 198 and 199.

When a patterned fabric with an all-over design is used for slipcovers, little or no matching is required. If a patterned fabric with a one-way design is used, be careful to lay the pieces in the correct direction on the fabric. Patterned fabrics may be matched at the seamline on the upper edge of the skirt, if desired, following the technique for boxed cushions (page 203).

Center large motifs in a print fabric on the top and the bottom of the cushion. For best results, also align the design so it continues down the back of the furniture, onto the cushion, and down the skirt.

In addition to the pieces cut from the muslin pattern, you will need a 3" (7.5 cm) tacking strip cut on the straight of grain. This strip is used to secure the slipcover to the furniture with T-pins, tacks, or staples. Cut the length of the tacking strip equal to the distance around the furniture at the upper edge of the skirt.

Cut fabric strips for the welting as on page 205. Measure the seamlines that will have welting to determine the total length of the bias strips you will need to cut.

Tips for Laying Out and Cutting the Slipcover Fabric

Center large motifs, such as floral clusters, on the back, sides, cushions, and on the top of the arms.

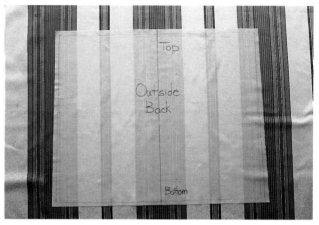

Center the prominent stripe of a striped fabric on the center placement line of the outside and inside back pieces and on the cushion pieces. Decide in which direction the stripes will run on the arms; usually it is preferable to have the stripes run in the same direction as the stripes on the skirt.

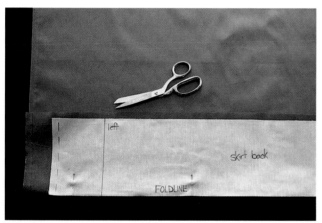

Cut the skirt pieces for a self-lined skirt, placing the foldline at lower edge of skirt on a crosswise fold of the fabric. Self-lined skirts hang better than single-layer skirts with a hem.

Cut arm pieces, right sides together, using the first piece as the pattern for cutting the second piece.

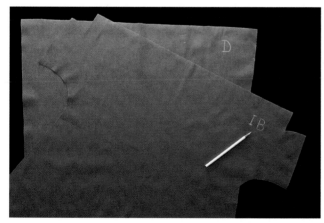

Mark names of pieces on wrong side of fabric, using chalk. Abbreviations like "D" for deck, "IB" for inside back, and "OA" for outside arm may be used.

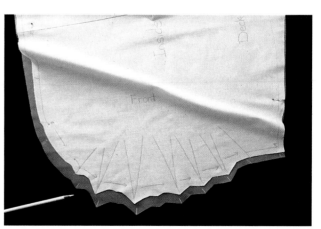

Transfer all markings, including notches and dots, from the muslin pieces to the slipcover fabric.

Sewing the Slipcover

Although the slipcover for your piece of furniture may be somewhat different from the style shown, many of the construction steps will be the same. It will be helpful for you to lay out the pieces and think through the sequence for sewing the seams of your slipcover. The labeled notches on adjoining seams will help you see how the pieces are to be joined together. To minimize the handling of bulky quantities of fabric, stitch any small details, such as darts, before assembling the large pieces.

For durable seams, use a strong thread, such as long-staple polyester, and a medium stitch length of about 10 stitches per inch (2.5 cm). Because slipcovers have several thicknesses of fabric at intersecting seams with welting, use a size 90/14 or 100/16 sewing machine needle.

Add welting to any seams that will be subjected to stress and wear, because welted seams are stronger than plain seams. For decorative detailing, welting can also be added to seams such as around the outside back and at the upper edge of the skirt. On furniture with front arm pieces, welting is usually applied around the front arm as a design detail. To prevent welted seams from puckering, take care not to stretch either the welting or the fabric as the seam is stitched. When a welted seam will be intersected by another seam, remove ½" (1.3 cm) of cording from the end of the welting to prevent bulk at the seamline.

For a chair, apply a zipper to one of the back seams of the slipcover. For a sofa, apply zippers to both back seams.

How to Sew a Slipcover with a Pleated Front Arm

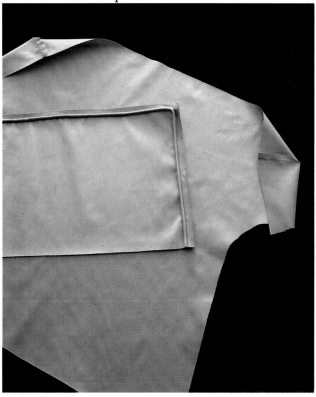

1) Stitch darts at upper corners of inside back. If welting is desired, apply it to upper and front edges of outside arm, pivoting at corner.

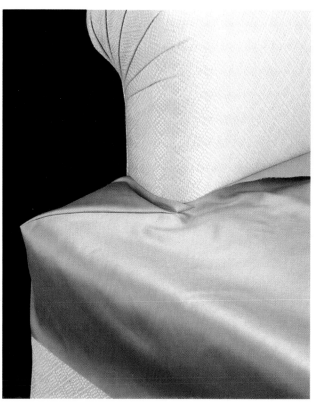

2) Stitch darts at outer front corners of deck; stop stitching ½" (1.3 cm) from raw edge at inner corner.

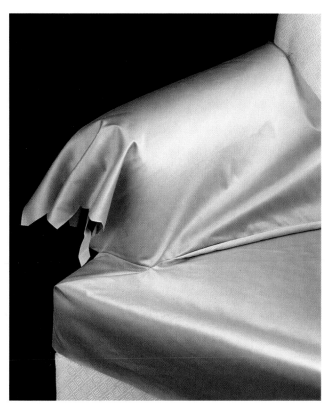

3) Stitch deck to front of arm and inside arm; this can be stitched as two separate seams.

4) Pin pleats in place at front and back of arm. Check the fit over arm of chair. Baste in place on seamline.

(Continued on next page)

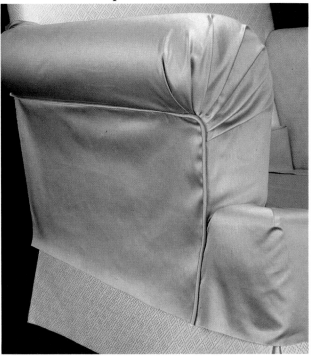

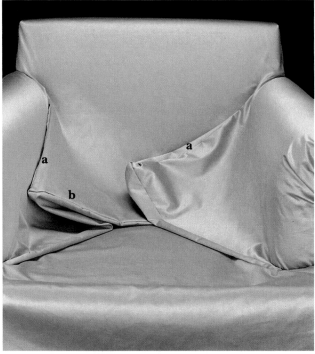

5) Stitch the horizontal and vertical seams, joining outside arm to inside arm; pivot at corner.

6) Pin inside arms to inside back on both sides **(a)**. Pin lower edge of inside back to back edge of deck **(b)**. Make tucks in seams at corners, if necessary, so pieces fit together. Stitch seams.

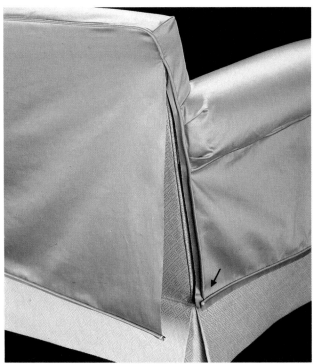

7) Apply welting around sides and upper edge of slipcover unit (page 205); curve ends of welting into seam allowance ½" (1.3 cm) from the lower edges (arrow). Join slipcover unit to outside back, leaving seam open for zipper application. Apply welting to lower edge.

8) Stitch skirt pieces together, leaving seam at back corner unstitched for zipper insertion; press seams open. Fold skirt in half lengthwise, wrong sides together; press.

9) Press pleats for pleated skirt. Or for gathered skirt, stitch gathering stitches by zigzagging over a cord as on page 169; for skirt with bunched gathers, stitch gathering stitches between the markings.

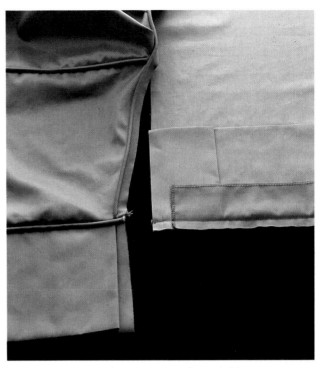

10) Pin tacking strip to upper edge of skirt on wrong side. Join the skirt to adjoining pieces; for gathered skirt, pull up gathers to fit. Apply zipper (page 197). Sew cushions (pages 199 to 201).

11) Apply slipcover to furniture. Secure tacking strip to furniture by pinning into upholstery with T-pins.

12) Push extra fabric allowance into crevices around the deck and inside back. Stuff 2" (5 cm) strips of polyurethane foam into crevices around deck to keep fabric from pulling out. Insert cushions.

How to Sew a Slipcover with Front Arm Piece

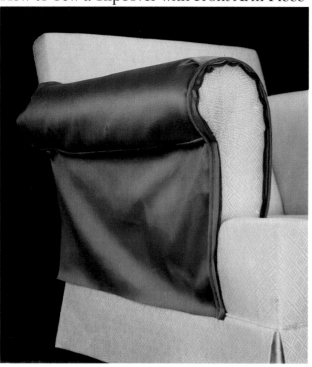

1) Stitch darts at upper corners of inside back. Apply welting to the upper edge of inside arm, if desired. Stitch horizontal seam, joining the outside arm to the inside arm. Pin and baste tucks at front edge of inside/outside arm. Apply welting to front edge of inside/outside arm.

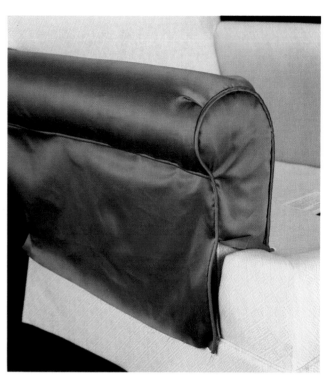

2) Stitch the front arm piece to the front edge of inside/outside arm; stop stitching 2" (5 cm) from outer end of front arm piece.

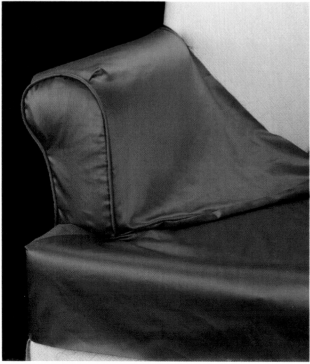

3) Follow the steps on page 193. Pin pleats in place at back of arm; baste in place on seamline.

4) Complete vertical seam at front edge of outside arm. Finish the slipcover as on pages 194 and 195.

How to Apply the Zipper

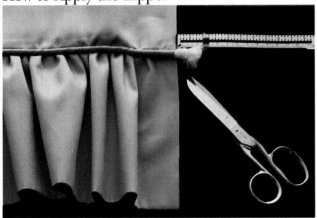

1) Pull the cording out slightly from ends of skirt opening; trim off ends 1" (2.5 cm). Pull seam to return cording to original position.

2) Press under seam allowances on zipper opening. Place open zipper on welted side of seam, so welting just covers zipper teeth and with zipper tab at lower edge. Pin in place; fold in seam allowance at lower edge of skirt to miter. Fold up end of zipper tape.

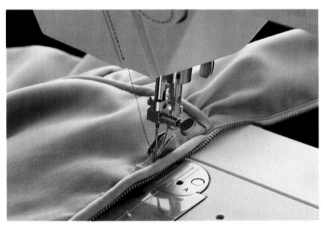

3) Edgestitch on skirt, using zipper foot, with zipper teeth positioned close to folded edge. Stitch in the ditch of the welted seam.

4) Close zipper. Place remaining side of zipper under seam allowance, with folded edge at welted seamline. Pin in place; fold in seam allowance at lower edge of skirt to miter. Fold up end of zipper tape.

5) Open zipper. Stitch ⅜" (1 cm) from folded edge, pivoting at top of zipper.

Pleated skirt. Follow steps 1 to 5, above, except break stitching at upper edge of the skirt. On skirt, stitch through lower layer of box pleat; stitch as close as possible to seam at upper edge of skirt.

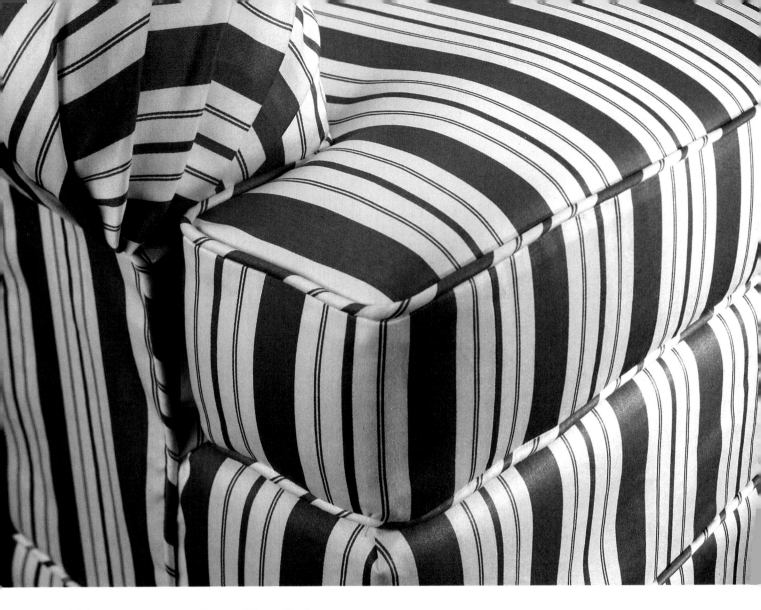

Slipcovers for Cushions

You can make slipcovers for cushions on benches or window seats, as well as on sofas or chairs. Often cushions have welting at the edges, which adds strength to the seams. Plain welting (page 120) is most commonly used, but gathered welting (page 122) or twisted welting (page 124) may also be used.

To make it easier to insert the cushion, install a zipper across the back of the slipcover, extending around about 4" (10 cm) on each side. For cushions that are exposed on three sides, install a zipper across the back of the slipcover only. Use upholstery zippers, which are available in longer lengths than dressmaker zippers. The tab of the zipper will be concealed in a pocket at the end of the zipper opening. This is an upholsterer's technique that gives a professional finish.

✂ Cutting Directions

For a boxed cushion, cut the top and bottom pieces 1" (2.5 cm) larger than the cushion size to allow for seam allowances. T-cushions are pin-fitted, using muslin, to ensure accurate cutting. Cut two zipper strips, each the length of the zipper tape; the width of each zipper strip is equal to one-half the thickness of the cushion plus 1" (2.5 cm) for seam allowances. Cut a boxing strip the length of the cushion front plus twice the length of the cushion side; the width of the boxing strip is equal to the thickness of the cushion plus 1" (2.5 cm) for seam allowances. Seam strips together, as necessary. Cut welting strips for plain welting (page 205) or gathered welting (page 122). To match patterns on cushion see page 203.

YOU WILL NEED

Decorator fabric.

Zipper, about 8" (20.5 cm) longer than back edge of cushion.

Fabric and cording for fabric-covered welting; or twisted welting.

How to Cut the Fabric for a T-cushion

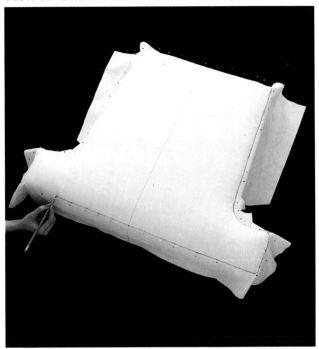

1) Cut muslin about 4" (10 cm) larger than top of cushion; mark grainline at center of fabric. Place muslin over cushion; pin along seamlines, smoothing out fabric. Mark seamlines along pin marks.

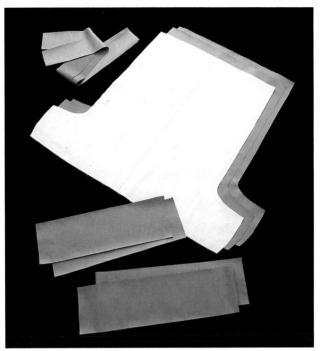

2) Remove muslin. True seamlines, using straightedge. Fold muslin in half to check that piece is symmetrical; make any necessary adjustments. Add ½" (1.3 cm) seam allowances. Cut cushion top and bottom from slipcover fabric. Cut zipper and boxing strips, opposite. Mark wrong side of fabric pieces, using chalk.

How to Sew a Slipcover for a Boxed Cushion

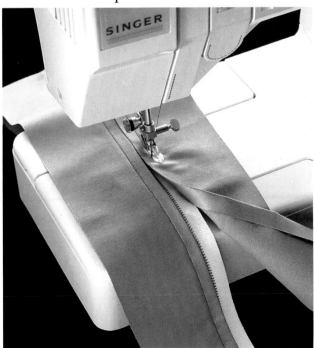

1) Press under ½" (1.3 cm) seam allowance on one long edge of each zipper strip. Position folded edges of strips along center of zipper teeth, right sides up. Using zipper foot, topstitch ⅜" (1 cm) from folds.

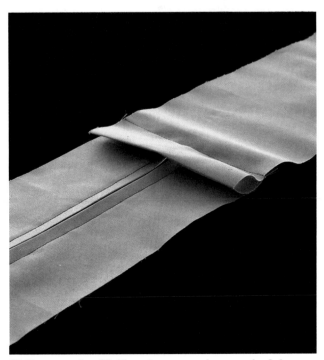

2) Press under 2" (5 cm) on one short end of the boxing strip. Lap the boxing strip over the zipper strip to cover zipper tab. Stitch through all layers 1½" (3.8 cm) from folded edge of boxing strip.

(Continued on next page)

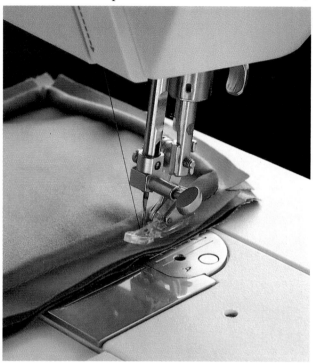

3) Make and apply plain welting as on page 205; gathered welting as on pages 122 and 123, steps 1 to 7; or twisted welting as on pages 124 and 125, steps 1 to 5. Stitch welting to right side of top and bottom pieces.

4) Place boxing strip on slipcover top, right sides together; center zipper on back edge. Start stitching 2" (5 cm) from zipper end, crowding cording. Clip corners as you come to them; stop stitching 4" (10 cm) from starting point.

5) Clip to mark seam allowances at ends of boxing strip. Stitch boxing strip ends together. Trim excess fabric; finger-press seam open. Finish stitching boxing strip to slipcover top.

6) Fold boxing strip, and clip seam allowance to mark lower corners; be sure all four corners are aligned with corners on slipcover top. Open zipper.

7) Place boxing strip and slipcover bottom right sides together. Match clips of boxing strip to corners of slipcover bottom; stitch. Turn right side out.

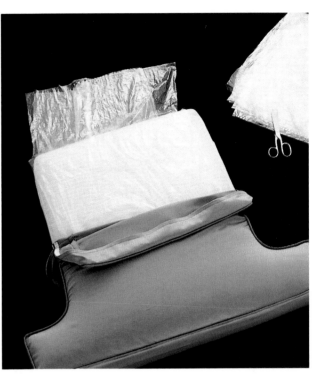

8) Fold cushion to insert it into slipcover. If necessary, wrap cushion with plastic to help slide it into slipcover, then remove plastic.

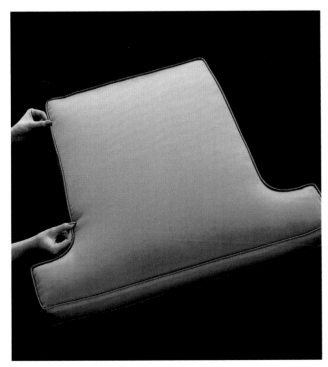

9) Stretch cover from front to back. Close zipper. Smooth cushion from center to edges. Stretch welting taut from corner to corner to square the cushion.

Alternative zipper placement. Install zipper across the back of the slipcover, without extending it around the sides, if slipcover will be exposed on three sides.

Boxed Cushions with Welting

To update any room in the house, make new covers for loose cushions on chairs, benches, or window seats. Boxed cushions may be firm or soft, depending on the foam used. Foam is available in several thicknesses and densities. Use firm or medium density foam for seat cushions; select soft density foam for back cushions. Wrap the foam with bonded polyester batting to keep the cover from shifting and to soften the look of boxed cushions.

Install a zipper as for slipcovers for cushions (page 198). Or install a zipper across only the back side for cushions that will be exposed on three sides (page 201).

✂ Cutting Directions

Cut top and bottom pieces 1" (2.5 cm) larger than finished cushion size to allow for seam allowances. Cut foam same size as top and bottom pieces for a firm, tight fit. Cut two zipper strips, each the length of the zipper tape; each zipper strip is half the thickness of finished cushion plus 1" (2.5 cm) for seam allowances. Cut boxing strip the length of cushion front plus twice the length of cushion side. Cut welting strips 1½" (3.8 cm) wide, with length 2 times the circumference of the cushion plus seam allowances.

YOU WILL NEED

Decorator fabric for top, bottom, boxing strips, and welting.

Upholstery bonded polyester batting to wrap all sides of cushion.

Foam in desired density and thickness.

Upholstery zipper, about 8" (20.5 cm) longer than back width measurement of cushion.

5/32" cording, 2 times the circumference of the cushion plus seam allowances.

How to Measure for and Cut a Boxed Cushion

1) Measure width and depth of cushion area to determine the size of finished cushion. Determine thickness of foam.

2) Cut fabric and foam. Mark the wrong side of fabric pieces with chalk.

How to Match Patterns on a Boxed Cushion

1) Cut cushion top, boxing strip, and bottom to match pattern at front seamlines. For reversible cushion, match pattern from cushion top, down boxing strip, and continue to the back.

2) Notch corners of boxing strip. Join boxing strip to cushion top and bottom, stitching front edge first. Then stitch along other sides of cushion.

Decorative Welting

Just as piping is used in garments to outline a fashion detail, welting is used in home decorator sewing to define or finish seams. Welting is fabric-covered cording, sewn into a seam to provide extra strength and a decorative finishing touch. Welting is the term used in upholstery and home decorating, and piping is the fashion term; however, the two terms are often interchanged.

Fabric strips for welting may be cut on the bias or the straight grain. For more economical use of the fabric, they are cut on the straight grain. Straight-grain welting is preferred for fabrics that are not tightly woven because bias welting can stretch too much, resulting in an uneven, wavy appearance.

For firm fabrics that must be shaped around curves, bias welting works better than straight-grain welting because it does not wrinkle. Bias welting strips do not have to be cut on the true bias. Cutting the strips at an angle less than 45° gives the flexibility of bias grain but requires less yardage. For stripes and plaids, bias welting does not require matching.

To determine how wide to cut the fabric strips, wrap a piece of fabric or paper around the cording. Pin it together, encasing the cording. Cut ½" (1.3 cm) from the pin. Measure the width, and cut strips to match.

Double welting is glued in place as a finishing treatment to cover seams and raw edges in nonsewn items, such as the edges where two fabrics meet on padded headboards or upholstered walls.

Cording Sizes

5/32" is the usual cording for pillows, cushions, and slipcover seams. Cut fabric strip 1½" (3.8 cm) wide.

8/32" is slightly larger for similar applications. This size is appropriate for gathered welting. Cut fabric strip 1¾" (4.5 cm) wide.

12/32" is jumbo cording that can be used for tiebacks and for decorative finishing. Cut the fabric strip 3¾" (9.5 cm) wide.

22/32" is used for pillows, tiebacks, and tablecloth edgings. It provides weight for a better hang at the bottom of bedspreads and comforters. Cut fabric strip 4½" (11.5 cm) wide.

How to Cut and Make Bias Strips

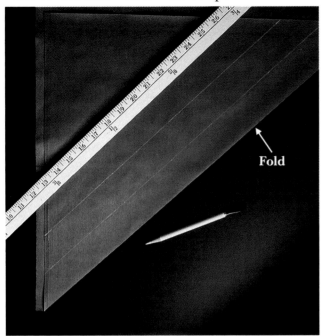

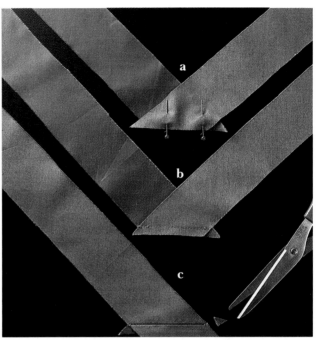

1) Cut bias strips. Determine bias grainline by folding fabric diagonally so selvage aligns with crosswise cut. For ¼" (6 mm) cord, mark and cut 1⅝" (4.2 cm) strips parallel to bias grainline. Cut wider strips for thicker cord.

2) Pin strips at right angles, right sides together, offset slightly **(a)**. Stitch ¼" (6 mm) seams **(b)**, and press open, making one continuous strip equal in length to perimeter of pillow plus 3" (7.5 cm). Trim seam allowances even with edges **(c)**.

How to Make and Apply Welting

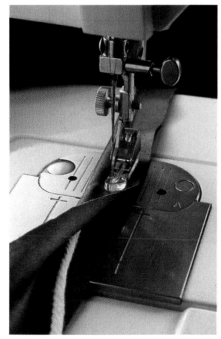

1) Center cord on wrong side of bias strip. Fold strip over cord, aligning raw edges. Using zipper foot on right side of needle, stitch close to cord, gently stretching bias to help cording lie smoothly around pillow.

2) Pin the cording to the right side of the pillow front, with raw edges aligned. To ease corners, clip seam allowances to stitching at corners.

3) Attach welting on right side with raw edges aligned. Begin stitching 2" (5 cm) from end of welting; stitch on bastestitching line. To ease at rounded corners, clip seam allowances to bastestitching.

Cushion Ties

Attach cushions to chairs with traditional fabric ties. Ties prevent cushions from sliding, and add a decorative accent to chairs.

Make ties to suit the style of the chair and cushion. Experiment with different sized fabric strips tied around the chair posts, to determine the appropriate length and width of the ties. Trim the fabric strip to desired size to use as a pattern.

✂ Cutting Directions

Cut each tie 1½" (3.8 cm) longer and 1" (2.5 cm) wider than the fabric pattern, allowing ½" (1.3 cm) for seam end and 1" (2.5 cm) for knotting the finished end. Cut two ties for each post where the ties will be attached.

How to Make Cushion Ties

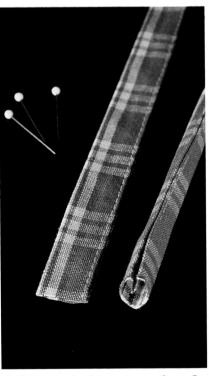

1) Make two ties for each post where ties will be attached. Press under ¼" (6 mm) on long edges of each tie. Press tie in half lengthwise, wrong sides together, pressed edges even; pin.

2) Edgestitch along open edge of ties. Leave both ends of tie open. Tie a single knot at one end of tie, enclosing the raw edges in the knot.

3) Pin unfinished ends of ties to right side of cushion front at marks. Pin cushion front to back, right sides together. Stitch, backstitching over ties. Finish cushion and tie to chair post.

Cushion Tabs

Hook and loop tape tabs make a cushion extremely easy to attach and remove, and because they are small and inconspicuous they blend in well with furniture.

The length of the tab depends on the size of the rung or post that the tab goes around. Measure accurately because the tabs must fit snugly. Tabs may be hand-stitched to existing cushions because they do not need to be stitched in a seam.

✂ Cutting Directions

Cut tabs just long enough to go around chair post and overlap by 1" to 1½" (2.5 to 3.8 cm), plus ½" (1.3 cm) for seam; twice the finished width, plus ½" (1.3 cm).

Cut hook and loop tape 1" to 1½" (2.5 to 3.8 cm) long for each tab.

How to Make Cushion Ties with Hook and Loop Tape

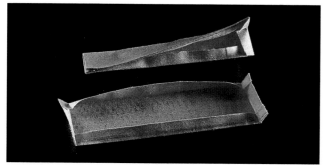

1) Make one tab for each corner. Press under ¼" (6 mm) on each edge of tab. Press tab in half lengthwise, wrong sides together. Edgestitch all four sides of tab.

2) Cut hook and loop tape for each tab. Separate hook and loop sides. Attach opposite sides of tape to opposite sides of tab. Stitch around all four sides of hook and loop tape.

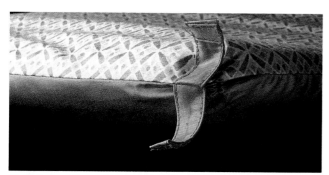

3) Stitch pillow front to back. Before stuffing, pin center of tab to seam at cushion corners. Place all tabs in same direction; stitch and backstitch.

4) Finish cushion. Attach cushion to chair or bench by fastening hook and loop tabs around posts, overlapping ends to secure.

Slipcovers for Folding Chairs

Slipcovers for folding chairs are an easy and affordable way to dress up an old steel folding chair. For special occasions, for a change of seasons, or simply for some fun in home decorating, folding-chair slipcovers are attractive and versatile. They can work with any decorating scheme from contemporary to country, depending upon fabric choice and styling options. And they offer a practical solution to the age-old problem posed by large gatherings: attractive yet portable and stowable temporary seating.

Folding chairs come in a variety of shapes and sizes, quite similar but not exactly the same. To make a well-fitting slipcover, make a custom-fitted pattern out of muslin. Start with four rectangles of fabric cut approximately to size, then drape and pin them to the chair to fine-tune the shape. Once this muslin has been fitted, use it as a pattern for cutting the slipcover.

When you make the actual slipcover, add a decorative bow tied across the back, or add contrasting piping or ruffles or creative touches of your own.

YOU WILL NEED

3 yd. (2.75 m) unbleached muslin, 42" (107 cm) wide, for pattern.

Folding chair.

Marker or pencil, pins, shears, double-stick tape.

Heavy weight, such as books or gallon (3.78 L) bottle of water.

Decorator fabric.

Muslin pattern layout. Mark muslin for rough pattern pieces; cut on solid lines. Mark dotted center lines. Mark arrows on skirt pattern piece, 6" (15 cm) and 12" (30.5 cm) on each side of center line.

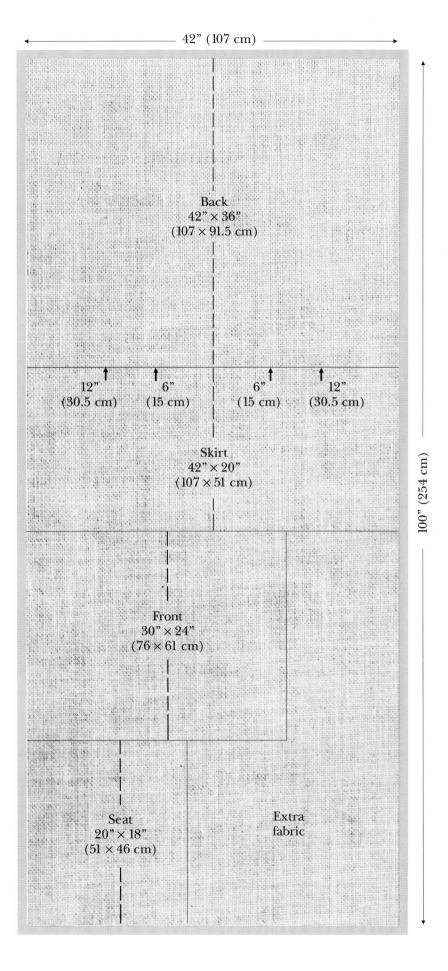

42" (107 cm)

Back
42" × 36"
(107 × 91.5 cm)

12"
(30.5 cm)   6"
(15 cm)   6"
(15 cm)   12"
(30.5 cm)

Skirt
42" × 20"
(107 × 51 cm)

Front
30" × 24"
(76 × 61 cm)

Seat
20" × 18"
(51 × 46 cm)

Extra
fabric

100" (254 cm)

How to Make a Folding Chair Slipcover

1) Pin back and front pattern pieces together for 4" (10 cm) on either side of the center marks. Pin horizontally from center toward sides, using a 1/2" (1.3 cm) seam allowance.

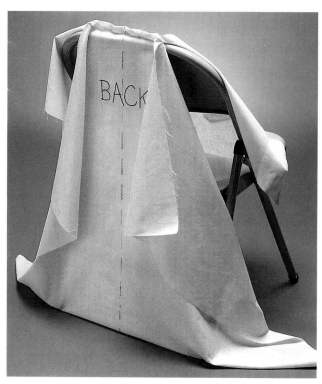

2) Drape pinned pattern over chair, matching center lines to center of chair back. Secure pattern at top of chair back with double-stick tape. Tuck pattern under back legs; keep grainline straight.

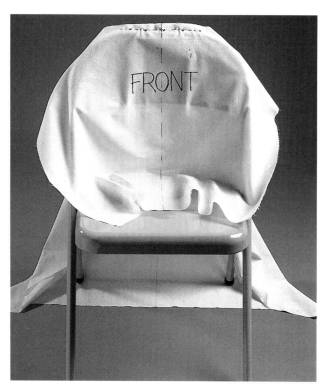

3) Push front pattern piece toward back edge of seat at bottom to allow enough ease for sitting. Secure pattern to chair with double-stick tape at center of seat and both corners.

4) Drape back pattern around curve of chair. Drape smoothly, keeping grainline perpendicular to floor. Pin along edge of chair to indicate seamline. Repeat for other side.

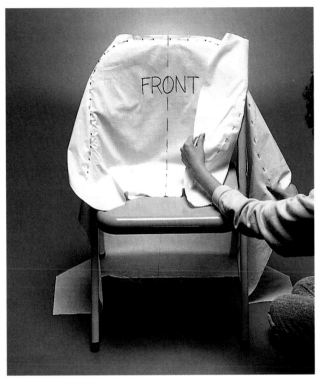

5) Drape front pattern around curve of chair. Pin along edge of chair to indicate seamline. Pin back pattern to front pattern along seamlines, adjusting to fit chair smoothly and maintain grainline.

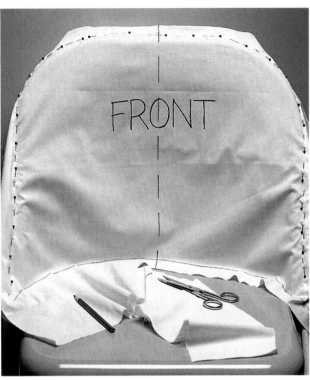

6) Trace edge of the chair seat at bottom of front pattern. Trim to 1" (2.5 cm) beyond traced outline.

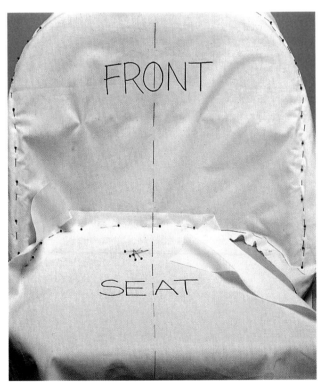

7) Secure seat pattern to chair at center front with double-stick tape. Pin back of seat pattern to bottom of front pattern, stopping where the front and back pieces meet.

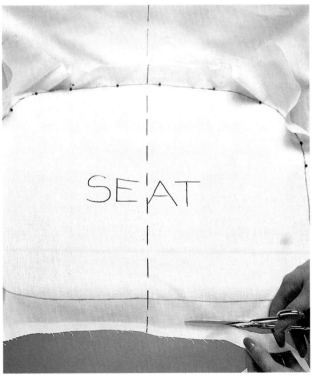

8) Trace outline of chair seat onto seat pattern. Add ¼" (6 mm) to front edge of seat pattern to allow for the rounded front edge of chair. Trim to 1" (2.5 cm) beyond outline.

(Continued on next page)

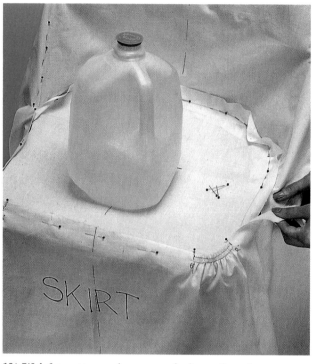

9) Gather or pleat skirt pattern between 6" and 12" (15 and 30.5 cm) marks on each side of center line. Draw up each set of gathers to 3" (7.5 cm).

10) Weight pattern pieces on chair so they do not move; a gallon (3.78 L) of water or stack of books works well. Match center lines of seat and skirt patterns. Pin skirt to seat ending where all four pieces meet.

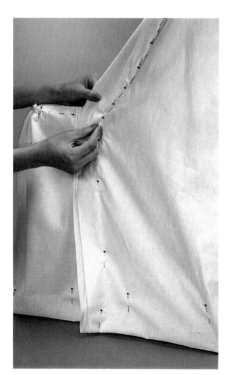

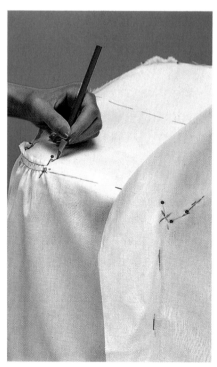

11) Turn up and pin hem to the desired length. Pin skirt to back pattern at sides. Examine fit of muslin on chair and make any necessary adjustments. Pattern should fit snugly, without pulling.

12) Mark seamlines between pins on all pieces. Mark placement for gathers on seat and skirt patterns. Mark all pieces with an "X" at point where all four pattern pieces meet at sides.

13) Remove pins and release gathers. Lay pieces flat. Mark seamlines. Fold pieces along centers. Compare markings on each half. Make any necessary adjustments so pattern is symmetrical.

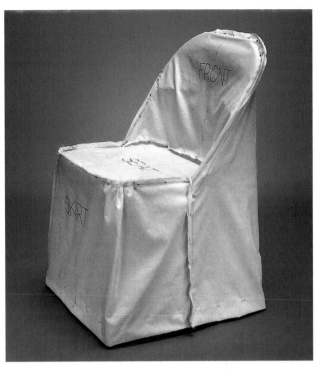

14) Trim hem allowance on skirt to 2" (5 cm) for a finished 1" (2.5 cm) double-fold hem.

15) Repin, and try pattern on chair. Adjust the fit, seamlines, and placement marks, as necessary. Add ½" (1.3 cm) seam allowances; trim excess fabric. Try pattern on chair again, if desired.

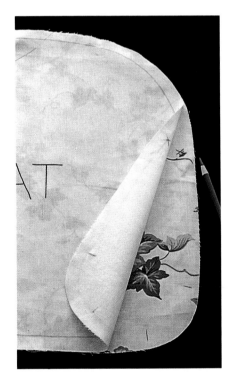

16) Cut chair cover from decorator fabric, using the muslin pieces as a pattern. Transfer markings.

17) Cut two pieces for ties, each 7" (18 cm) wide and 42" (107 cm) long. Fold in half lengthwise, right sides together. Fold one end to form triangle; cut on fold. Stitch cut side and bias end; turn and press.

18) Stitch front to seat along back edge of seat between Xs **(a)**. Stitch back to skirt at side seams, inserting tie in seam **(b)**. Gather skirt between markings; stitch front/seat to back/skirt **(c)**. Stitch hem.

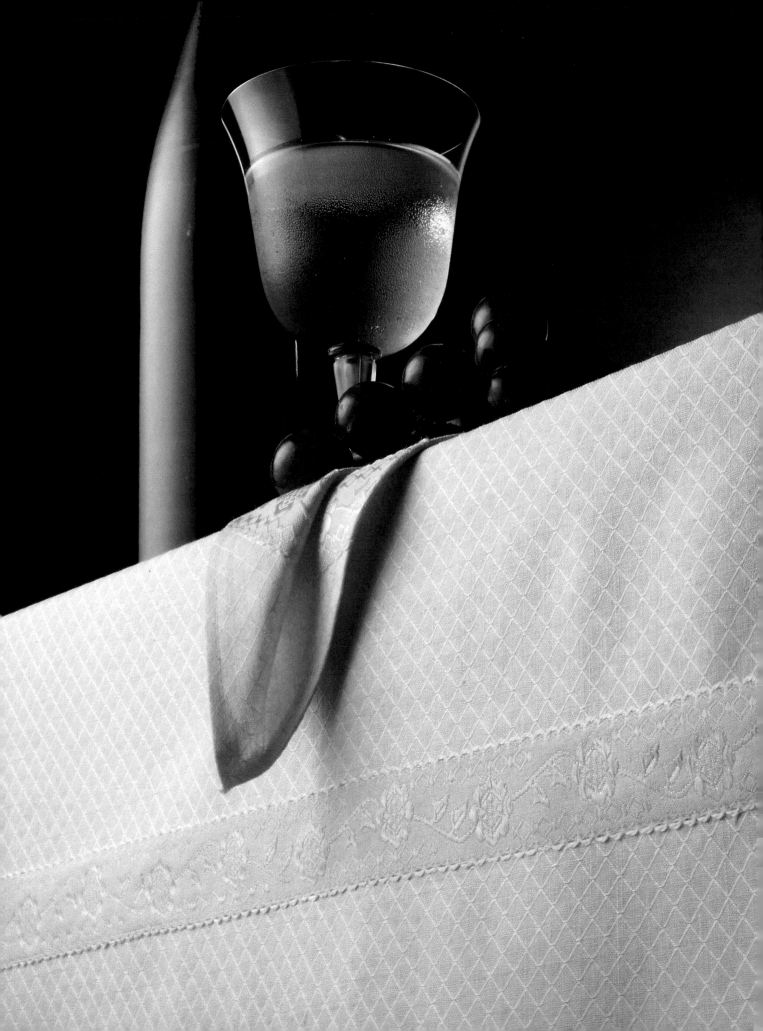

Tables

Placemats & Table Runners

Placemats and table runners protect tabletops and add color and style to table settings. Use them over tablecloths, or alone to show off the beauty of wood and glass tables. The sewing techniques for placemats and table runners are very similar.

Select fabric for mats and runners that is durable and stain-resistant, if possible. Permanent-press fabrics offer easy care. Lightweight cotton is good for everyday use, and linen, for special occasions. Avoid large prints.

Make sure ribbon trim is also washable. Fabric may be machine-quilted using the procedures described on pages 311 to 313.

Finish edges of tabletop projects with a wide banding or ribbon (page 31) or bias binding. To make bias binding, cut and join bias strips as shown on page 205. Use bias tape maker (page 32) or fold strip in half lengthwise, wrong sides together, and press. Open binding and press cut edges toward center.

Tips for Binding Placemat Edges

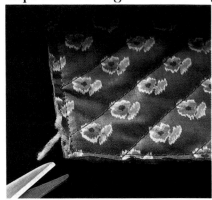

Quilted fabrics. Before applying binding, stitch placemat ¼" (6 mm) from edge. Trim batting from hem area to reduce bulk in bound edge.

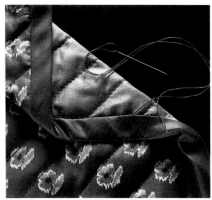

Slipstitched edges. Open out bias binding. Pin right side of binding to front of mat, raw edges even. Stitch on foldline. Turn binding to back of mat and slipstitch.

Topstitched edges. Open out bias binding. Pin right side of binding to back of mat, raw edges even. Stitch on foldline. Turn binding to front of mat and topstitch.

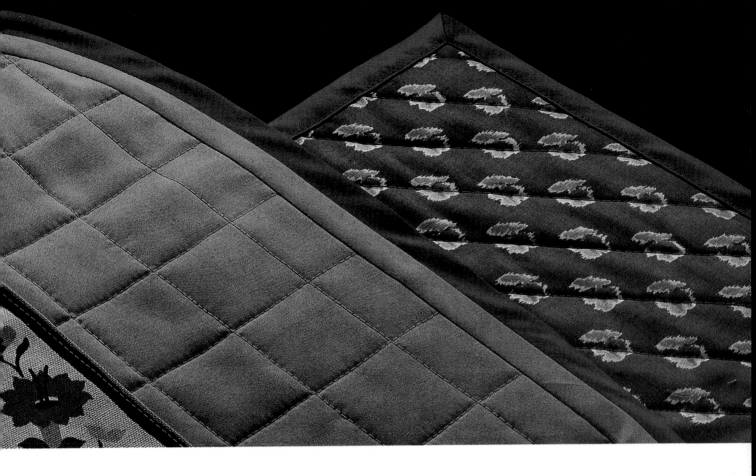

Placemats can be lined, underlined with fusible interfacing, made of quilted fabric, or sewn double for extra body. Two common finished sizes of placemats are 18" × 12" (46 × 30.5 cm) and 16" × 14" (40.5 × 35.5 cm). Choose the best size for your table and place settings.

Table runners are usually 12" to 18" (30.5 to 46 cm) wide; make them wider if they will be used as placemats. Drop lengths vary from 8" to 12" (20.5 to 30.5 cm). Table runners may be cut on either the lengthwise or the crosswise grain of the fabric, but less piecing of fabric is required if they are cut on lengthwise grain. Make a solid channel-quilted table runner or the pieced holiday star table runner on page 294.

Square corners. Start at center of edge; fold binding over edge. Stitch to corner. Pin binding to next edge, folding diagonally at corner. Begin stitching at miter. Finish ends, right.

Oval mats. Shape corners of mat using a dinner plate as a guide. Before applying bias binding, shape binding to curves with a steam iron.

Finishing ends. Cut bias binding 1" (2.5 cm) beyond the end. Turn under ½" (1.3 cm); finish stitching to end of binding. Slipstitch.

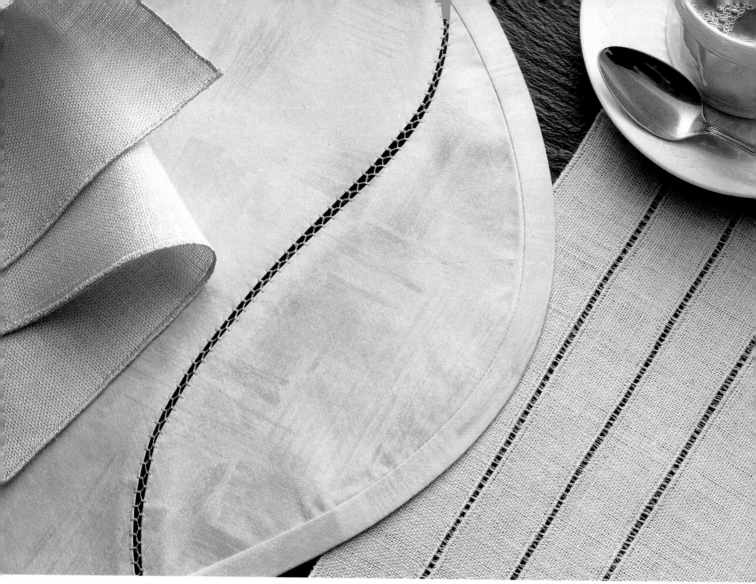

Fagoted Placemats

Fagoting is used to create an open, lacelike effect. Placemats and table linens are ideal places to feature fagoting. There are two methods for fagoting, each giving a different appearance. In the first method, curved or straight seamlines are stitched with an open-toe presser foot, using the fagoting stitch or three-step zigzag stitch. The placemat shown above left, made using this method, is oval-shaped and bound with bias strips (page 217).

In the second method, a tacking or fringe presser foot and the zigzag stitch are used for straight seamlines only. The width of the fagoting varies from ⅛" to ⅜" (3 mm to 1 cm), depending on the tacking foot; ⅜" (1 cm) fagoting may increase the finished size of the garment slightly. If the bar on the tacking foot is not centered on the foot, use a zigzag stitch with a right-needle position to center the stitches over the bar.

The placemat shown above right, made using the second method, is square, with satin-stitched edges.

Select the thread and needle according to the weight of the fabric. Cotton machine embroidery thread and a size 70/9 or 80/11 needle will work well for lightweight to mediumweight fabric; rayon thread and a size 80/11 needle may be used if extra sheen is desired. Topstitching thread or buttonhole twist and a size 90/14 needle are recommended for fagoting on mediumweight to heavyweight fabric.

Loosen the needle thread tension, if necessary, so the bobbin thread does not show on the right side of the fabric. Experiment with the stitches on your sewing machine and make a test sample, checking the tension adjustments and stitch length; the shorter the stitch length, the more filled-in the fagoting space.

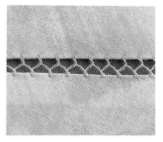

Fagoting stitched using open-toe presser foot.

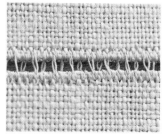

Fagoting stitched using tacking presser foot.

How to Stitch Fagoted Seams Using the Open-toe Foot

1) Trim seam allowances to ¼" (6 mm); finish edges. Press under the seam allowance plus ¹⁄₁₆" (1.5 mm). Baste one folded edge, right side up, to water-soluble stabilizer. Mark a line on stabilizer ⅛" (3 mm) beyond fold. Baste adjoining folded edge to stabilizer at marked line.

2) Center open area under open-toe presser foot. Stitch edges together, using fagoting stitch or 3-step zigzag, barely catching alternate edges as you stitch. Remove stabilizer; press.

How to Stitch Fagoted Seams Using the Tacking Foot

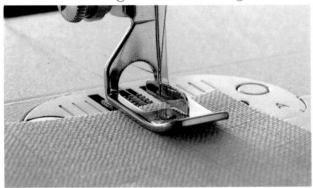

1) Attach tacking foot; place needle thread to back of foot. Set zigzag stitch width so needle barely stitches over bar on foot. If bar is not centered on foot, set machine for zigzag stitch with a right-needle position so stitches are centered over bar. Set stitch length and loosen needle thread tension.

2) Stitch seam, right sides together, so center of zigzag stitches is ⅝" (1.5 cm) from raw edge.

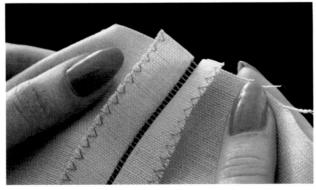

3) Remove fabric from machine carefully to prevent threads from drawing up. Finish seam allowances. Pull layers apart firmly. Press seam open.

4) Attach open-toe presser foot. Set the machine to balanced tension. Stitch on each side of fagoting, from right side, using satin stitch or other decorative stitch; pull fabric flat as you stitch. If short stitch length is used, the seam allowances may be trimmed close to the stitching.

Table Linens with Mitered Corners

Table linens with wide hems and mitered corners are elegant and easy to make. Use the same hemming technique for tablecloths, placemats, and napkins. Any of these items can be customized with fabric painting, following the instructions on pages 240 to 245.

Make tablecloths the desired width by joining fabric widths as necessary, using full widths in the center and partial widths on the lengthwise edges. Straighten the crosswise ends of the fabric to square the corners. Use French or overedge seams, or use selvage edges (page 28) to eliminate seam finishing, if seaming is necessary.

Select the width and finish of the hem to complement the weight and texture of the fabric. Mitering is the neatest way to square corners, because it covers the raw edges and eliminates bulk.

Determine the amount of fabric needed for the tablecloth by dividing the total width of the tablecloth by the width of your fabric less 1" (2.5 cm). Multiply this figure, which is the number of panels needed, by the total length of the tablecloth. Divide this number by 36" (91.5 cm) to get the total yards (meters) required. Allow for about 1" (2.5 cm) hems, depending on the size of the project.

Determine the amount of fabric for placemats as on page 217. To make napkins you will need 1 yard (0.95 m) of 36" (91.5 cm) fabric for 17" (43 cm) napkins. You may wish to vary the size of napkins.

How to Make Mitered Corners

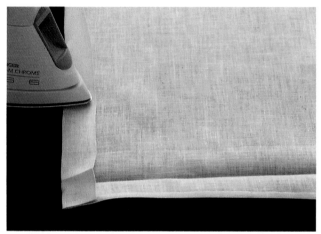

1) Stitch a scant ¼" (6 mm) from edges of fabric. Fold the edges to wrong side; press just beyond the stitching line. Press under desired hem depth on each side of fabric.

2) Open out corner; fold diagonally so pressed folds match. Press diagonal fold.

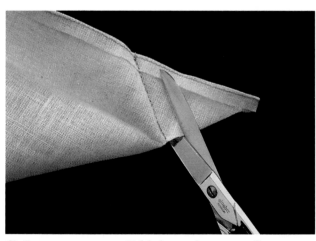

3) Open out corner. Fold through center of corner, right sides together. Stitch on diagonal foldline from step 2. Trim fabric from corner to ¼" (6 mm) from stitching. Press seam open.

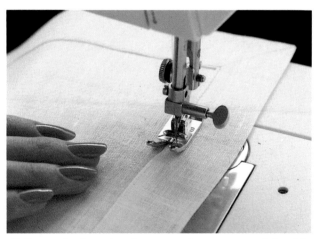

4) Press the hem in place, turning corners right side out. Stitch hem, pivoting at corners; use decorative thread, such as rayon or metallic thread, if desired.

Satin-stitched Tablecloth

Satin stitching can be used to apply appliqués, outline cutwork, stitch decorative design lines, or finish edges. The tablecloth below utilizes all of these applications. Choose a mediumweight linen for this square tablecloth with satin-stitched hem. Choose designs from appliqué, cutwork, and embroidery patterns.

To sew the satin stitch, set the machine for a zigzag stitch and a short stitch length, so the stitches lie close to each other, concealing all the fabric under the stitches. Satin stitches can be any stitch width desired; generally, the smaller the design, the narrower the stitch width.

Adjust the tension so the bobbin thread does not show on the upper side of the fabric. Use an open-toe presser foot or special-purpose presser foot for sewing satin stitching. The groove on the bottom of the foot provides space for the stitches, so the fabric feeds through the sewing machine evenly.

Machine embroidery thread is recommended for satin stitching. Cotton embroidery thread has a subtle sheen, rayon embroidery thread, a more pronounced sheen.

Satin stitching may be corded, using one to three strands of pearl cotton or topstitching thread. A cording foot is helpful, because it guides the cord under the stitches automatically. However, if a cording foot is not available for your sewing machine, the cord can be guided by hand.

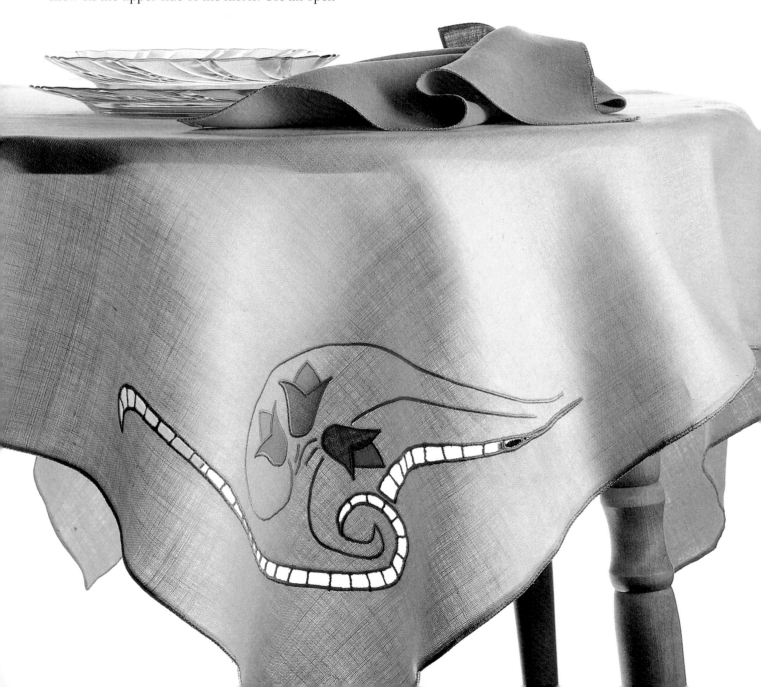

Setting the Stitch Length

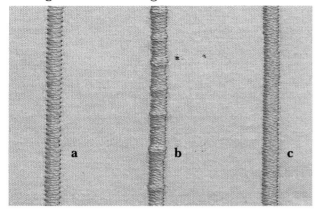

Set the stitch length for short stitches. Place a stabilizer under a fabric scrap, and stitch to check stitch length. If stitches are too long **(a)**, the fabric shows between the stitches. If stitches are too short **(b)**, the stitches pile up or overlap, and the fabric does not feed smoothly. Perfect satin stitches **(c)** are evenly spaced and lie next to each other without overlapping.

Two Ways to Sew an Edge Finish Using Satin Stitching

Folded edge. Press the edge under ½" (1.3 cm). If using a lightweight fabric, place tear-away stabilizer under fabric, aligning it with fold. Stitch along the folded edge so needle stitches just over fold. Turn corners or curves, and remove stabilizer. Trim excess fabric close to stitches.

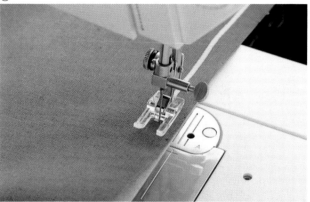

Single layer. Place 1" (2.5 cm) strip of tear-away or water-soluble stabilizer under edge. Satin stitch ½" (1.3 cm) from raw edge to prevent stretching at edge. Turn corners or curves, and remove stabilizer. Trim fabric at edge, close to stitches.

How to Sew Corded Satin Stitching

1) Satin stitch, above. Place pearl cotton in hole of cording foot. Stitch over cord along outer edge, using narrow zigzag stitch. Stop one stitch width away from corner, with needle down at inner edge; stitch in place for a few stitches.

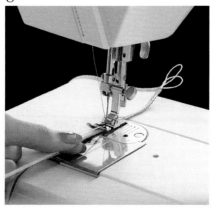

2) Pivot fabric. Make a loop in cord and stitch in place for a few stitches. Continue zigzag stitching over cord for a few inches (2.5 cm). Pull on ends of cord to eliminate the loop.

3) Trim end of cord at starting point so cord ends meet. Overlap stitching ½" (1.3 cm).

Finishing Touches

Accent with Trimming

The addition of a trim may be all that is needed to create a decorator look or embellish a special treatment. Fringe, tassels, braid, silk cord, lace, ribbons, and bows are custom trimmings that add fancy finishing touches throughout the home. Use them on window treatments, valances, and tiebacks as well as on pillows, cushions, and duvets.

Trimmings should be compatible with the mood of the room as well as the weight and care of the fabric. Silky braids and tassels are perfect partners with elegant high-gloss fabrics. Eyelet and lace edgings are essential to a romantic, feminine look. Be sure that washable trimmings are used on washable items.

To mark placement lines for trimmings, use a water-soluble marking pen or a marking pen with lines that evaporate. If pins distort the trim when it is temporarily positioned for stitching, use glue stick to hold the trim in place. If a project lacks interest after it is finished, an applied trim can save it.

Allow extra trim for mitering corners. To be sure that the miter is perfect, you may want to test the trim in place and then baste it in position before stitching, especially when a patterned braid or eyelet needs matching at the corners.

1) Edgings have one raw edge and one finished edge. Lace and eyelet edgings may be flat or preruffled and pregathered. The unfinished edge is stitched in a seam or under a hem. If used on the surface, the raw edge may be covered with a ribbon or braid.

2) Twisted cords are available with an attached woven banding that can be stitched in a seam allowance.

3) Loop fringe has continuous, uncut loops attached to a band heading. The heading may be stitched or glued onto a hem.

4) Tasseled tiebacks are decorative twisted cords with tassels for holding draperies or curtains open.

5) Tasseled fringe has small tufts or tassels attached to a heading. The heading may be stitched or glued onto a hem.

6) Fringe is made of loose strands knotted through a finished heading. The heading may be stitched or glued onto a hem.

7) Ribbons are available in a wide range of colors and widths for every decorative application. Grosgrain is a fine, narrow corded weave. Satin is a smooth weave with sheen. Velvet has dense pile weave on one side. Taffeta is crisp, shiny ribbon with plain, plaid, or moiré finish. Ribbons are stitched, glued, or fused onto the surface.

8) Gimp is a narrow decorative braid with a loop or scroll design in one or two colors, used to cover seams and raw edges. It may be glued or stitched in place.

9) Braid has several strands or cords braided together to form a flat surface trim. It is applied on the surface of an item, not in a seam, and is either stitched, glued, or fused in place.

10) Band trims have two finished edges. They are applied the same way as braid.

Trimming Ideas

Tie a wide ribbon and a narrow ribbon of contrasting colors in large bow for tieback or ties on chair seats.

Sew or fuse braid or banding along drapery edges. Use purchased trim, or cut stripes or strips from fabric.

Use flat braid down the sides or along the bottom edge of roller shades.

Use narrow ribbon as bows to tie quilts and comforters.

Apply silky cord on edges of pillows.

Use straight and looped fringe as traditional trims on edges of Austrian valances.

Apply lace on ruffled edges for quick hem on duvets, dust ruffles, and tablecloths.

Sew flat lace or eyelet on edges of pillow shams over solid colors.

Glue or sew braid or banding on edges of lampshades.

Sew six tucks down center of duvet cover; press three each way. Sew a row of lace edging down outside edges of tucks. Repeat on pillow shams.

Tie chair seat cushions in place with bows.

Use bows on curtain tiebacks.

Use bows to accent table toppers or swags.

Bows & Knots

One of the easiest ways to accent a decorating scheme or give a new look is with large, soft bows or knots. At the window, use bows or knots to trim the corners of swags, to shape drapery or curtain panels into pouffed tiers, and to tie valances into draped scallops for a swag or cloud effect. Streamers, 16" to 20" (40.5 to 51 cm) long, give a luxurious effect.

In addition, bows or knots are a quick alternative to more tailored curtain and drapery tiebacks. To use as tiebacks on ruffled curtains, slit the panel next to the ruffle and seal the cut edges with liquid fray preventer; tie a bow through the slit, so the ruffle is not crushed. Sew a small plastic ring to the center of the bow, or knot the section to use as a tieback. You can also use bows or knots to trim lampshades and to anchor seat cushions on chairs.

The speediest bows or knots can be sewn from one continuous tube of fabric. Cut the tube into appropriate sections as needed. For best results, use lightweight fabric with a crisp finish. To add body to limp fabrics, apply soft fusible interfacing to the wrong side of the fabric before cutting and sewing.

How to Sew a One-piece Bow or Knot

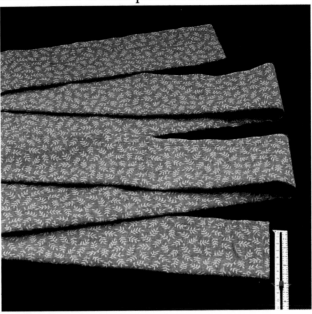

1) Cut strips 7" (18 cm) wide for 3" (7.5 cm) wide bows or knots, and 9" (23 cm) wide for 4" (10 cm) wide bows or knots. Cut strips as long as possible, so multiple bows or knots can be cut from each strip. Fold strip in half lengthwise, right sides together. Sew seam on one long edge. Turn right side out, and press.

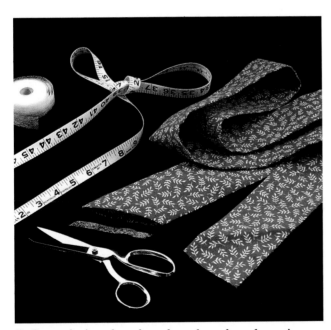

2) Cut strip into bow-length or knot-length sections. Determine length of sections by tying tape measure into bow or knot for desired effect. Cut ends of sections at an angle. Fold raw edges into tube, and press. Fuse or glue openings closed.

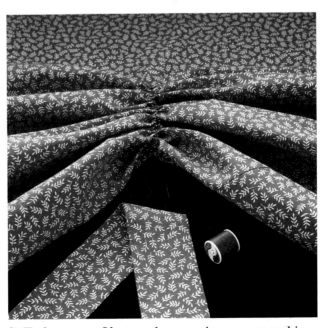

3) Tack center of bow or knot section to seat cushions and tie. Or, for tiebacks or swags, tie bow before attaching.

Bow
Picture Hangers

These attractive bows are used to accent a painting or portrait. They add interest to the wall at a higher level than most room furnishings, and they draw the eye upward, visually adding height to a room. Originally used to support the weight of pictures, bow picture hangers are now used as decorative, nonfunctional accessories.

Bow picture hangers are an excellent use for the long, narrow side cuts of fabric that are frequently left over after sewing other projects. For best results, use a fabric that has body, so the bow will hold its shape. Chintz and moiré are frequently used for crisp bows.

Bow picture hangers can be made to any size. The instructions that follow are for a picture hanger about 50" (127 cm) long.

✄ Cutting Directions
Cut one 11" × 34" (28 × 86.5 cm) piece of decorator fabric for bow, two 7" × 54" (18 × 137 cm) pieces for tails, and two 3" × 5" (7.5 × 12.5 cm) pieces for ties. These measurements include ½" (1.3 cm) seam allowances.

YOU WILL NEED

Decorator fabric.

Small plastic curtain ring.

How to Sew a Bow Picture Hanger

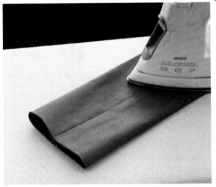

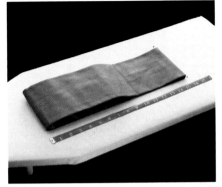

1) Fold bow piece in half lengthwise, right sides together; stitch long edges. Press seam open. Turn right side out. Press, centering seam on back of bow.

2) Stitch short ends, right sides together. Turn right side out. Fold in half, with seam at one end; pin-mark foldline. Stitch across the width of the bow, through all layers, 10" (25.5 cm) from seam.

3) Flatten bow, with stitching lines and marked foldline in the middle of the bow. Stitch through all layers at middle.

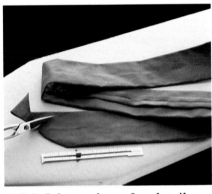

4) Stitch long edges of each tail, right sides together; press seam open. Center seam on back; mark points 2" (5 cm) up from lower edge at sides. Draw lines from marks to ½" (1.3 cm) from raw edge at the center. Stitch on marked lines; trim excess fabric.

5) Turn tails right side out; press, centering seams on back. Press under ¾" (2 cm) at upper edge of one tail; trim ¾" (2 cm) from remaining tail. With right sides up, place tails together as shown.

6) Fold both tails over 4" (10 cm) from fold at upper edge. Stitch through all layers ¼" (6 mm) from first fold.

7) Fold in raw edges of tie pieces to make ties 1¼" × 5" (3.2 × 12.5 cm); press. Pinch bow at center. Hand-stitch one tie over center of bow, turning under raw edge.

8) Pull remaining tie through the previous tie. Pinch tails 4" (10 cm) from upper edge. Hand-stitch tie around tails, turning under raw edge.

9) Stitch curtain ring on back of bow for hanging on wall.

Fabric Screens

Fabric screens are decorative and functional. A simple screen instantly blocks an unattractive view, fills an empty corner, or separates a conversation or sleeping area. It is also an elegant way to show off an unusual fabric.

Decorative folding screens with removable dowels for mounting fabric panels are available at stores selling unfinished furniture, or you may construct wooden frame panels and hinge them together.

If the fabric has no obvious right or wrong side, such as lace and a woven plaid or stripe, it can simply be hemmed on the sides. Fabrics with an obvious right and wrong side need to be made double or with a contrasting lining, because both sides of the fabric may show.

✂ Cutting Directions

For hemmed panels, measure from top of upper dowel to bottom of lower dowel; add allowance for rod pockets and double headings at the top and bottom. The rod pocket is 2 times the diameter of the dowel.

The cut width of the fabric panel depends on the fabric. Generally, 1½ times the fullness is sufficient and will not distort a print; add 2" (5 cm) to each panel for side hems. Small prints and solids may use more fullness.

For a lined panel, measure from the top of the upper heading to the bottom of the lower heading. Add 1" (2.5 cm) for seam allowances. Cut decorator fabric and lining same size.

YOU WILL NEED

Folding screen with removable dowels for fabric insertion.

Decorator fabric and optional lining, as determined by type of fabric.

How to Sew a Fabric Screen

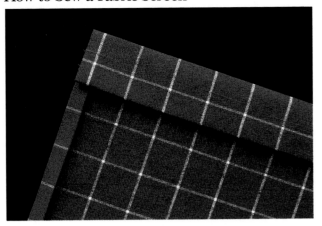

1) Press under double ½" (1.3 cm) side hems. On ends, turn under ½" (1.3 cm), then heading and rod pocket allowance. Stitch side hems, then rod pockets and headings.

2) Slip the dowels into the rod pockets; attach panels to the screen.

How to Sew a Lined Fabric Screen

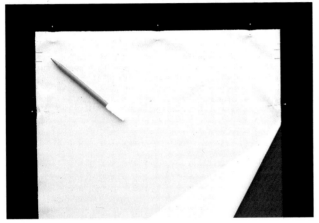

1) Pin right sides of decorator fabric and lining together with all edges even. On the lining, mark the heading and opening for rod pocket, allowing for ½" (1.3 cm) seam at upper and lower edges.

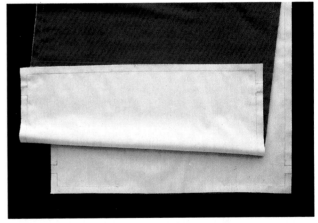

2) Stitch all four sides in ½" (1.3 cm) seam, leaving openings for upper and lower rod pockets on both sides of panel. Leave an 8" (20.5 cm) opening at lower edge for turning right side out.

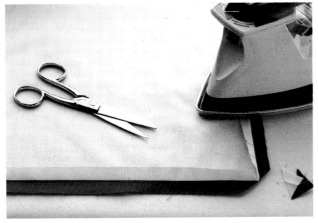

3) Trim corners diagonally. Press lining seam allowances toward lining. Turn panel right side out. Press edges.

4) Stitch rod pockets on upper and lower edges, stitching across panel at opening. Edgestitch the 8" (20.5 cm) opening closed at the lower edge. Slip dowels into rod pockets; attach panels to screen.

Upholstered Walls

An upholstered wall is a dramatic finishing touch that adds a soft, sculptured look to a room. The batting absorbs sound and covers imperfections.

Plaids or stripes will call attention to a floor or ceiling that is not squared. Stripes must be carefully stapled to keep them looking straight. It is easy to staple fabric to wood and plasterboard walls, but staples will not penetrate metal corner pieces. Before starting, remove switch plates and outlet covers. Do not remove moldings or baseboards because double welting will cover fabric edges.

✂ Cutting Directions

Cut fabric lengths as figured in chart, right. Do not trim selvages unless they show through the fabric.

Measure around doors, windows, and ceiling and floor lines to determine the amount of double welting needed. You will also need double welting from floor to ceiling for each corner. Cut 3" (7.5 cm) welting strips equal to this measurement.

YOU WILL NEED

Decorator fabric for upholstered walls.

Staple gun, ¼" (6 mm) staples, ⅝" (1.5 cm) polyester upholstery batting; or ¼" (6 mm) foam; pushpins; single-edged razor blades; hot-glue gun; white glue.

Amount of Fabric Needed

Cut Length	in. (cm)
1) Measurement from floor to ceiling plus 3" (7.5 cm)*	=
Cut Width	
1) Width of fabric minus selvages	=
2) Fabric widths: Width of each wall divided by width of fabric**	÷
Welting	
1) Welting length (see Cutting Directions)	
2) Divided by width of fabric	÷
3) Number of strips times 3" (2.5 cm)	=
Total Fabric Needed	
1) Cut length (figured above)	
2) Fabric widths (figured above) for all walls	×
3) Fabric needed for all walls	=
4) Fabric for welting	+
5) Number of yd. (m) needed: Total width needed divided by 36" (100 cm)	yd. (m)

*Allow extra for pattern repeat; do not subtract for windows and doors unless they cover most of the wall.

**Round up to the nearest whole number.

How to Upholster a Wall

1) Staple batting every 6" (15 cm), leaving 1" (2.5 cm) gap between batting and edge of ceiling, corners, baseboard, and moldings. Butt edges. Cut out batting around switch and outlet openings.

2) Seam fabric panels together for each wall separately, matching motif carefully (page 25). Avoid placing seams next to a door or window.

3) Start hanging fabric from top, turning under ½" (1.3 cm) and stapling every few inches (cms). Begin at a corner where matching is not critical. Do not cut around windows and doors.

4) Anchor fabric in corners, pulling taut and stapling close to corner so staples will be covered with welting. Trim excess fabric. Start next panel at corner.

5) Staple along baseboard, pulling and smoothing fabric taut to remove any wrinkles. Trim excess fabric along baseboard with single-edged razor blade.

6) Mark outside corners of windows and doors with pushpins. Cut out openings with diagonal cuts into corners. Turn under raw edges, and staple around molding.

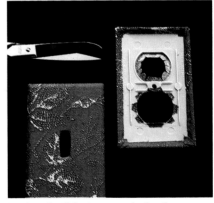

7) Make double welting (page 33). Run hot glue about 12" (30.5 cm) at a time along seam on back of welting. Carefully push welting into position to cover staples.

8) Press welting into corners and around openings. Use screwdriver to force welting into corners. Glue dries in about one minute. After it dries, peel off any excess.

9) Apply fabric to switch plates and outlet covers, using white glue diluted with water. Clip and trim around openings. Turn raw edges to back of plate, and glue.

Decorating with Lace

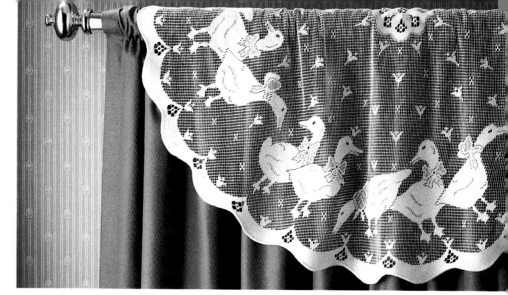

Valances. Drape circular lace panel over decorative pole rod for a timesaving valance. Use purchased round tablecloth, or cut circle from allover lace. No hems are necessary.

Tieback curtains. Stitch rod pocket heading on lace panel. Insert rod, and hang panel. Tie bow or tieback around lace. To make a bishop's sleeve curtain, use lace panel that is about 24" (61 cm) longer than measurement from rod to floor. Attach one or two tiebacks, and puff up lace panel to create bishop's sleeve effect. Allow lower edge to puddle gracefully onto floor.

Pillows. Slipcover pillows with tie-on lace cases to refresh a solid-color pillow. Cut lace sections to size of pillow plus ½" (1.3 cm) for seams. Stitch lace square on three sides. Use ribbon to tie fourth side closed.

Tied panels. Thread satin or grosgrain ribbon through tops of lace panels. To hang panels, tie bows or knots over decorative curtain or shower rod.

Lampshades and shutters. Gather lace over lampshade frame. Staple lace panels behind shutter openings or to the frame of a folding screen.

Table toppers. Cut a lace circle, or purchase a round lace tablecloth. Trim edge with ruffled wide-lace trim, or divide edge into 6 to 8 sections and gather into swags. To show off lace pattern most effectively, layer lace over solid-color or printed floor-length cloth.

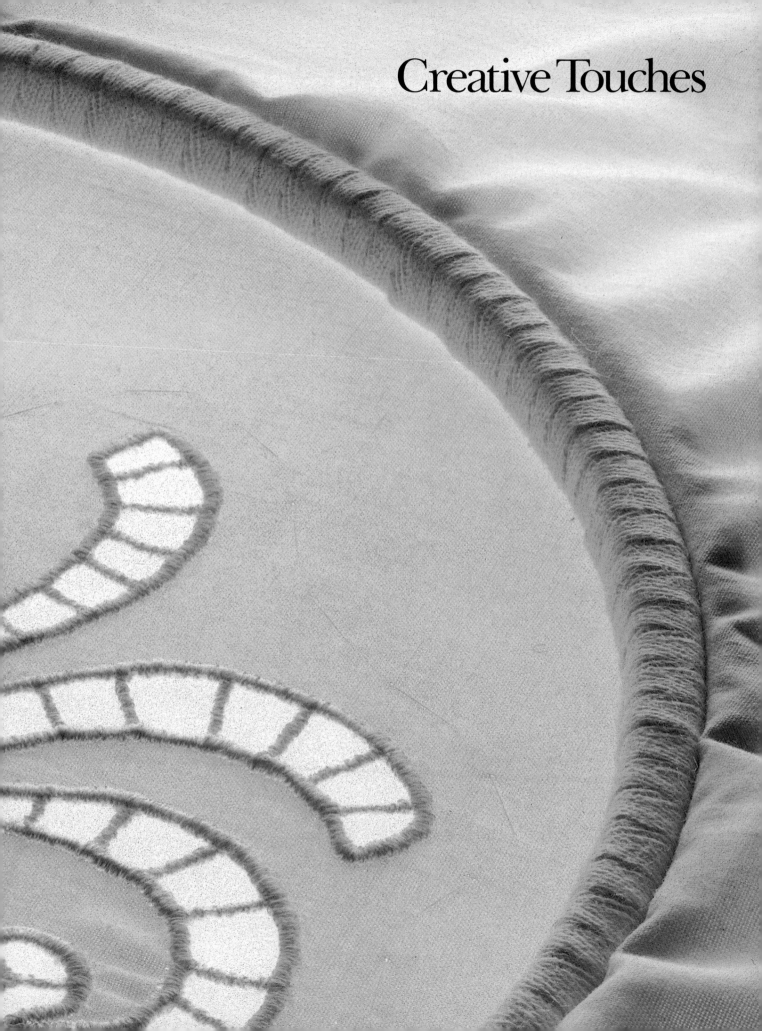

Fabric Painting

Fabrics can be painted to add an artistic touch to accessories for the home. Projects such as the shower curtain at left can be painted to complement the color scheme of a room. Paints can be applied to either woven or knit fabrics. Mediumweight to heavyweight wovens are easier to paint, because they do not shift during painting. Remove any sizing from the fabric by washing it before painting.

Use textile paints, applying them with synthetic brushes. For a variety of interesting designs, a number of other tools, such as kitchen or sewing utensils, can be used to apply paint. Water-repellent fabrics can be painted with water-based enamel; check the fabric recommendations on the label.

It is important to practice the painting techniques on scraps of the fabric or on paper before painting on the actual fabric. Protect the work surface by covering it with a sheet of plastic. Heat-set the paints according to the manufacturer's directions. Most heat-setting processes require a temperature of 325°F (163°C) for three minutes to remove all the moisture from the paint. Usually paint is heat-set by pressing with an iron. After the paints have been heat-set, use the care method recommended for the fabric.

Flanged pillow shams have been sponged with a natural sea sponge, using textile paints. Apply masking tape inside the border while sponging to define the edges of the flange.

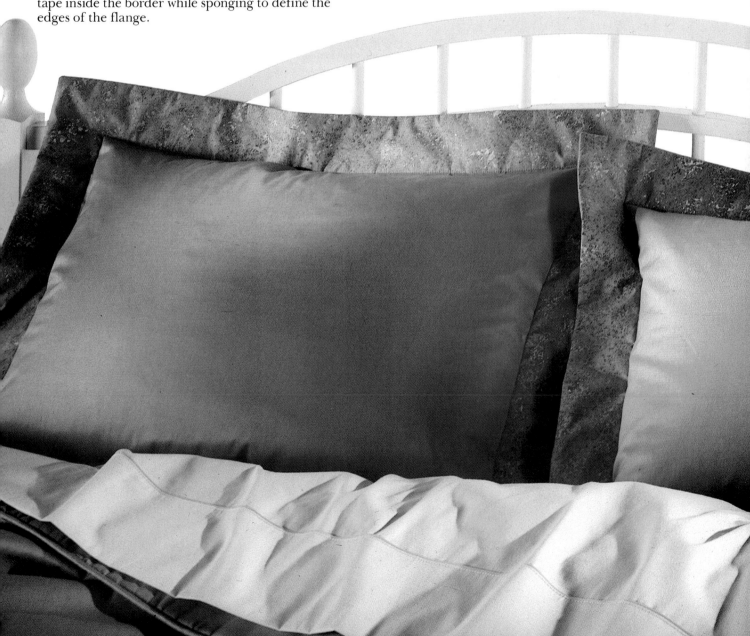

How to Paint Fabric in an All-over Design

1) Wet fan brush; blot excess water on a sponge or paper towel. Work bristles so fan is separated into small fingers. Dip into paint ¼" (6 mm), taking care that bristles remain separated into fingers.

2) Make several brush strokes about 1" (2.5 cm) in length on fabric, applying *light* pressure and using one color of paint. Refill brush with paint, as needed, and vary direction of brush strokes, as desired.

How to Paint Fabric in a Randomly Spaced Design

1) Wet fan brush; blot excess water on a sponge or paper towel. Coat brush with paint. Make large, curving brush strokes, 3" to 5" (7.5 to 12.5 cm) in length.

2) Wash brush; using second color of paint, make curved brush strokes, about 2" (5 cm) in length, using method in steps 1 and 2, above.

3) Wash brush. Apply a different color of paint, making fewer brush strokes than with first color.

4) Repeat step 3 for each color that is used. By layering more colors in the design, more depth is achieved.

3) Apply third color, using a medium round brush. Make small, curving brush strokes, about 1" (2.5 cm) in length; overlap some of the larger strokes.

4) Use Monoject® tool to add squiggles, as on page 244. Dip wooden end of brush in a different color of paint; add dots of paint on fabric.

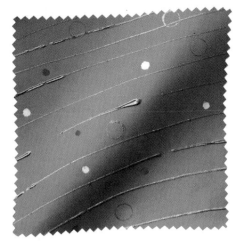

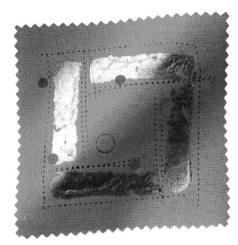

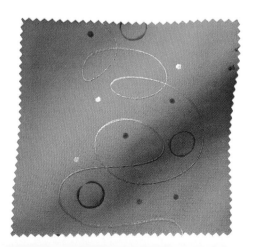

Creative Painting Techniques

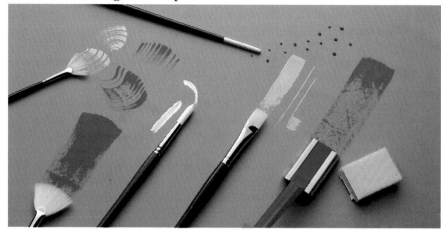

Brushes of different types and sizes are used to create different effects. Variety can also be achieved by changing the size of the brush strokes and the number of repetitions.

Sponges can print many designs. Use precut sponges, or cut shapes, using scissors or artist's knife. Dip sponge into paint. Remove excess paint, using spatula or brush.

Monoject® tool is used for swirled designs. Place tip of #412 Monoject tool into 1" (2.5 cm) of paint and pull plunger to suction paint into tube; fill one-quarter full. Wipe tip clean. Keeping tip on surface of fabric and holding tool, as shown, use *slight* pressure to eject paint. Make squiggles at beginning and end of line to control flow.

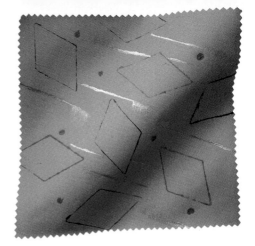

Kitchen utensils, such as wire whisk, noodle lifter, pastry edger, and cookie cutters, can be used. Bend bottom of wire whisk for a flat spiral printing surface. Do not use utensils for preparing food after using them with paint.

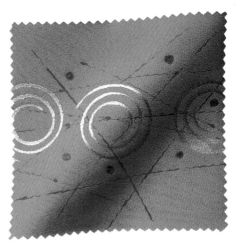

Sewing tools, including tracing wheel, thread spools, thimble, and overlock spool holders, may be used; apply paint sparingly. When using tracing wheel, coat the entire wheel with paint.

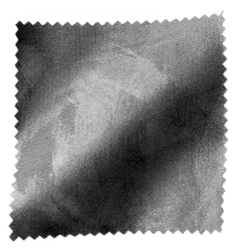

Paint pad can be used for an all-over mottled design. Apply small amount of paint to end of damp pad. Apply paint to fabric in light strokes; continue until pad is dry. Brush over strokes, using pad, to mute them; allow to dry. Repeat, using additional colors of paint, if desired, blending colors into the background for muted effect; use brighter colors first.

Screen Printing

Screen printing allows you to apply a variety of designs to fabric. In screen printing, ink is forced through a fine screen onto the fabric. The sharp, clear, screen-printed designs are quick to produce. It is important to practice screen printing on test fabric to become familiar with the technique and materials.

A special type of screen is used for screen printing. Screens are easy to construct from stretcher bars and polyester mesh. A stencil, cut from Con-Tact® self-adhesive vinyl, is then placed on the screen; when the ink is applied to the screen, it passes through the open cutouts in the stencil.

Use water-based textile inks that are transparent or opaque. The ink may be heat-set, following the manufacturer's directions, for permanent designs that will withstand laundering and dry cleaning.

YOU WILL NEED

For constructing the screen:

Four stretcher bars, at least 5" (12.5 cm) longer than design.

10 xx multifilament polyester mesh.

Masking tape; duct tape, 2" (5 cm) wide; heavy-duty stapler and ¼" (6 mm) staples.

For printing the fabric:

Con-Tact® self-adhesive vinyl, artist's knife, and cutting mat.

Water-based textile inks that are transparent or opaque, in sufficient quantity for entire project.

Fabric, prewashed, cut to desired size, and pressed.

Squeegee, ½" (1.3 cm) narrower than inside measurement of frame.

Plastic sheets large enough to protect work area, newsprint, paper towels, terry towel.

Designs can be adapted from a wallpaper border or other source to make coordinating accessories, such as the duvet cover and window shade. You can vary the scale of a design by enlarging it, using a photocopy machine. Mix larger and smaller designs to add interest to a project.

How to Construct a Screen for Screen Printing

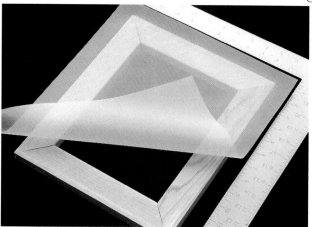

1) Assemble frame from stretcher bars, making sure corners fit tightly and are squared. Cut mesh 1" (2.5 cm) larger than frame on all four sides. Center mesh over frame, aligning grainlines with sides of frame.

2) Apply masking tape to mesh, about ½" (1.3 cm) from outer edges of frame. Smooth tape, pressing from center of frame to ends.

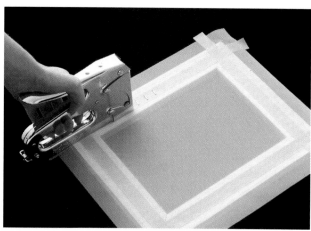

3) Staple mesh to frame on one side through masking tape, working from center to ends; place the staples perpendicular to edge of frame, or at a slight diagonal.

4) Staple mesh to opposite side of frame, pulling mesh tight. Repeat for other two sides. Staple corners.

5) Trim excess mesh. Apply duct tape over masking tape and staples, wrapping tape around sides of frame.

6) Apply duct tape to upper side of screen to form a border, or trough, applying about ½" (1.3 cm) of tape to mesh and remainder of tape to frame. Stencil design must fit within taped area.

How to Prepare the Design for Screen Printing

1) Draw or photocopy desired design; design may be enlarged or reduced, using photocopy machine.

2) Hold design up to light source, such as light table or window, and trace design onto paper backing of self-adhesive vinyl.

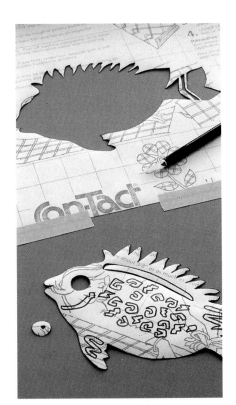

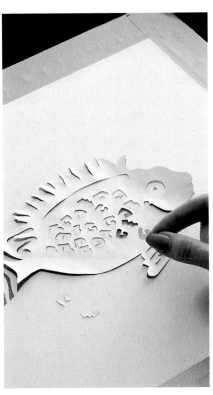

3) Cut self-adhesive vinyl on design lines, using artist's knife.

4) Remove paper backing carefully. Apply vinyl to underside of screen, overlapping duct tape border. Apply cutout details, if any.

5) Turn screen over and press down firmly on mesh; take care to secure cut edges of stencil.

How to Screen Print the Fabric

1) Place plastic sheet over work area, including table and floor. Hang a clothesline to dry prints, if desired.

2) Place terry towel on table over plastic sheet; the padded surface helps to produce a better print. Place sheet of newsprint over towel. Place fabric, right side up, over newsprint. Position screen over fabric.

3) Place 2 to 3 tablespoons (30 to 45 ml) of ink along vinyl next to design area or along border. Applying firm, even pressure, use squeegee to pull ink back and forth across screen until ink is evenly distributed. Too many repetitions cause ink to soak through fabric; too few cause design to look uneven and incomplete.

4) Lift screen slowly to a low angle, taking care that ink does not run onto fabric; carefully peel off fabric. Between prints, rest the screen so one edge is slightly elevated, and rest the squeegee on a stand or lid. Set the screen-printed fabric aside to dry, or hang on a clothesline.

How to Clean the Screen

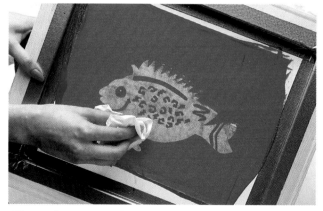

Clogged screen. Wipe top of screen gently, using dry facial tissue, if print is uneven or incomplete.

Final cleanup. Remove stencil from screen; wash screen as soon as printing is finished, using soft cloth. Wash off stencil and affix to waxed paper for reuse, if desired.

Troubleshooting Problems in Screen Printing

Print is uneven or incomplete. Too much time may have been taken between prints, or ink may be too thick, causing clogged screen. Thin ink, if necessary, following manufacturer's directions. Wipe clogged screen, opposite.

Ink runs into fabric along edges of design. Ink was thinned too much, or stencil was not pressed firmly to the screen at edges of design.

Print has uneven patches of color. Ink was applied unevenly, or squeegee was not pulled across screen enough times.

Ink soaks into fabric. Too much ink was used, or the squeegee was pulled across screen too many times.

Transparent Appliqués

One or more layers of sheer fabric can be used to make an elegant transparent appliqué which can be added to sheer curtains or table linens. The sheer fabric is placed on the wrong side of the background fabric; the layers are stitched together along the design lines, and the background fabric is trimmed away from the right side to create sheer openings.

How to Apply a Transparent Appliqué

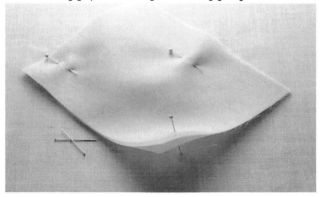

1) Mark placement of appliqué. Place background fabric right side down. Pin one or more layers of sheer fabric to background fabric, right side down, inserting pins at placement points of design. Remove pins from right side of fabric.

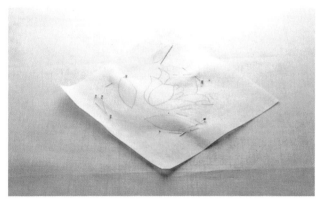

2) Cut tear-away stabilizer at least 2" (5 cm) larger than area to be appliquéd. Trace design onto stabilizer; if using an asymmetrical design, trace the mirror image. Position stabilizer over sheer fabric layers, matching placement points of design; pin in place. Baste stabilizer to garment through all layers. Remove pins.

3) Stitch three rows of straight stitches on outer design lines from wrong side, using short stitch length. Trim background fabric within design areas close to stitching. Insert a pin into background fabric layer; lift and clip a few threads, making an opening that allows for easier trimming without cutting sheer fabric.

4) Stitch three rows of straight stitches on remaining design lines, from wrong side. Trim away one or more sheer layers from right side of fabric, within design areas, using a pin to separate sheer layers for easier trimming.

5) Set machine for closely spaced zigzag stitches; set stitch width, as desired. Loosen needle thread tension, if necessary, so bobbin thread will not show on right side. Satin stitch around appliqué, as for cutwork (pages 256 and 257).

6) Remove tear-away stabilizer. Trim excess sheer fabric outside design area, from wrong side, close to the stitching.

Cutwork

Cutwork detailing has open, cutout design areas that are outlined with satin stitching. Cutwork is often used on fine linens.

Cutwork designs are available, but stencil designs may also be used for cutwork. Both cutwork and stencil designs include bars or bridges, which connect the cutout areas of the cutwork and add stability. If you design your own cutwork, be sure to place bars at frequent intervals. In selecting or planning a cutwork design, keep in mind that it is easier to stitch around large shapes than to follow intricate designs. Select a

closely woven fabric that does not ravel easily, such as batiste, chambray, or lightweight linen. All-purpose thread may be used to stitch along the design lines and reinforce the cutout areas; however, for the satin stitching, cotton or rayon machine embroidery thread is recommended. Use a size 70/9 or 80/11 needle.

Stitch the cutwork on the fabric before cutting out the garment section whenever possible. To prevent puckering, place water-soluble stabilizer under the fabric and place the fabric in an embroidery hoop.

How to Sew Cutwork

1) Trace mirror image of design on water-soluble stabilizer that is cut larger than embroidery hoop. Baste stabilizer to wrong side of fabric. Position fabric in hoop; place stabilizer side up.

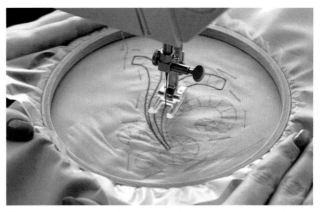

2) Remove presser foot to position hoop under the needle; attach open-toe presser foot. Reinforce outline of design by stitching three rows of straight stitches on design lines, using short stitch length; do not stitch bars.

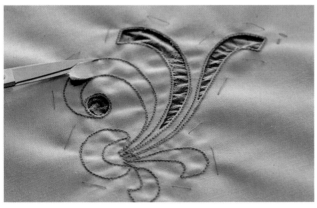

3) Remove fabric from hoop. Cut away fabric in open areas of design 1/16" (1.5 mm) from reinforcement stitches, using embroidery or appliqué scissors; do not cut through the stabilizer. Place fabric, stabilizer side up, in hoop.

4) Stitch three rows of straight stitches on design lines for bars, stitching bars to outer edge of previous rows of outline stitching; second row of stitching can be stitched using reverse setting. Clip threads carried from one design area to another.

5) Place fabric in hoop right side up. Set machine for zigzag stitching, with stitch width just wide enough to cover straight stitches of bars. Satin stitch over bars.

6) Adjust stitch width so it is wide enough to cover straight stitches and raw edges. Satin stitch cutwork openings so needle stitches just over edge of fabric (pages 256 and 257); work from center of design out, stitching small details first. Remove stabilizer; press, wrong side up, on padded surface.

How to Satin Stitch Corners and Curves of Cutwork

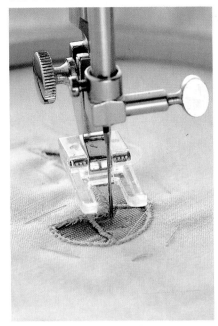

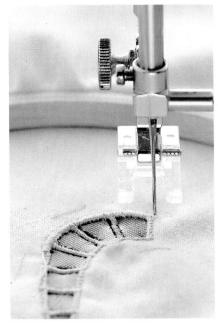

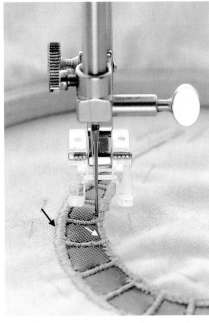

Inside corners. Stitch one stitch past edge of opening, stopping with needle down in stabilizer at inner edge of satin stitching; raise presser foot. Pivot and satin stitch next side of opening, covering previous stitches at corner.

Outside corners. Stitch past corner a distance equal to width of satin stitch, stopping with needle down at outer edge of satin stitching; raise presser foot. Pivot and satin stitch next side of opening, covering previous stitches at corner.

Curves. Raise presser foot and pivot fabric frequently, pivoting with needle down at longest edge of satin stitching (arrows).

How to Satin Stitch Inside Points of Cutwork

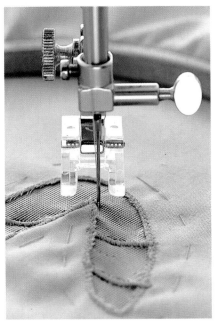

1) Stitch one stitch past the edge of opening, stopping with needle down in stabilizer at inner edge of satin stitching; raise presser foot.

2) Pivot fabric to an angle slightly less than 90°. Stitch two to four stitches, stopping when stitches just cover previous stitches; stop with needle down on inner edge of satin stitching. Raise presser foot.

3) Pivot fabric; continue satin stitching next side of opening.

How to Satin Stitch Outside Points of Cutwork

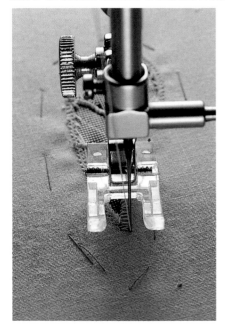

1) Stitch past point a distance equal to width of satin stitch, stopping with needle down at outer edge of satin stitching; raise presser foot.

2) Pivot fabric to an angle slightly less than 90°. Stitch two to four stitches, stopping when stitches just cover previous stitches; stop with needle down on outer edge of satin stitching. Raise presser foot.

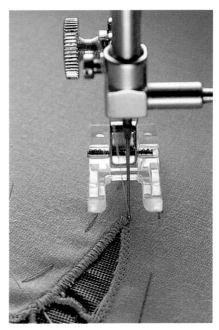

3) Pivot fabric; continue satin stitching next side of opening.

How to Satin Stitch Tapered Outside Points

1) Stitch past point a distance equal to width of satin stitch, stopping with needle down at inner edge of satin stitching; raise presser foot.

2) Pivot fabric slightly. Continue stitching, gradually narrowing stitch width to 0 and stopping directly in front of point.

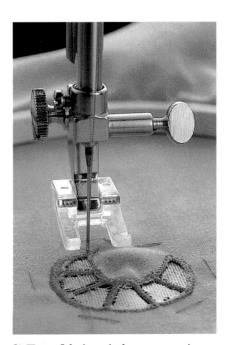

3) Turn fabric; stitch over previous stitches, gradually widening stitch width to original width and stopping at inner edge of satin stitching when stitches meet the finished side of opening. Pivot fabric slightly. Satin stitch next side of opening.

Monograms

Although the automatic monogram stitch patterns on computerized sewing machines are convenient and easy to stitch, you may want to create different sizes or styles of monograms, using free-motion machine embroidery.

Monograms can either be drawn directly onto the fabric or onto a piece of water-soluble stabilizer. If you are monogramming a bath towel or sweater, it is easier to draw the monogram on water-soluble stabilizer than it is to draw it on the textured fabric; the stabilizer is then placed over the fabric to use as a guide for stitching. Draw a horizon line under each letter and keep it horizontal as you stitch so the stitching will automatically taper in the right places.

Use a narrow, wooden hoop or a spring hoop for monogramming. Wooden hoops with fixing screws hold the fabric more tightly, but spring hoops are available in the small sizes needed for areas such as pockets, cuffs, and collars. It is helpful to place tear-away stabilizer under the hoop to prevent the fabric from puckering.

You can use either 30-weight or 40-weight machine embroidery thread for monogramming; the 30-weight thread is a little heavier and fills in faster than 40-weight thread.

Practice stitching the upper case "M" and lower case "e", because these two letters include all the techniques required for the other letters in the alphabet. When you monogram, think of the sewing machine needle as a pencil. Start to stitch each letter at the same place you would start writing it with a pencil.

The size of the letter determines the stitch width; the larger the letter, the wider the stitch width. The widest stitch width setting on the sewing machine works well for 2" (5 cm) letters, but a medium stitch width should be used for smaller letters.

How to Stitch an Upper Case "M" Monogram

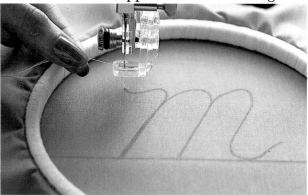

1) Draw an upper case "M" about 2" (5 cm) high on fabric; draw horizon line under letter. Place fabric in embroidery hoop. Set stitch width to 0. Draw up bobbin thread at top of "M"; stitch in place a few times to secure stitches. Set stitch width to the widest setting.

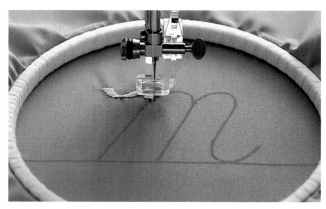

2) Satin stitch up to the first stem of the letter, using short zigzag stitches; keep horizon line horizontal as you sew.

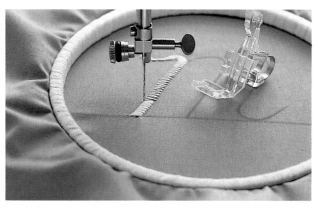

3) Stitch down the first stem of the letter, using longer zigzag stitches, to prevent a buildup of stitches on the stem. Satin stitch back over the stem, using short, closely spaced zigzag stitches. (Darning foot was removed to show detail.)

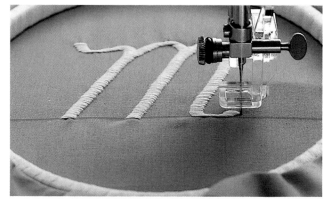

4) Continue satin stitching to second stem of letter; repeat step 3 for second stem. Satin stitch remainder of letter. Set stitch width to 0 and secure stitches.

How to Stitch a Lower Case "e" Monogram

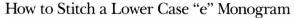

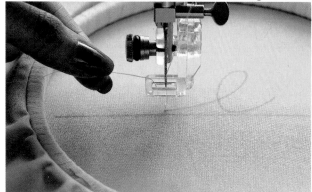

1) Draw lower case "e" about 1" (2.5 cm) high on fabric; draw horizon line under letter. Place fabric in embroidery hoop. Set stitch width to 0. Draw up bobbin thread at left side of "e"; secure stitches. Set stitch width to a medium setting.

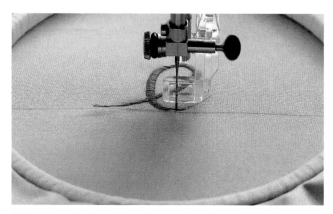

2) Satin stitch, using short, closely spaced zigzag stitches; stitch on the outside of loop so center of loop does not become too small. Keep the horizon line horizontal as you sew. Set the stitch width to 0 and secure stitches.

Tips for Monogramming

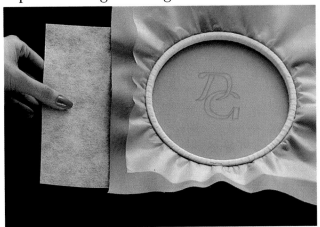

Trace letters on water-soluble stabilizer. Place the stabilizer on right side of fabric; position in hoop. Place tear-away stabilizer under hoop during stitching. Remove both stabilizers after stitching.

Change direction of the horizon line, such as placing it on the diagonal, so tapering of letter changes position for a different look.

Change direction of the horizon line within a letter for added emphasis.

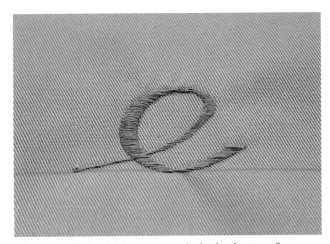

Change stitch width as you stitch the letters for an interesting effect. Change the width when sewing side stitch or at top of letter so width change is less noticeable and flows with the letter.

Stitch larger letters first with narrower stitches; then repeat stitching with wider stitches if raised or padded effect is desired.

Use wide stitch width for large letters and a narrower stitch width for small letters.

Floral Monograms

The floral monogram is made up of small flowers and leaves, and is sewn using free-motion embroidery techniques. This monogram can be added to bed linens or towels for a personal touch.

Letter styles that have smooth, curved lines are more appropriate for floral monograms than block styles. Select dark and light colors of thread to stitch the flowers and a green thread for the leaves.

How to Make Free-motion Floral Monograms

1) Draw 2" or 2½" (5 or 6.5 cm) letter on fabric with water-soluble marking pen. Draw small dots on each side of letter about ¼" (6 mm) apart; dots may be placed closer together on curves. Place fabric in the embroidery hoop.

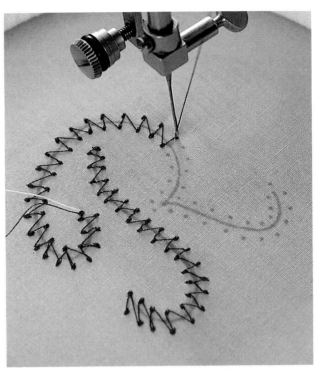

2) Set zigzag stitch to narrow width. Stitch in place on dot five or six times, using a dark-colored thread. Move across marked line to next dot; stitch in place. Continue until all dots are stitched, to make centers of flowers. Clip thread tails, but do not clip threads between dots.

3) Set machine for straight stitch; change to lighter-colored thread. Stitch around center of one flower; continue until all flowers are stitched. Clip thread tails, but do not clip threads between flowers.

4) Change to green thread. Using the straight stitch setting on machine, stitch leaves in curved motion, stitching in and out between the flowers.

Decorating
with Quilts

Selecting Fabrics

Fabric is usually selected after a quilt design and color scheme have been chosen, although a special piece of fabric may help create a design idea or establish color for a quilt. Many kinds of fabric can be used for a quilt, but a primary consideration is fiber content.

Fabric of 100 percent cotton is the best choice for quilts. Cotton fabric is easy to cut, sew, and mark; it is also easy to press, holds a crease well, and is available in a wide range of colors and prints. The quality and weight of cotton fabric is determined by thread count. The thread count is the number of threads per inch (2.5 cm) of fabric. In high-quality cotton fabric, the thread count is equal lengthwise and crosswise; this is called an even weave. Most quilting cottons are either 78-square or 68-square. Fabrics with lower thread counts are too lightweight.

Cotton/polyester blends resist wrinkling and abrasion, making them a suitable choice for frequently washed quilts. The different lengthwise and crosswise thread counts in cotton/polyester blends cause a different amount of stretch along the lengthwise and crosswise grains, which can make it more difficult to piece fabrics accurately. Also, when stitched, cotton/polyester blends tend to pucker more than 100 percent cotton fabrics.

Choose good-quality fabrics that are compatible with the function of your quilt. If you are making a comforter for a child's bed, the quilt will be subject to hard and constant use; select fabrics that can withstand wear and frequent washing. If you are making a wall hanging, the durability of the fabric is less important.

Types of Quilting Fabrics

Quilting fabrics include calico, muslin, and other broadcloths. They are mediumweight, closely woven fabrics of 100 percent cotton or of a cotton/polyester blend. Calico (1) and other printed fabrics are available in a variety of patterns and colors. Muslin (2) is off-white or white, and is usually used for the background pieces in a pieced design, for the plain blocks, or for a quilt backing. Broadcloth (3) is a plain-weave fabric and is generally a solid color. Hand-dyed fabrics (4) are 100 percent cotton and are available in gradations of solid colors. These fabrics can be purchased from some quilting stores and from mail-order sources. Chintz (5) is a tightly woven fabric with a glazed finish and is usually 100 percent cotton. The shiny or glossy finish gives chintz its unique character, but it may wash out after a few launderings. The finish may cause the fabric to pucker when stitched. Pins and stitching may leave permanent holes, so care must be taken when piecing or basting quilts made from chintz fabrics.

Selecting Backing Fabrics

Select a backing fabric that has the same care requirements as the fabrics in the quilt top. Fabrics of 100 percent cotton are the best choice for machine quilting, because they do not pucker as much as cotton/polyester blends.

Some fabrics are manufactured specifically for quilt backing. They are 100 percent cotton and are available in 90" and 108" (229 and 274.5 cm) widths, so they usually do not require piecing. These fabrics are available in light-colored prints on white backgrounds and a few solid colors. If the quilt will be finished with a mock binding (pages 314 and 315), choose a backing fabric that will coordinate with the quilt top.

Sheets are not a good choice for the backing fabric, because the permanent-press finish may cause skipped stitches and pucker the fabric.

Tips for Selecting Backing Fabrics

Solid-colored fabric accentuates the quilting stitches; printed fabric tends to hide the stitches.

Backing fabric should not show through to the quilt top when the batting has been sandwiched between the layers. If it does show through, change to a lighter-colored backing fabric.

Preparing the Fabric

If you plan to wash the quilt, test dark or vivid-colored fabrics for colorfastness to determine whether the dye bleeds to light-colored fabrics or colors the water. If colors do bleed, repeat the test; if a fabric still bleeds, it is probably not colorfast.

Fabrics can be preshrunk by machine-washing them using a mild soap, such as dishwashing soap. Do not use soap intended for fine woolens; it may yellow cotton fabrics. Machine-dry the fabric, using a warm setting.

Preshrinking fabrics removes excess dyes and chemical finishes used in the manufacturing process. Most cotton fabrics shrink 2 to 3 percent when washed and dried, so if they are not preshrunk, the fabrics may pucker at the stitching lines and the finished size of the quilt may change the first time it is washed. After preshrinking, you may want to press the fabric, using spray starch, to make cutting and stitching easier.

Fabric is not always woven with the threads crossing at 90° angles; however, it is usually not necessary to straighten the grainline. Minor variations in the grainline do not change the overall look of a quilt block and straightening the grainline may waste as much as 4" (10 cm) of a piece of fabric.

How to Test Fabric for Colorfastness

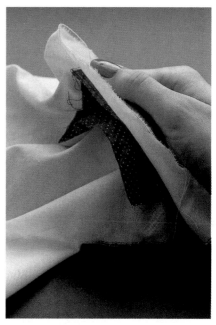

1) Fill jar or glass with warm water and a few drops of mild soap, such as dishwashing soap.

2) Cut 2" to 6" (5 to 15 cm) square of fabric. Place in water. Allow to soak until the water has cooled slightly. Swish fabric.

3) Place wet fabric on sample of light-colored fabric for the quilt; blot dry. If dye transfers to light-colored fabric, repeat the test; if fabric still bleeds, it is probably not colorfast.

Selecting Batting

Batting is the middle layer of a quilt. The loft, or thickness, of the batting determines the warmth or springiness of the quilt. Batting is purchased according to the amount of loft desired (opposite).

The most widely used fibers for batting are cotton and polyester, or a blend of the two. Cotton batting gives a flat, traditional appearance when quilted. Polyester batting gives a puffy look and is more stable and easier to handle than cotton batting. Cotton/polyester batting combines the flat appearance of cotton with the stability and ease in handling of polyester.

Two types of batting are frequently used: bonded and needlepunch. Bonded batting is made by layering fibers and then adding a finish to hold the fibers together and make the batting easier to handle. Quilting stitches may be placed as far apart as 5" (12.5 cm). Needlepunch batting is made by layering the fibers and then passing them through a needling machine to give a dense, low-loft batting. It is firm, easy to handle, and warm. Most needlepunch batting is polyester.

The fibers in batting may migrate, or move, affecting the appearance of the quilt. Bonded batting is treated to help control fiber migration. There are two forms of fiber migration: bunching and bearding.

Bunching is the migration of fibers within a quilt, causing thick and thin areas. Bunching can be controlled by placing the quilting stitches ½" to 1" (1.3 to 2.5 cm) apart.

Bearding is the migration of fibers through the surface of the quilt. Polyester batting tends to beard, and these fibers may pill. Cotton batting may beard, but the fibers break off at the surface. To help prevent bearding, use a closely woven fabric for the quilt top and backing. If using a batting that may beard, avoid dark-colored fabrics, because the bearding is more noticeable on these fabrics. If bearding does occur, clip the fibers close to the surface of the quilt; do not pull the batting through the fabric. After clipping the fibers, pull the quilt top away from the batting so the fibers return to the inside of the quilt.

Batting is available in a wide range of sizes, although the selection in certain fibers and construction types may be limited. Polyester battings have the widest range of sizes and lofts. Batting should extend 2" to 4" (5 to 10 cm) beyond the edges of the quilt top on all sides, to allow for the shrinkage that occurs during quilting.

Batting is packaged for standard-size quilts. It is also available by the yard and in smaller packages for clothing and craft projects.

Guidelines for Selecting Batting

Fiber Content	Appearance of Finished Quilt	Characteristics	Spacing of Quilting Stitches
Cotton	Flat	Absorbs moisture, cool in summer and warm in winter	½" to 1" (1.3 to 2.5 cm)
Polyester	Puffy	Warmth and loft without weight, nonallergenic, moth and mildew-resistant	3" to 5" (7.5 to 12.5 cm)
Cotton/polyester Blend	Moderately flat	Combines characteristics of cotton and polyester	2" to 4" (5 cm to 10 cm)

Tips for Selecting Batting

Low-loft bonded cotton or cotton/polyester batting is easiest to handle.

Medium-loft adds texture to the finished quilt. The higher the loft, the more difficult to machine-quilt.

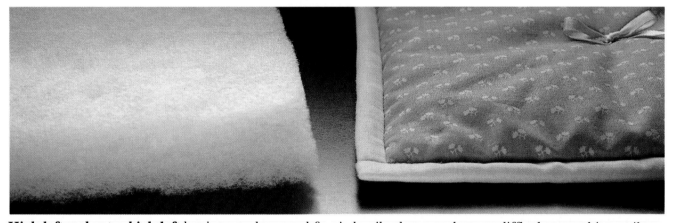

High-loft and extra-high-loft battings are best used for tied quilts, because they are difficult to machine-quilt.

Batting Thickness

Low-Loft	⅛" to ⅜" (3 mm to 1 cm)
Medium-loft	½" to ¾" (1.3 to 2 cm)
High-loft	1" to 2" (2.5 to 5 cm)
Extra-high-loft	2" to 3" (5 to 7.5 cm)

Packaged Batting Sizes

Crib	45" × 60" (115 × 152.5 cm)
Twin	72" × 90" (183 × 229 cm)
Full	81" × 96" (206 × 244 cm)
Queen	90" × 108" (229 × 274.5 cm)
King	120" × 120" (305 × 305 cm)

Notions & Equipment

A few carefully selected notions can make quilting easier and help improve your accuracy in cutting, marking, and sewing.

Quilting can be done entirely on a straight-stitch conventional sewing machine. Choosing the correct type of sewing machine accessories, such as presser feet and needle plates, can help improve your results.

Measuring & Cutting Tools

See-through rulers (1) serve as both a measuring tool and a straightedge for cutting with a rotary cutter.

Measurements are visible through the ruler, so you can cut without marking. Many sizes and types of see-through rulers are available. A ruler 6" × 24" (15 × 61 cm) is recommended, because it is versatile.

Features of rulers vary widely. Some rulers are printed with measurements in two colors to show clearly on both light and dark fabrics. Some have a lip on one edge to hook onto the edge of the cutting mat for easier alignment. Some are printed on the underside to prevent distortion and increase accuracy; if the lines and numbers are molded on the underside, it will help prevent slippage. Square rulers, and rulers with 30°,

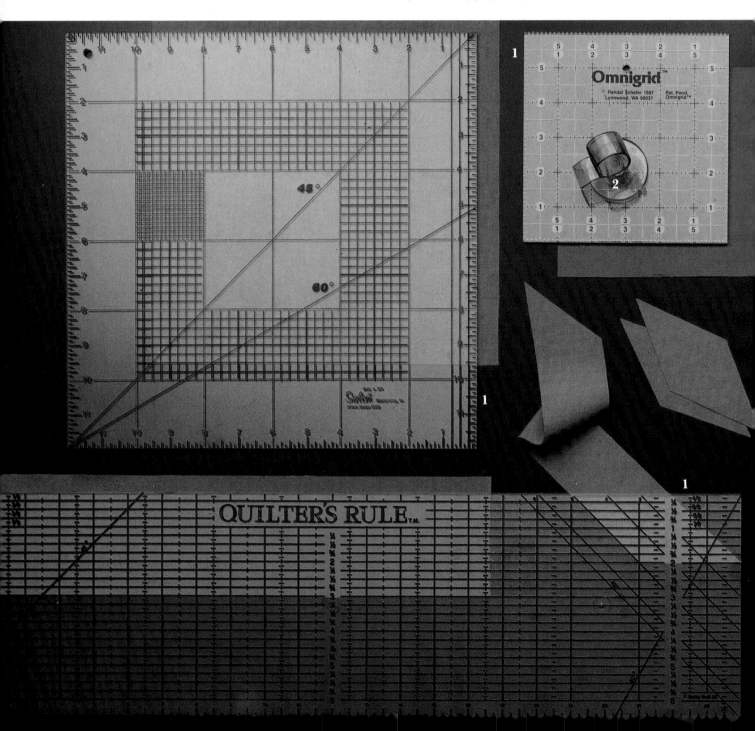

45°, and 60° angle lines, are available. Choose rulers that have the features most important for the type of quilting you are planning to do.

Suction rings **(2)** and suction handles **(3)** are available to help in positioning a ruler.

Rotary cutters **(4)** allow you to cut smooth edges on multiple layers of fabric quickly and easily. The cutters are available in two sizes: the smaller size works well for cutting curves or a few layers of fabric; the larger size works well for cutting long, straight edges or many layers of fabric.

Cutting mats **(5)**, made especially for use with rotary cutters, protect the blades and the table. They may be plain, or printed with a grid and diagonal lines. A mat printed with a grid is helpful for cutting right angles. Mats come in a variety of sizes. Choose a mat at least 22" (56 cm) wide to accommodate a width of fabric folded in half.

Sewing scissors **(6)** and shears **(7)** are used for cutting shapes and clipping threads. X-acto® knives **(8)** are used for cutting cardboard, paper, and plastic templates for pieced or appliquéd designs.

Marking Tools

The markings on a quilt should last only as long as you need them, and you should be able to remove them easily and thoroughly without damaging the quilt. Always test markers on fabrics to see how long the markings last and to be sure they can be removed. Mark lightly; it is more difficult to remove markings that are embedded in the fibers.

A special fabric eraser (1) can be used to remove light lead pencil (2) marks without abrading or leaving marks on the fabric. Oil-free and wax-free colored pencils (3) may also be used for marking. Choose a color close to the fabric color; or choose silver, because it shows on most fabrics. Remove marks before pressing the fabric or washing it in hot water; heat may set pencil marks. White water-soluble pencils (4) are available for marking dark fabrics; remove marks with a damp cloth. Soapstone pencils (5) are made of pressed talc and marks can be rubbed off or wiped off with water.

Chalk wheels (6) are available in a variety of shapes and colors; marking is fine and accurate. Chalk-wheel marks brush off easily, are washable, and will not stain.

A variety of plastic sheets (7) is available for making your own templates. Precut templates (8) are available for marking traditional quilting designs.

Sewing & Quilting Tools

For ease in stitching, thread should be of good quality. For piecing, use 100 percent cotton (1) or all-purpose sewing thread (2); match thread color to the darker fabric or use a neutral color, such as black, cream, or gray, to blend. For basting, use a fine, white cotton basting thread (3), or white all-purpose thread; the dye from dark thread could rub off on fabrics.

For quilting, 100 percent cotton thread is usually the best choice. Fine, .004 mm, or size 80 monofilament nylon thread (4), which comes in smoke or clear, is good for quilting and for invisibly stitching appliqués, because it blends with all colors. Cotton quilting thread (5) without a finish may be used for machine quilting; however, quilting thread with a special glacé finish should not be used for machine quilting. Quilting thread may either match or contrast with the fabric.

Insert a new sewing machine needle (6) before beginning a quilting project. For piecing and appliqué, use a size 70/9 or 80/11; for machine quilting, use a size 80/11 or 90/14 needle, depending on the thickness and fiber content of the batting.

Safety pins (7) are essential for pin-basting a quilt; 1" (2.5 cm) rustproof pins work well for most quilting projects. Use milliners needles (8) for thread-basting, because they are long and have small, round eyes. Use glass-head quilting pins (9), because they are long, 1¾" (4.5 cm), and strong.

Sewing Machine Equipment

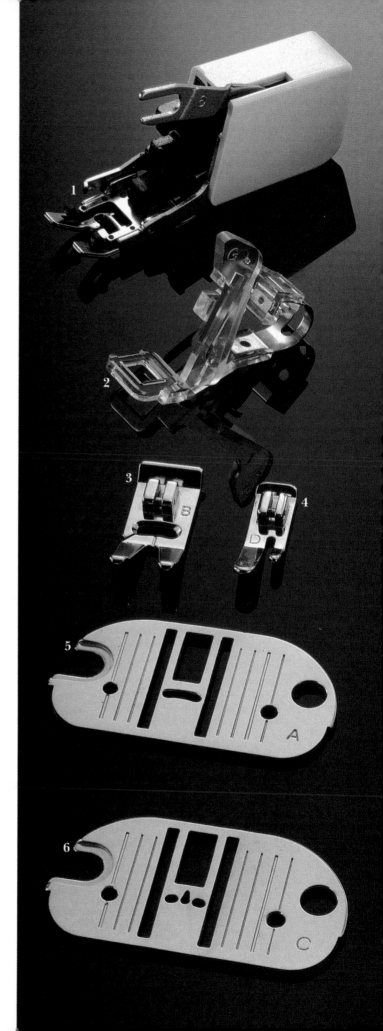

A straight-stitch conventional sewing machine is used for quilting. The stitch length should be easy to adjust, because you start and end lines of stitches by gradually increasing or decreasing the stitch length.

An entire quilt can be made using only the straight stitch, but several additional features, common on most sewing machines, expand your quilting options. A blind-hem stitch can be used for attaching appliqués. Feed dogs that can be covered or dropped allow you to do freehand quilting.

Presser Feet

Special presser feet are not necessary for machine quilting, but they can improve your results. For machine-guided quilting, an Even Feed™ foot (1) is recommended for pucker-free stitching. The feed dogs on the Even Feed foot work with the feed dogs of the sewing machine to pull layers of fabric through at the same rate of speed. For freehand quilting, you can either use a darning foot (2) or stitch without a foot, depending on the sewing machine.

Use a general-purpose foot (3), or a special-purpose foot for zigzag and blindstitching. A straight-stitch foot (4) can improve the quality of stitches, particularly when piecing fabrics with the narrow seam allowances that are standard in quilting.

Needle Plates

Use a general-purpose needle plate (5) with the general-purpose or special-purpose foot for zigzag and blindstitching. Use a straight-stitch needle plate (6) with the straight-stitch foot for straight and uniform seams and quilting lines. The small hole in the needle plate keeps the fabric from being pushed down into the sewing machine as you stitch. Also use the straight-stitch needle plate with the Even Feed foot for machine-guided quilting and with the darning foot for freehand quilting.

Basic Piecing Techniques

The designs in this section are for basic, traditional quilt patterns, and range from simple squares to more complex curves and appliqués. With the exception of curves and appliqués, the pieces are cut using template-free methods.

The techniques for setting up the sewing machine and for cutting, stitching, and pressing the fabrics are the same for most pieced designs.

Accuracy is critical to successful piecing. A small error can multiply itself many times, resulting in a block or a quilt that does not fit together properly. Check the accuracy of your cutting and stitching frequently. You may want to practice cutting and stitching techniques on a small project before using them on a large project.

Cutting Techniques

The quick-cutting techniques that follow are both timesaving and accurate. Instead of cutting each piece of the quilt individually, stack several layers of fabric and cut them into crosswise strips. The pieces are then cut from these strips, eliminating the need for templates.

Determine the grainline by folding the fabric in half and holding it by the selvages. Then shift one side until the fabric hangs straight. It is not necessary to straighten quilting fabrics that are off-grain or to pull threads or tear fabrics to find the grainline.

Good-quality cutting equipment helps ensure that every piece you cut is exactly the right size and that all the pieces fit together perfectly. Use a rotary cutter with a sharp blade and a cutting mat with a printed grid.

Tape three or four thin strips of fine sandpaper across the width of the bottom of a see-through ruler, using double-stick tape. This prevents the ruler from slipping when you are cutting fabric.

How to Cut Fabric Strips

1) Fold fabric in half, selvages together. Hold selvage edges, letting fold hang free. Shift one side of fabric until fold hangs straight. Fold line is straight of grain.

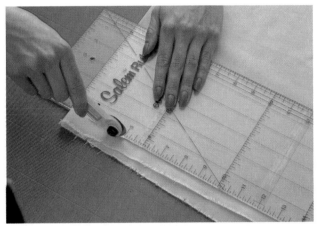

2) Lay fabric on cutting mat, with fold along a grid line. Place ruler on fabric close to raw edge at 90° angle to fold. Trim along edge of ruler, taking care not to move fabric. Hold ruler *firmly*; apply steady, firm pressure on blade. Stop when rotary cutter gets past hand.

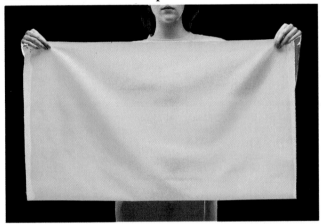

3) Leave blade in position; reposition hand ahead of blade. Hold firmly and continue cutting. Make sure the fabric and ruler do not shift position.

4) Place ruler on fabric, aligning trimmed edge with appropriate measurement on ruler. Hold ruler firmly; cut as in steps 2 and 3. After cutting several strips, check fabric to be sure it is still on-grain, as in step 1.

Stitching Techniques

For pieced quilts, seam allowances are traditionally ¼" (6 mm); stitch accurate seam allowances, so all pieces will fit together exactly. If you have a seam guide on your sewing machine, check the placement of the ¼" (6 mm) mark by stitching on a scrap of fabric. If your machine does not have a seam guide, mark one on the bed of the machine with tape.

Use a stitch length of about 15 stitches per inch (2.5 cm). A shorter stitch length may be necessary for stitching curves and is used for securing stitches at the ends of seams. Adjust thread tensions evenly, so the fabric does not pucker when stitched.

Chainstitching is a timesaving technique for piecing. Seams are stitched without stopping and cutting the threads between them. After all the pieces are stitched together, the connecting threads are clipped and the seams are finger-pressed.

Although some quilters prefer working on one block at a time for the satisfaction of completing a block quickly, it is more efficient to sew an entire quilt top in units. Chainstitch together all the smallest pieces from all the blocks; then combine them to create larger units.

How to Chain and Assemble Pieces

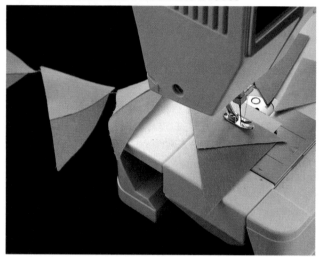

1) Start with smallest pieces; stitch together without backstitching or stopping between pieces, to make a chain of two-piece units. Clip threads between units; finger-press seams.

2) Add more pieces to units, if necessary for quilt block design, chainstitching them together. Clip threads and finger-press.

3) Chainstitch units together to create larger units. Clip threads and finger-press.

4) Stitch larger units together to form quilt block. Press with iron.

Pressing Techniques

Seams are usually pressed to one side in quilts. When pressing seams to one side, it is best to press them to the darker fabric to prevent show-through.

Do not press seams with an iron until a unit or block has straight of grain on all four sides. Always remove all markings from the fabrics before pressing, because the heat from the iron may set marks permanently. When pressing seams, use steam rather than pressure, to prevent the layers from imprinting on the right side. A heavy pressing motion can distort the shape and size of the pieces. Press the blocks first from the wrong side; then press them again lightly from the right side.

The quilt should not be pressed after it is completed because pressing will flatten the batting.

Tips for Pressing

Finger-press individual seam allowances; pressing with an iron can distort bias seams. Press with iron only after a unit or block has straight of grain on all four sides.

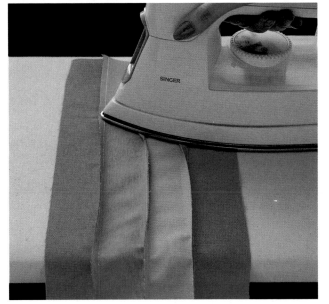

Press long seams with iron by placing strips across, rather than lengthwise on, ironing board, to prevent distorting grainline as you press.

Sewing Designs with Squares

Many quilts are made from nine-patch quilt blocks. A Nine-patch block may be made from one-piece squares or pieced squares. A Double Nine-patch block alternates one-piece squares and checkerboard pieced squares. Each of the checkerboard squares is made from nine smaller squares.

There are two ways to assemble a nine-patch quilt block, the traditional method and the strip-piecing method. The traditional method works well when using larger pieces of fabric, such as 4½" (11.5 cm) squares. The strip-piecing method is used primarily when making quilt blocks with intricate designs,

because the piecing can be done quickly without handling small pieces of fabric. A double nine-patch quilt block may be assembled using both the strip-piecing and traditional methods.

The instructions for the Nine-patch quilt block (page 282) and the Double Nine-patch quilt block (page 283) make 12" (30.5 cm) finished blocks. A single block is ideal for a pillow top. Quilt the block first. For the easiest project, use machine-guided quilting (page 311) and make a basic pillow (page 117). You may also add a ruffle (page 30) or welting (page 120) to the pillow.

How to Cut Squares

1) Cut strips of fabric (page 277) the width of one side of square plus ½" (1.3 cm) for seam allowances. Stack three or four strips, matching edges exactly; place ruler on fabric near selvages at 90° angle to long edges of strips. Trim off selvages.

2) Place ruler on fabric, aligning short edge of fabric with appropriate measurement on ruler. Cut to same width as strips, holding ruler firmly.

How to Sew a Nine-patch Quilt Block Using Traditional Piecing

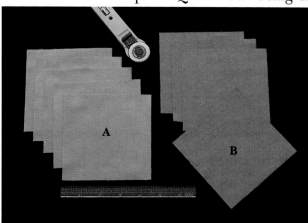

1) Cut five 4½" (11.5 cm) squares from Fabric A. Cut four 4½" (11.5 cm) squares from Fabric B.

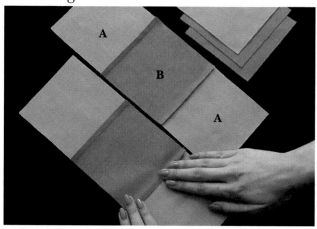

2) Stitch one square of Fabric A and one square of Fabric B, right sides together, using ¼" (6 mm) seam allowances. Stitch another square of Fabric A to other side of Fabric B. Finger-press seam allowances toward darker fabric. Repeat to make two A-B-A units.

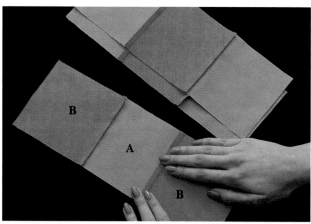

3) Stitch one square of Fabric A and one square of Fabric B, right sides together. Stitch another square of Fabric B to other side of Fabric A. Finger-press seam allowances toward darker fabric.

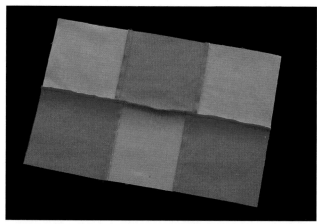

4) Stitch one A-B-A unit to the B-A-B unit, on long edges, right sides together; match seamlines and outside edges, keeping seam allowances toward darker fabric.

5) Stitch remaining A-B-A unit to the other long edge of B-A-B unit, as in step 4.

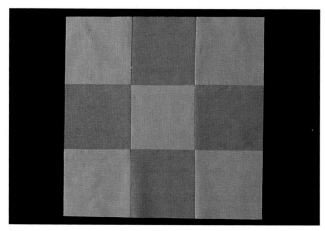

6) Press long seam allowances to one side; then press from right side.

How to Sew a Double Nine-patch Quilt Block Using Strip-piecing

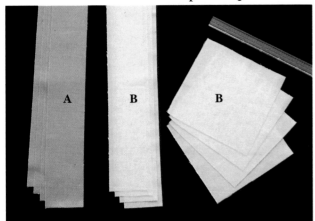

1) Cut two scant 1⅞" (4.7 cm) strips from Fabric A and from Fabric B; cut strips in half to make four 22" (56 cm) strips. Cut four 4½" (11.5 cm) squares from Fabric B.

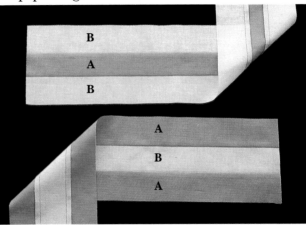

2) Stitch one B-A-B unit and one A-B-A unit, right sides together, using ¼" (6 mm) seam allowances. Press seam allowances toward darker fabric.

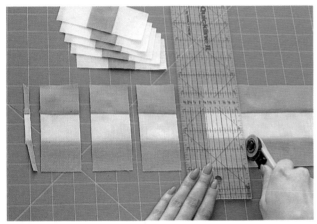

3) Trim short edge of each pieced unit at 90° angle. Cut ten scant 1⅞" (4.7 cm) strips from A-B-A unit. Cut five scant 1⅞" (4.7 cm) strips from B-A-B unit.

4) Stitch one A-B-A unit to one B-A-B unit on long edges, right sides together. Then stitch A-B-A unit to other long edge of B-A-B unit, right sides together, to form checkerboard.

5) Repeat step 4 for remaining checkerboard units. Press each seam toward side with two darker squares.

6) Stitch checkerboard units and plain units to form a nine-patch quilt block, as in steps 2 to 6, opposite.

Sewing Designs with Rectangles

Rectangles are used in many block designs. Strip-piecing methods are frequently used to piece designs created from rectangles. Streak O' Lightning is one of the easiest of all quilt blocks to strip-piece. Rail Fence uses the same piecing methods, but the strips are narrower.

Log Cabin is one of the most popular and variable traditional designs. Quick-cutting and quick-piecing methods can be used for the Log Cabin block.

Choose fabrics carefully for all three designs, as they define the overall pattern in the quilt top. For example, in the Streak O' Lightning design, choose a light color and a dark color. In the Rail Fence design, where two of the fabrics will define the zigzag pattern on the quilt top, light-to-dark color progressions can be effective.

For the Log Cabin design, three fabrics can be a light color and three a dark color; the center square should be a solid, contrasting, or complementary color.

The instructions for Streak O' Lightning and Rail Fence quilt blocks are used when only one quilt block is needed, such as in a sampler quilt or a pillow top. However, when making a quilt top from these designs, it is easier to sew an entire row of squares in a horizontal-vertical-horizontal arrangement the width of the quilt top and then join the rows together.

The instructions for the Streak O' Lightning quilt block (below), the Rail Fence quilt block (page 286), and the Log Cabin quilt block (page 287) make 12" (30.5 cm) finished blocks.

Make a pillow top out of one block, as suggested on page 280.

How to Make a Streak O' Lightning Quilt Block

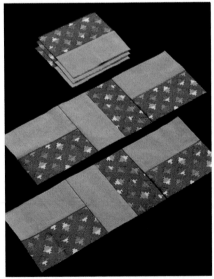

1) Cut one 2½" (6.5 cm) strip (page 277) from each of two different fabrics. Stitch strips, right sides together, on long edge. Press seams to one side. Cut nine 4½" (11.5 cm) squares from unit at 90° angle to seams.

2) Stitch three squares together in a horizontal-vertical-horizontal sequence, as shown. Repeat with three more squares. Keep fabrics in same sequence, from left to right and from top to bottom, throughout quilt. Press seams to same side.

3) Stitch remaining three squares in a vertical-horizontal-vertical sequence. Press seams in opposite direction from other rows. Stitch rows together, with the vertical-horizontal-vertical row in middle. Press seams to one side.

How to Make a Rail Fence Quilt Block

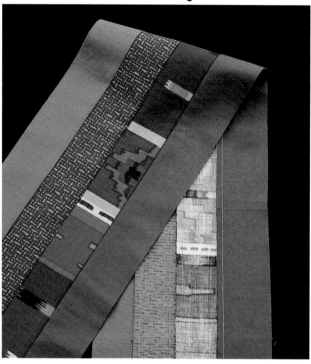

1) Cut one 2" (5 cm) strip (page 277) from each of four different fabrics. When strips are stitched together, outside strips define zigzag pattern. Stitch strips, in sequence, right sides together, along length. Press seam allowances to one side.

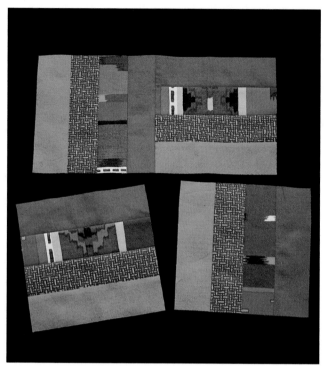

2) Cut four 6½" (16.3 cm) squares from unit, at 90° angle to seams. Stitch two squares together, in vertical-horizontal arrangement, as shown. Press seam allowances to one side.

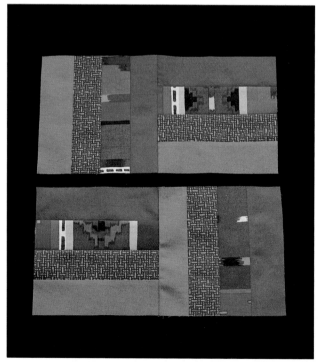

3) Stitch remaining two squares together in horizontal-vertical arrangement, as shown; keep fabrics in same sequence from left to right and from top to bottom throughout quilt. Press seam allowances in opposite direction from first row.

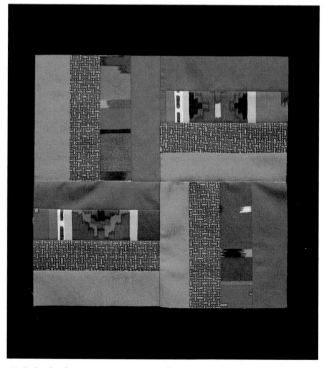

4) Stitch the two rows together, matching seamlines. Press seam allowances to one side.

How to Make a Log Cabin Quilt Block

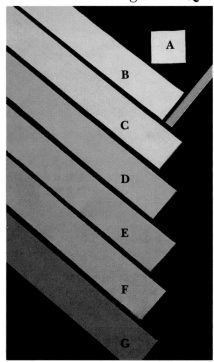

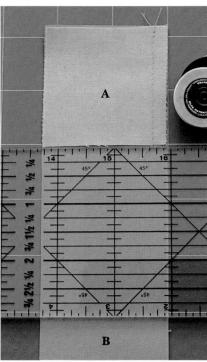

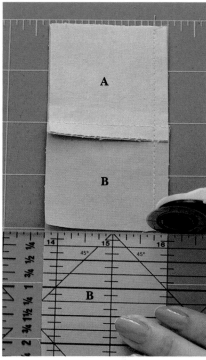

1) Cut one scant 2¼" (6 cm) square from Fabric A. Cut one scant 2¼" (6 cm) strip (page 277) from each of six different fabrics. Label strips from B to G, as shown.

2) Place solid square on Strip B, right sides together. Stitch along one side. Trim strip even with square. Press seam allowance away from center square.

3) Place pieced unit on remaining length of Strip B, as shown. Stitch on long side. Trim strip even with bottom of pieced unit. Press seam allowance away from center square.

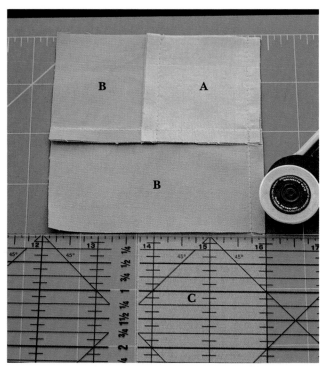

4) Place three-piece unit on Strip C at 90° angle to most recent seam. Stitch on long side. Trim strip even with bottom of pieced unit. Press seam allowance away from center square.

5) Place four-piece unit on remaining length of Strip C at 90° angle to most recent seam. Continue in this manner, stitching two strips of each color to pieced unit in sequence. Press seam allowances away from center square.

Sewing Designs with Triangles

Triangles are frequently used for quilt blocks. There are two methods for cutting and sewing triangles: the quick-cutting method with traditional piecing and the grid-piecing method.

The quick-cutting method allows you to cut several layers of fabric at one time. Some right triangles are cut with the grainline on the long side and some with the grainline on the short side. The grainline should be on the outside edges of each unit so the edges are stable and will not stretch when units are stitched together. The triangles are then assembled using a traditional piecing method.

The quick-cutting method is used to cut the right triangles for the Flying Geese quilt block (pages 290 and 291); avoid using a fabric with a one-way design. Flying Geese strips may be used for sashing or borders,

or sewn together to make an entire quilt, as in the crib quilt, opposite.

The grid-piecing method (page 292) allows you to cut and piece the triangles in one operation. It is used whenever two triangles are stitched together to make a square, commonly referred to as a *triangle-square*, as in the Pinwheel quilt block (page 293). The grid-piecing method is especially useful when piecing small triangles.

The following instructions for the Flying Geese quilt block (pages 290 and 291) and the Pinwheel quilt block (page 293) make 12" (30.5 cm) finished blocks.

Use a single block to make an easy quilted pillow for a beginning project, as suggested on page 280.

How to Cut Right Triangles Using the Quick-cutting Method

Triangles with short sides on grainline. Cut squares (page 281) with sides the length of finished *short* side of triangle plus ⅞" (2.2 cm). Cut half as many squares as number of triangles needed. Stack three or four squares, matching edges exactly. Place ruler diagonally across stack, holding ruler firmly; cut.

Triangles with long side on grainline. Cut squares (page 281) with sides the length of finished *long* side of triangle plus 1¼" (3.2 cm). Cut one-fourth as many squares as number of triangles needed. Place ruler diagonally across stack, holding ruler firmly; cut. Place ruler diagonally across stack in other direction; cut.

How to Make a Flying Geese Quilt Block

1) Cut three 5¼" (13.1 cm) squares of one fabric. Cut through squares diagonally in both directions so long side of each large triangle is on grainline.

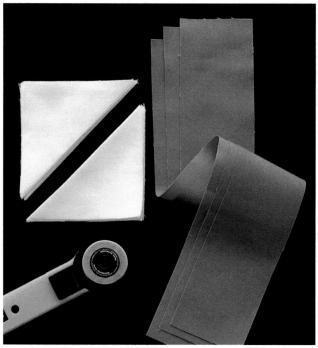

2) Cut twelve 2⅞" (7.2 cm) squares of second fabric. Cut through squares diagonally in one direction so short sides of each small triangle are on grainline. Cut three 1⅞" × 12½" (4.7 × 31.8 cm) strips of third fabric.

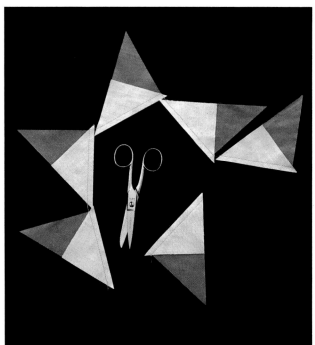

3) Stitch long side of one small triangle to short side of one large triangle, right sides together, using ¼" (6 mm) seam allowances and matching corners at base of large triangle; take care not to stretch bias edges. Repeat, using chainstitching, for remaining units; clip apart.

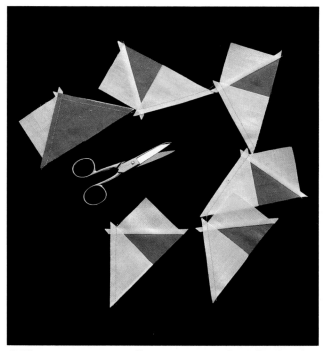

4) Finger-press seam allowances toward small triangle. Stitch a small triangle to other short side of large triangle, right sides together, matching corners at base of large triangle. Take care not to stitch a tuck in first seam. Repeat, using chainstitching, for remaining units; clip apart.

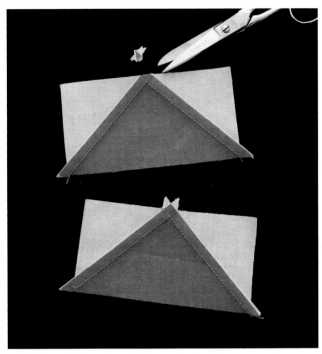

5) Press seam allowances toward small triangles. Trim points.

6) Place two units right sides together, matching top of one unit to bottom of other, so large triangles are pointing in same direction. Stitch, with point of large triangle on top, to make sure stitching goes through point. Repeat, using chainstitching, for remaining units; clip apart.

7) Stitch three units together to make a pieced strip of six units. Repeat for a second pieced strip. Press seam allowances toward bases of large triangles.

8) Stitch one long strip between two pieced strips; stitch remaining long strips at sides of block. Press seam allowances toward long strips.

How to Make Triangle-squares Using the Grid-piecing Method

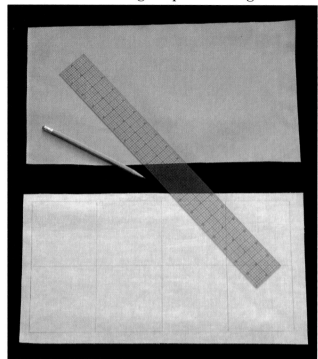

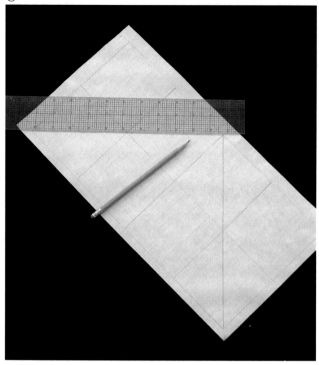

1) Cut one rectangle from each of two different fabrics. Draw grid of squares on wrong side of lighter-colored fabric, making grid squares ⅞" (2.2 cm) larger than finished triangle-square; each square of grid makes two triangle-squares.

2) Draw diagonal lines through the grid, as shown.

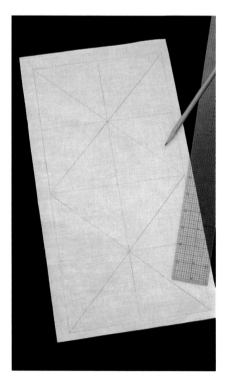

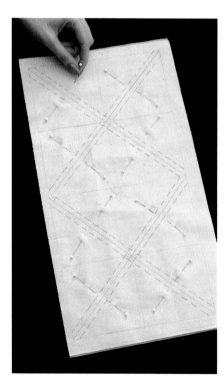

3) Draw diagonal lines through the grid in opposite direction.

4) Mark dotted stitching lines ¼" (6 mm) on both sides of all diagonal lines. Pin the fabrics, right sides together.

5) Stitch on dotted lines. Cut on all solid lines to make triangle-squares. Press seam allowances toward darker fabric. Trim points.

How to Make a Pinwheel Quilt Block

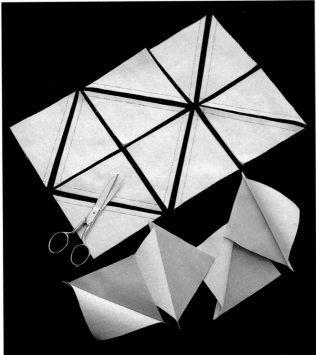

1) Cut one 7¾" × 15½" (20 × 40 cm) rectangle from each of two different fabrics. Draw 3⅞" (9.7 cm) grid, as in step 1, opposite. Draw the diagonal lines, stitch, and cut as in steps 2 to 5, opposite, to make 16 triangle-squares.

2) Stitch two triangle-squares, right sides together, as shown. Repeat with two more triangle-squares. Press seam allowances toward lighter fabric. Stitch two units together to form pinwheel, matching points. Keep seam allowances in alternating directions to eliminate bulk at points. Repeat for three more pinwheels.

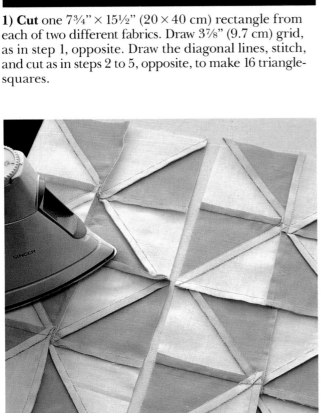

3) Stitch two pinwheels together. Repeat with two remaining pinwheels. Press seam allowances in alternating directions.

4) Stitch remaining seam to form block. Press seam allowances to one side. Release stitching at centers of pinwheels to make seam allowances lie flat, if necessary, as on page 297, step 10.

Sewing Designs with Diamonds

Diamonds are frequently used to make star designs. Select fabric that has an all-over print or is a solid color rather than fabric with a one-way design or stripes, so you do not have to be concerned about the direction of the design when stitching the pieces together.

Cut diamonds carefully to ensure that the angles are accurate. The cutting directions, opposite, are for diamonds that have 45° angles. Other diamond shapes used in quilting require templates for accurate cutting.

Because diamonds are cut on the bias, take care not to stretch the edges when stitching.

The instructions for the Eight-pointed Star quilt block (opposite) make a 12" (30.5 cm) finished block.

To make a holiday table runner, sew five blocks together, end to end, to form a 60" (152.5 cm) length; stitch-in-the-ditch-quilt and channel-quilt as on pages 311 to 313. Bind as on pages 314 to 317.

How to Cut Diamonds

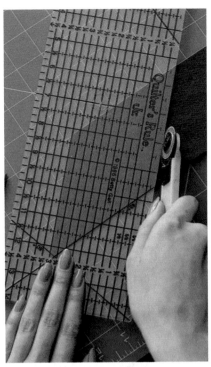

1) Cut strips (page 277) the width of finished diamond plus ½" (1.3 cm). Stack three or four strips, matching edges exactly. Place on cutting mat, along grid line.

2) Place ruler at 45° angle to long edge of fabric; hold ruler firmly, and cut.

3) Shift ruler on fabric, aligning fabric edge with measurement mark that is equal to width of strip; hold firmly, and cut. Check accuracy of angle frequently.

How to Make an Eight-pointed Star Quilt Block

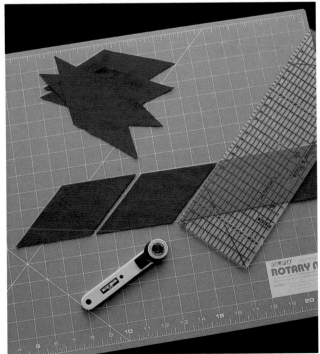

1) Cut eight 3" (7.5 cm) diamonds from one 3" (7.5 cm) strip of fabric, above, for star.

2) Cut four 4" (10 cm) squares and one 6¼" (15.7 cm) square of background fabric. Cut large square in half diagonally; then cut diagonally in other direction, to make four right triangles.

(Continued on next page)

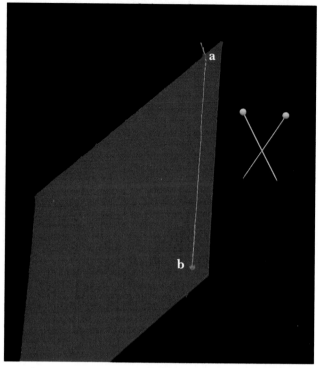

3) Mark wrong side of quilt pieces where ¼" (6 mm) seams will intersect, placing dots at right-angle corner of each triangle, both wide-angle corners of each diamond, and one corner of each square.

4) Align two diamonds along one side, right sides together, matching inner points **(a)** and dots **(b)**. Stitch from inner point exactly to dot; backstitch. Repeat for remaining diamonds.

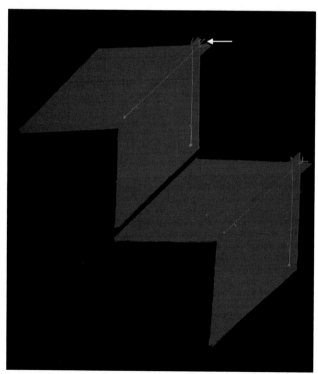

5) Stitch two 2-diamond units, right sides together, as in step 4, folding seam allowances in opposite directions (arrow). Repeat for remaining units.

6) Place two 4-diamond units right sides together. Pin, matching inner points at center. Fold seam allowances of each four-diamond unit in opposite directions to minimize bulk; stitch between dots, securing seams at ends. Do not press.

7) Align short side of triangle to a diamond, right sides together, matching edges at outer point **(a)** and dots at inner point **(b)**. Stitch from outer edge exactly to dot, *with diamond side up*; backstitch.

8) Align remaining side of triangle to adjoining diamond, and stitch seam as in step 7, *with triangle side up*. Repeat for remaining triangles, stitching them between every other set of points on the star.

9) Align squares to diamonds between remaining points of star, matching edges at outer point **(a)** and dots at inner point **(b)**; stitch *with diamond side up*, as in step 7. Align the remaining sides of squares and diamonds, stitching *with square side up*.

10) Release stitching within seam allowances at center of star, so seam allowances will lie flat. Press from wrong side, working from center out.

Types of Machine Quilting

Quilting holds the three layers of a quilt together, and adds design interest. Machine quilting is fast compared to hand quilting. You can quilt a project using the sewing machine in one-fourth to one-third the time it would take to do it by hand.

Machine quilting is strong, and the well-defined lines accentuate the quilting pattern. Machine stitches are tighter and compress the batting more than hand-quilting stitches, creating more depth and texture.

Plan the quilting design to cover the surface uniformly. Whether you choose to quilt close together or far apart, keep your quilting evenly spaced across the entire top. Heavily quilted areas tend to shrink more than lightly quilted areas.

There are three basic types of quilting: tied (**a**), machine-guided (**b**), and freehand (**c**).

Tying is a quick and easy way to finish a quilt. It is also the best way to maintain the loft of a thick batting. Traditionally, quilts were tied by hand with yarn or heavy thread, but a similar look can be achieved by using a sewing machine.

In machine-guided quilting, the feed dogs and presser foot guide the fabric. This method is used for long, straight rows of stitches.

In freehand quilting, the fabric is guided by hand; the feed dogs and presser foot are not used. Freehand quilting takes the most practice. A beginner may want to start with machine-guided quilting.

In both machine-guided and freehand quilting, the stitching is an integral part of the quilt design and should be planned carefully. Quilting should reinforce or complement the piecing or appliqué design, and it should also form an appealing design on the back of the quilt.

Marking the Quilting Design

Quilting designs should be marked on the quilt top, unless the design follows the piecing or appliqué lines.

Test the marking tools on the fabrics in the quilt top before marking. Be sure the marks can withstand handling, folding, and rolling, and that they can be thoroughly brushed, erased, or washed away after quilting.

It is easier to mark the quilt top before the layers are basted together. Place the quilt top on a hard, flat surface and draw or trace the design accurately with a clear, thin line.

If you are using a template to mark the design on a border, mark the corners first. If a design of repeating motifs does not fit, adjust the length of several motifs as necessary. You can use a single motif at the corners of the border or mark intersecting lines of channel quilting (page 311) to form a grid.

Guides used for marking quilting lines are rulers and plastic templates.

How to Mark a Quilting Design

1) Press quilt top; place on hard, flat work surface, with corners square and sides parallel. Tape securely, keeping quilt top smooth and taut.

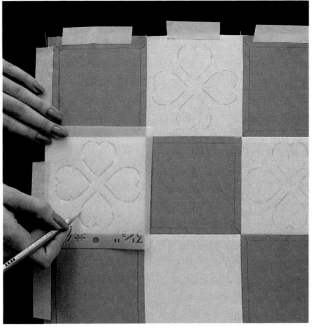

2) Mark quilting design, using ruler or template as a guide, beginning in corners. Mark distinct, thin lines, using as light a touch as possible.

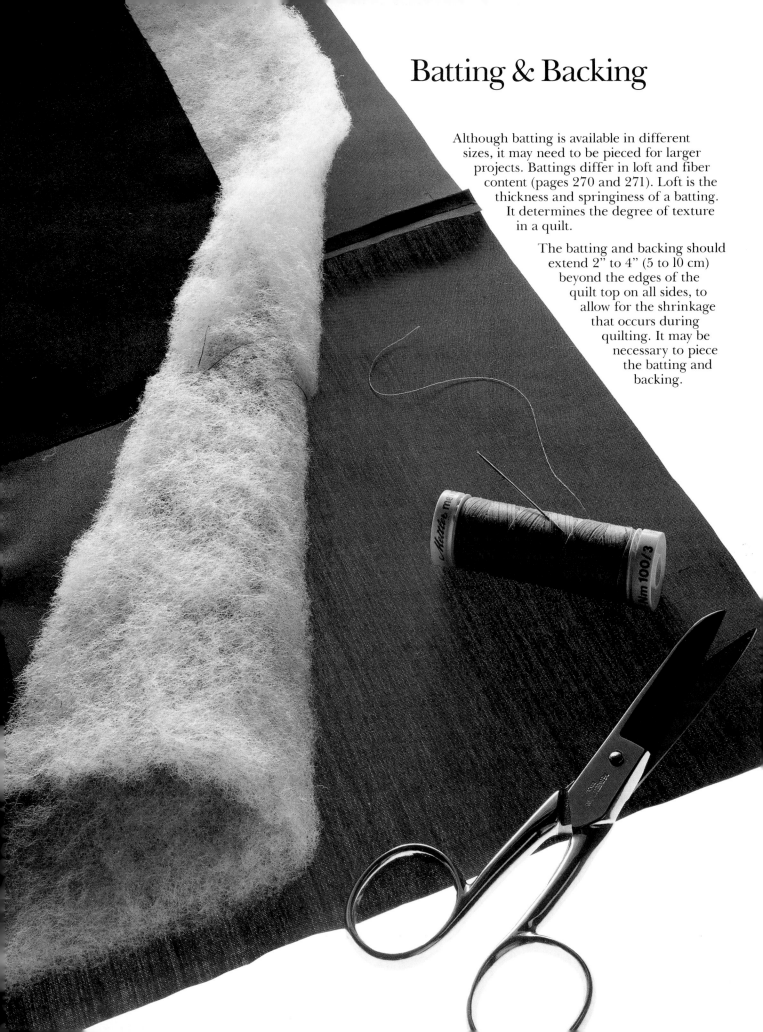

Batting & Backing

Although batting is available in different sizes, it may need to be pieced for larger projects. Battings differ in loft and fiber content (pages 270 and 271). Loft is the thickness and springiness of a batting. It determines the degree of texture in a quilt.

The batting and backing should extend 2" to 4" (5 to 10 cm) beyond the edges of the quilt top on all sides, to allow for the shrinkage that occurs during quilting. It may be necessary to piece the batting and backing.

How to Piece Batting and Backing Fabric

Batting. 1) Overlap two pieces of batting, 1" to 2" (2.5 to 5 cm).

2) Cut with shears through both layers, down the center of overlapped section.

3) Remove trimmed edges. Butt batting edges, and whipstitch by hand to secure.

Backing. Cut selvages from fabric. Piece fabric as necessary. Stitch, using a stitch length of 12 to 15 stitches per inch (2.5 cm) and ¼" (6 mm) seam allowances. Press seam allowances to one side or open.

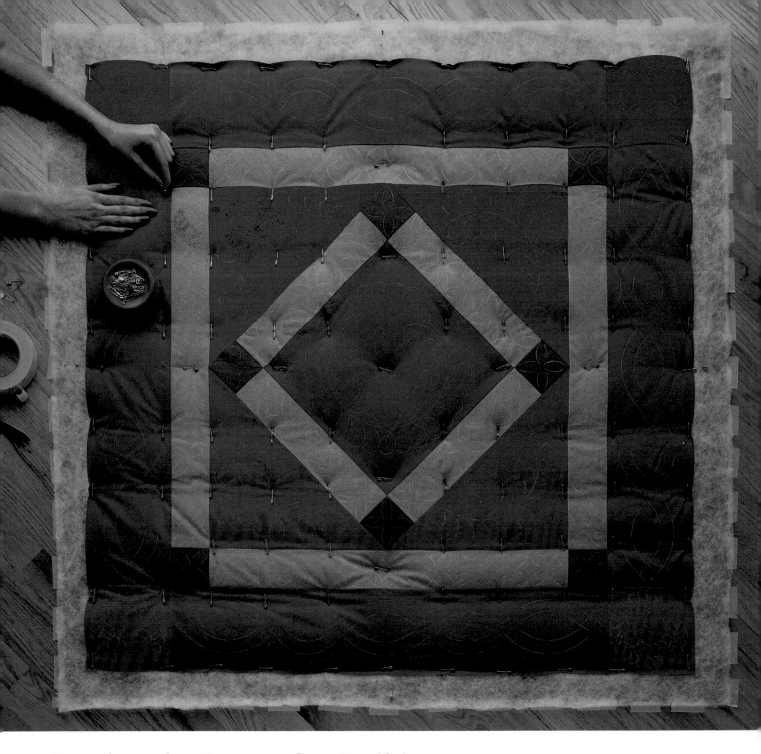

Basting the Layers for Quilting

Basting keeps the three layers of the quilt from shifting during the quilting process. Traditionally, quilts were basted using needle and thread; however, safety-pin basting may be used instead. Lay the quilt out flat on a hard surface, such as the floor or a large table and baste the entire quilt. Or baste the quilt in sections on a table at least one-fourth the size of the quilt.

Press the quilt top and backing fabric flat before layering and basting. If basting with safety pins, use

1" (2.5 cm) rustproof steel pins. Steel pins glide through fabrics more easily than brass pins, and the 1" (2.5 cm) size is easier to handle.

If basting with thread, use white cotton thread and a large milliners or darning needle. Use a large running stitch, about 1" (2.5 cm) long. Pull the stitches snug so the layers will not shift. Backstitch at the ends to secure the stitching.

How to Baste a Quilt on a Surface Larger Than the Quilt

1) Fold quilt top, right sides together, into quarters, without creasing. Mark center of each side at raw edges with safety pins. Repeat for batting and backing, folding backing wrong sides together.

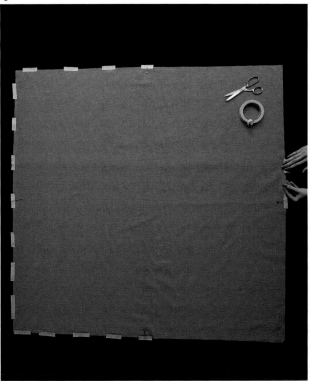

2) Unfold backing on work surface, wrong side up. Tape securely, beginning at center of each side and working toward corners, stretching fabric slightly. Backing should be taut, but not overly stretched.

3) Place batting on backing, matching pins on each side. Smooth, but do not stretch, working from center of quilt out to sides.

4) Place quilt top, right side up, on batting, matching pins on each side; smooth, but do not stretch.

(Continued on next page)

5) Baste with pins or thread from center of quilt to pins on sides; if thread-basting, pull stitches snug so layers will not shift. Avoid basting on marked quilting lines or through seams.

6) Baste one quarter-section in parallel rows about 6" (15 cm) apart, working toward raw edges. If thread-basting, also baste quarter-section in parallel rows in opposite direction, as shown in step 2, opposite.

7) Repeat step 6 for remaining quarter-sections. Remove tape from backing.

8) Fold edges of backing over batting and edges of quilt top to prevent raw edges of fabric from raveling and batting from catching on needle and feed dogs during quilting. Pin-baste.

How to Baste a Quilt on a Surface Smaller Than the Quilt

1) Fold and mark quilt as on page 303. Lay backing on table, wrong side up; let sides hang over edge of table. Tape raw edges of backing to tabletop. Clamp backing securely to table, stretching slightly, beginning at center of each side and working toward corners; place clamps about 12" (30.5 cm) apart.

2) Place batting on backing, matching pins on each side. Place quilt top right side up on batting, matching pins on each side; smooth, but do not stretch. Baste one quarter-section of quilt as in steps 5 and 6, opposite. Remove tape and clamps.

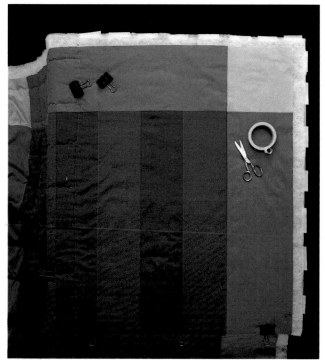

3) Move quilt to baste next quarter-section. Tape raw edges of backing to tabletop, stretching slightly; clamp all layers of quilt to edges of table. Baste quarter-section as in steps 5 and 6, opposite.

4) Repeat for remaining quarter-sections. Check for any tucks on backing; rebaste as necessary. Fold and pin-baste edges as in step 8, opposite.

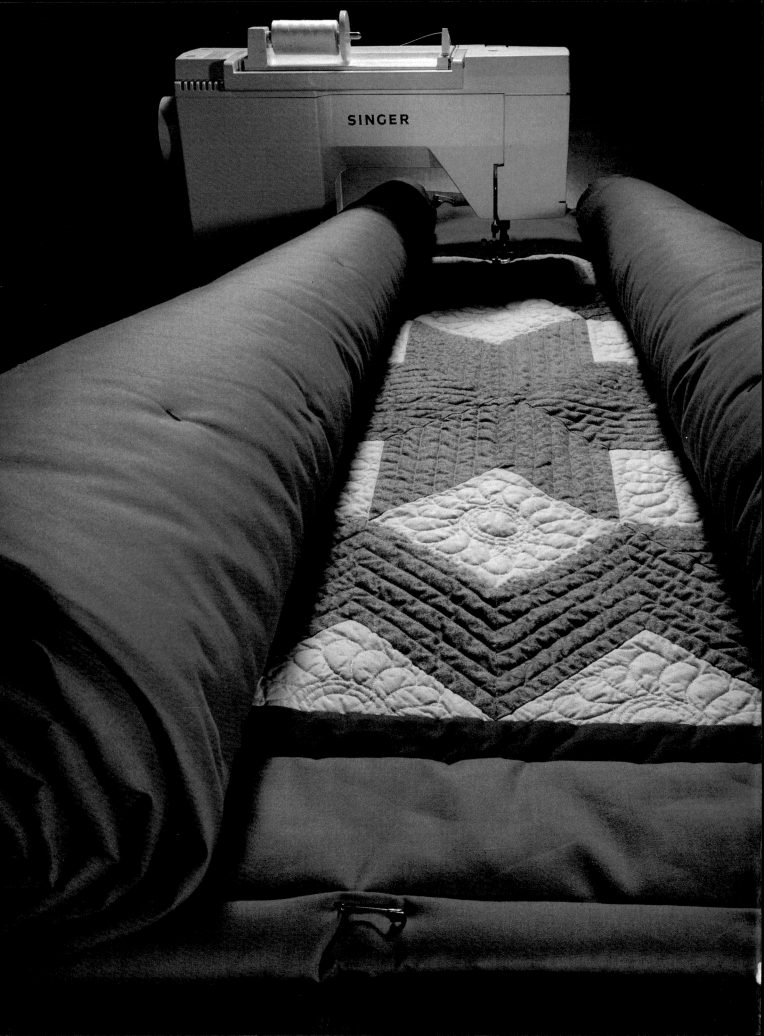

Machine-quilting Basics

When machine-quilting, it is necessary to roll or fold the quilt in order for it to fit under the sewing machine head and to prevent it from hanging over the edge of the table. You may want to expand your sewing surface to support the quilt. Always keep the largest section of quilt to the left of the needle as you stitch. As you quilt from the center toward the sides, there is less fabric to feed under the head of the machine, making the quilt easier to manage.

Cotton or monofilament nylon thread may be used for quilting (page 274). If using monofilament nylon thread, use it only in the needle and use a thread that matches the background fabric in the bobbin. Loosen the needle thread tension so the bobbin thread does not show on the right side.

When machine-quilting, stitch continuously, minimizing starts and stops as much as possible. Check for any tucks in the backing by feeling through the layers of the quilt ahead of the sewing machine needle. Prevent the tucks from being stitched by continuously easing in the excess fabric before it reaches the needle. If a tuck does occur, release stitches for 3" (7.5 cm) or more, and restitch, easing in excess fabric.

Quilting Sequence

Plan the stitching sequence before you begin to quilt. First quilt the longest or largest sections, working from the center toward the sides. For example, for a quilt with sashing, quilt the sashing strips before quilting the blocks, starting with the center strips and working toward the side strips. This helps anchor the layers throughout the quilt to prevent them from shifting.

Next, quilt the areas within the blocks that will not be heavily quilted, such as motifs. Then proceed to the smaller areas or those that will be more heavily quilted.

The sequence for quilting varies with the style of the quilt. For quilts with side-by-side blocks, anchor the layers throughout the quilt by stitching in the ditch between the blocks in vertical and horizontal rows. For a medallion quilt, stitch in the ditch along the border seam to anchor the layers; then quilt the central area.

How to Prepare a Large Quilt for Machine Quilting

1) Lay the quilt flat, right side up. For quilts with polyester batting, roll one side to within 2" or 3" (5 or 7.5 cm) of center basting line. If necessary, secure roll with large safety pins or plastic headband. For quilts with cotton batting, loosely fold one side into accordion folds; it will stay without pins.

2) Roll or fold other side, as in step 1, if the sewing surface is not large enough to hold remaining width of quilt flat.

3) Fold quilt loosely along length, accordion-style, into lap-size bundle. Place bundle on your lap.

4) Pull quilt up from lap, section by section, so it is level with needle as you stitch. Do not allow quilt to hang over back or side of sewing table.

Tips for Quilting

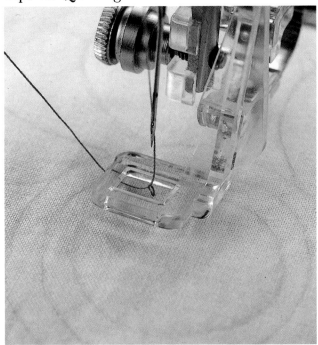

Draw up bobbin thread to the quilt top, by turning handwheel by hand, and stopping with needle at highest position. Pull on needle thread to bring the bobbin thread up through fabric.

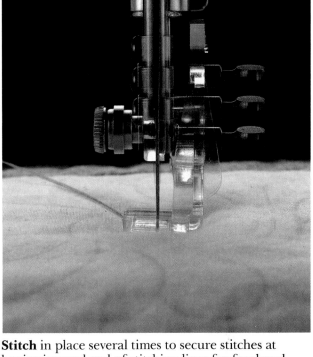

Stitch in place several times to secure stitches at beginning and end of stitching lines for freehand quilting. For machine-guided quilting, begin stitching with stitch length set at 0. Gradually increase stitch length for about ½" (1.3 cm) to desired stitch length. Reverse procedure at end of stitching line.

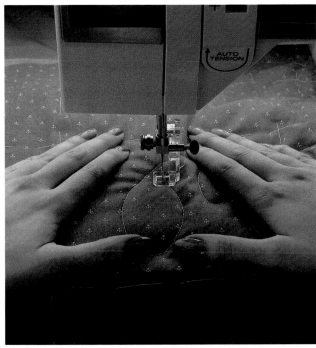

Freehand quilting. Position hands so they act as a hoop, encircling needle. Gently press down and pull outward to create tension on fabric. Move fabric with wrist and hand movements as you stitch. Rest elbows comfortably on sewing table while stitching; it may be helpful to elevate elbows on books.

Machine-guided quilting. Position hands on either side of presser foot. Gently press down and hold fabric taut to prevent layers from shifting, causing puckers or tucks. Ease any excess fabric under the presser foot as you stitch.

Machine-tying a Quilt

When using a high-loft batting, machine-tie the quilt to preserve the loft. A quilt can be machine-tied by using a zigzag or decorative stitch, or by attaching ribbons or yarns.

Mark the placement of the ties on the quilt top before basting it to the batting and backing. Stagger the rows of ties for greater interest and strength. Space the ties approximately 5" (12.5 cm) apart.

Three Ways to Tie a Quilt by Machine

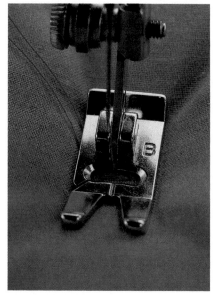

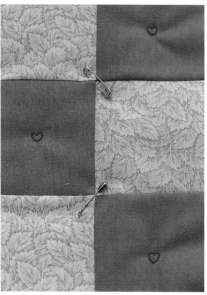

Zigzag stitch. Adjust stitch length and width to 0. Holding threads behind needle, stitch several times through all layers. Adjust stitch width to a wide setting; stitch 8 to 10 times. Return stitch width to 0; stitch several times. Clip threads.

Decorative stitch. Use a decorative stitch instead of a zigzag stitch to secure quilt layers; adjust stitch length and width for an attractive design. Stitch in place at beginning and end of decorative stitch.

Ribbon or yarn. Cut one 3" to 6" (7.5 to 15 cm) length of ribbon for each tie. Tie into bow. Center bow over placement mark; stitch bow in place, using zigzag stitch, left.

Machine-guided Quilting

Machine-guided quilting uses pressure from the feed dogs and presser foot to guide the three layers of fabric through the sewing machine. The Even Feed™ foot helps to prevent tucks when quilting.

Machine-guided quilting is used for stitching long lines of quilting. A straight stitch is most commonly used, but any stitch will work, including decorative stitches. Practice on a sample to determine the appropriate stitch length and width. Space the stitching lines according to the type of batting used (page 270).

Grid quilting (a) is stitched in evenly spaced lines. The quilting lines can be diagonal in both directions, or both vertical and horizontal. Diagonal quilting lines are marked, as on page 312. You may want to draw the

grid lines on paper before marking the actual quilt top to become familiar with the technique. The paper can be cut to the size of the quilt or in proportion to it.

Stitch-in-the-ditch quilting (b) emphasizes the pieced design, because it is stitched following the seamlines for the blocks, across length and width of quilt.

Outline quilting (c) also emphasizes the pieced design. It is stitched ¼" (6 mm) from the seamlines, outlining the pieces or blocks. Outline quilting can be either machine-guided or freehand.

Channel quilting (d) is stitched in evenly spaced lines. The quilting lines can be either diagonal, vertical, or horizontal. The quilting lines are marked using a ruler, as on page 299.

How to Grid-quilt on the Diagonal

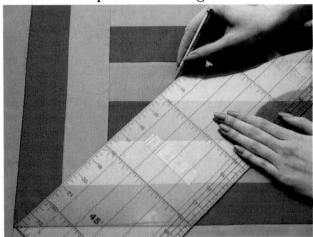

1) Tape quilt top to flat surface and mark quilting lines before basting quilt. Mark first line at an exact 45° angle to edge of design, starting at one corner; continue line to edge of design on opposite side.

2) Mark a line from end of previous line to opposite edge, keeping marked lines at 90° angles to each other and 45° angle to edge of design; continue marking lines in this manner until a line ends at a corner.

3) Mark a line, starting from another corner, if lines do not yet complete the grid design; continue marking lines to form a grid.

4) Mark additional quilting lines halfway between grid marks and parallel to previous lines, if smaller grid is desired.

5) Place quilt layers together and baste (pages 302 to 305). Stitch on marked lines, starting in one corner.

6) Stitch lines in same sequence as marked; turn fabric 90° at edge of design, pivoting with needle down.

How to Outline-quilt

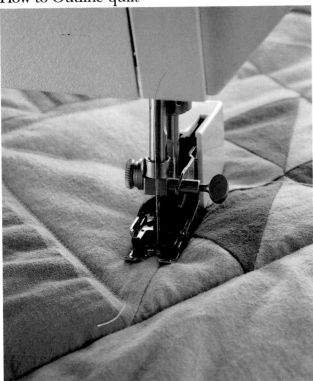

Stitch about ¼" (6 mm) from seamline, starting at corner. To prevent puckers and tucks, feed fabric under presser foot (page 309).

How to Stitch-in-the-ditch-quilt

Stitch in the ditch so stitches are hidden in the seam. To prevent puckers and tucks, feed fabric under presser foot (page 309).

How to Channel-quilt

1) Stitch lengthwise, on marked quilting line, at center of area to be quilted. Stitch parallel lines, working from center toward right side.

2) Turn quilt 180°. Stitch parallel lines, working from center toward right side, to complete quilting.

Binding a Quilt

There are two methods for finishing the edges of a quilt. For mock binding (top), fold the backing fabric over the raw edges to the quilt top. For double binding (bottom), attach a separate strip of binding fabric.

Mock binding is an easy way to finish the edges of a quilt and makes use of the excess backing fabric needed during basting and quilting. Choose a backing fabric that coordinates with the quilt top.

Double binding is cut on the straight of grain and has two layers of fabric to provide a durable edge. The binding can either match or complement the quilt top.

The instructions for mock binding (below) and double binding (pages 316 and 317) make ½" (1.3 cm) bindings.

How to Bind a Quilt with Mock Binding

1) Machine-baste through all layers of the quilt, ⅛" (3 mm) from raw edges of quilt top.

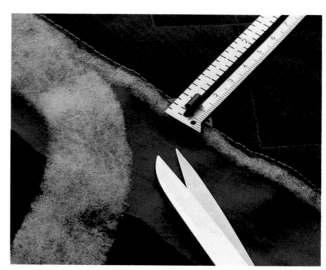

2) Trim batting only, ¼" (6 mm) from edge of quilt top, ⅜" (1 cm) from basting stitches.

3) Trim backing 1" (2.5 cm) from cut edge of batting.

4) Fold backing diagonally at corner of batting; press foldline.

5) Fold backing so edge of backing meets edge of batting; press.

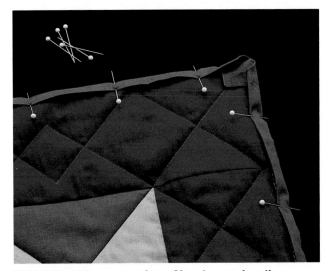

6) Fold backing over edge of batting and quilt top, covering stitching line; pin.

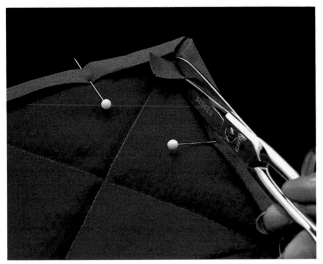

7) Cut out square of excess fabric at each corner. Pin corners.

8) Edgestitch along fold to secure. Remove basting stitches on quilt back. Slipstitch corners, if desired.

How to Bind a Quilt with Double Binding

1) Fold fabric in half on lengthwise grainline (page 277). Cut strips 3" (7.5 cm) on crosswise grainline.

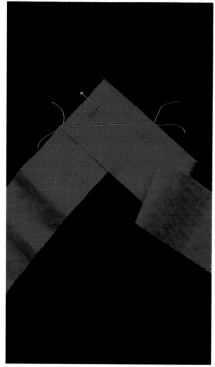

2) Pin strips, right sides together, at right angles; strips will form a "V." Stitch diagonally across strips.

3) Trim the seam allowance to ¼" (6 mm). Press seam open. Trim points even with edges.

4) Measure one side of quilt; cut binding this length plus 2" (5 cm). Mark binding 1" (2.5 cm) in from each end; divide section between pins in quarters; pin-mark. Divide side of quilt in quarters; pin-mark.

5) Fold binding in half lengthwise, wrong sides together. Place binding on quilt top, matching raw edges and pin-marks; binding will extend 1" (2.5 cm) beyond quilt top at each end.

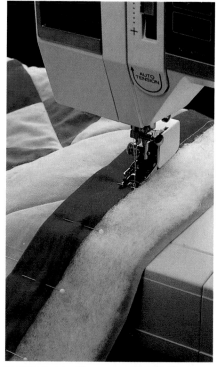

6) Stitch binding to quilt ¼" (6 mm) from raw edges of binding.

7) Cut excess batting and backing to ½" (1.3 cm) from stitching line.

8) Wrap binding around edge of quilt, covering stitching line on back of quilt; pin.

9) Stitch in the ditch on the right side of quilt, catching binding on back of quilt.

10) Repeat steps 4 to 9 for opposite side of quilt. Trim ends of binding even with edges of quilt top.

11) Repeat steps 4 to 7 for remaining two sides. Trim ends of binding to extend ½" (1.3 cm) beyond finished edges of quilt.

12) Fold binding down along the stitching line. Fold ½" (1.3 cm) end of binding over finished edge; press in place. Wrap binding around edge and stitch in the ditch as in steps 8 and 9. Slipstitch end by hand.

Index

Cy DeCosse Incorporated offers sewing
accessories to subscribers. For information
write:

Sewing Accessories
5900 Green Oak Drive
Minnetonka, MN 55343